HOME-BASED BUSINESS SERIES

how to start a home-based Landscaping Business

seventh edition

Owen E. Dell

Published by Taylor Trade Publishing
An imprint of The Rowman & Littlefield Publishing Group, Inc.
4501 Forbes Boulevard, Suite 200, Lanham, Maryland 20706
www.rowman.com

Unit A, Whitacre Mews, 26-34 Stannary Street, London SE11 4AB, United Kingdom

Distributed by NATIONAL BOOK NETWORK

British Library Cataloguing in Publication Information Available

Library of Congress Cataloging-in-Publication Data

Dell, Owen E., author.
How to start a home-based landscaping business / Owen E. Dell.—Seventh edition.
pages cm
Includes bibliographical references and index.
ISBN 978-1-4930-1171-1 (pbk.)—ISBN 978-1-6307-6097-7 (e-book) 1. Landscaping industry—Management. 2. New business enterprises—Management. 3. Home-based businesses—Management. I. Title.
SB472.5.D44 2015
635.9068--dc23

2015013253

The paper used in this publication meets the minimum requirements of American National Standard for Information Sciences—Permanence of Paper for Printed Library Materials, ANSI/NISO Z39.48-1992.

Printed in the United States of America

The information provided in this book is as accurate and complete as possible, but laws, rules, regulations, and policies change constantly and there is considerable variation in legal issues governing proper business practice from state to state, and especially outside of the United States. The author has made every effort to check all facts, but neither the author nor the publisher is responsible for the accuracy of the information contained herein, nor for the applicability of the information to the needs and situation of the reader or for the success or failure of the reader's existing or future business activities. The information provided is not guaranteed and is not intended to be used without checking with legal and other professional counsel and verifying specific circumstances as they apply to the reader's needs and in their particular jurisdiction.

Contents

Acknowledgments

Behind every book is a cast of unseen characters, those patient, helpful people who offer endless advice with no trace of the annoyance they must surely feel now and then, who spend weekends critiquing sloppy, half-formed manuscripts, and who are always there with encouragement, enthusiasm, and good cheer.

It was Lili Singer, the editor of *Southern California Gardener* magazine, who first said the right words to the right people to connect aspiring author with publisher and get this project going. Mark Wisniewski, landscape professional extraordinaire, spent untold hours on the manuscript and kept me out of a lot of trouble, I'm sure. Thanks also to my insurance agent of many years, Dart Whitmore, and to Lloyd Gibbs, intrepid CPA, who chewed up the sections on insurance and bookkeeping and spit them out in a much-improved form. I would be lost without my IT guru, Mac (no, that's not his stage name) Bakewell, who has helped me keep my information on computers up-to-date and relevant. Finally, to my friends, whom I haven't paid much attention to while this work was in progress: I can't remember your names or exactly what you look like, but I love you and really appreciate your patience. I'm sure we'll enjoy getting to know one another again. Truth be told, I'm grateful to so many people that it would take a chapter to fully acknowledge them all. So I will just say thanks to those who have given me so much, and also thanks to the Earth and its cargo of life, the greatest teacher of all.

Owen Dell
1993 and 2015

Preface to the Seventh Edition

I was a little over forty years old when I wrote the first edition of this book. At the time, somebody thought I was well-enough suited to the task of advising eager young (and not so young) aspirants to the landscaping business on how to start and run their own operations. I wasn't so sure, and I took on the project with mixed feelings of honor and blood-curdling terror. Writing a book isn't easy, and this one was no exception. I wanted to be certain that I offered the very best advice, and so I made a point of questioning everything I thought I knew from my years of experience running a small, home-based landscaping business. I spent a lot of time talking to fellow professionals, poring over books at the library (this was before the Internet made research a comfy home-based task), and relentlessly checking my facts. When all was said and done and the book went to press, I was pooped. I was also pretty sure I had done right by my future readers.

Then a marvelous thing happened. I began to get emails and letters from readers, thanking me for guiding them toward a successful career. What a heartwarming and unexpected payoff that has been! The flow of gratitude continues, over 20 years later, and my life is regularly enriched by touching, kind words from people who found in *How to Start a Home-Based Landscaping Business* the help they needed to embark on a career in this demanding field and build thriving small businesses and satisfying lives.

The day I began writing *How to Start a Home-Based Landscaping Business,* so long ago now, I had an instinct that people wanted someone to act as their guide, a friendly arm around their shoulder as they took on their daunting adventures. I wanted to be that guide, and I feel the same way today. So it is with the deepest gratitude for those who have supported me in this work, and with the deepest affection for new readers who are looking for a little support, that I present you with this revised and expanded edition of the book. I'm with you on your journey, and I look forward to hearing of your successes.

Owen Dell
June 2015

p.s. If you like this book, please tell the world by posting reviews at Amazon and other online retailers. It helps me to go on helping you. Thanks!

Introduction

In 1972 I was studying botany at the local junior college, going out into the mountains and deserts of the beautiful state of California, and looking at some of the most gorgeous natural places anyone has ever seen. As luck would have it, '72 was one of the great years for wildflowers, and we really got an eyeful. Having grown up in the inner city, I knew little about nature, or about gardens for that matter, and I was deeply moved by what I saw. Through that wonderful spring that I'll never forget, something grew inside me, something entirely new and remarkable.

Our class would troop out into the wilderness and we would spend a morning, a day, or a week steeping ourselves in the incredible elegance of it all. Then we would inevitably return to civilization, which looked more and more like a bad mistake carried out on a grand scale by some very inept people. As I began to see nature, I also began to see gardens, and what I saw was how vastly different the two were. Slowly, over that spring, I came to understand that gardens were important and could be made better than they were. I came to love nature, but I also came to love the idea of my playing a part in nature. I came to have a passion about the dream that had unfurled inside me like the first leaves of a sprouting bean—the dream of making landscapes more like nature.

My good friend Buddy was also in the botany class. Buddy was a Louisiana boy, fun loving and easygoing. He saw this dream, too, and we talked about it a lot. That summer, broke as always, we decided that we were going to quit school and become native plant landscapers. So, suddenly there we were, our meager funds invested in a '55 Ford pickup (light blue, no major dents, ran pretty good, $100), a few hand tools (from the swap meet mostly, another $50), and a couple of straw hats (Thrifty Drug Store, $2.29 each plus tax). No, we didn't have any work, but we felt great just the same.

A cup of coffee was still a dime at Sambo's Restaurant, and that was our lunch every day. We called it "Coffee Bean Soup" and drank lots of it, adding plenty of soothing "coffee whitener," the ingredients of which we avoided thinking about too much. We had Coffee Bean Soup and lots of laughs and not a whole lot more at first. No sensible person would have lasted a day with us.

We spent the last part of that first June and most of July driving around looking for piles of trash to haul, weeds to be cut down, anything that would get us a few dollars to pay for the next day's gas and a couple of beers in the evening. We did some pretty horrendous things. And we were having a great time.

Finally in late July we got a job building some retaining walls and a terraced garden for a kindly college professor up in the hills above Santa Barbara. I often think back on how trusting he was to let us do this, especially since our initial approach had been to ask him if we could haul away some rubbish. Still I guess we did something right, because he kept us busy right through September.

The first day we broke the gas main. August was the hottest on record. The soil was more like rock, and it never occurred to us to soften it with some water before trying to dig it. But we were doing it, that was the thing! And what a summer it was, so good to be alive. We were on our way!

We finished the job just as we began to feel a bit of fall in the morning air. And yes, the work we had done was beautiful; everyone agreed on that. On the last day at about 3:00 p.m., Buddy and I carried the last of our tools up to the faithful blue Ford and turned to look back down on our masterpiece. That moment with my wonderful friend and business partner, surveying our hard, fine work, will surely always guide me through the hard times, as it has so often in the past. We stood for I don't know how long, each thinking the same thought: If we could feel this good once a year, that would be reason enough to carry on. When we finally turned to each other, we both had tears in our eyes.

Landscaping has been good to me. I'm pretty comfortable these days. I have lots of work, and if I have Coffee Bean Soup for lunch, it's because I'm trying to lose a couple of pounds. I still think about quitting now and then; we all have bad days. But when I consider the other choices I might have made, I'm glad about my life.

I believe that if you want to put your green thumb to use, and if you learn to do things really right, you will be doing something brave and noble and fine. You will have a marvelous, challenging, and rewarding life. You will meet the finest and warmest people. You will see beauty every day, often beauty of your own making. And as you grow old, you can sit beneath the shade of trees you planted with your own hands.

If this is the life you want, I'll try to help you get a good start. Remember, don't come looking for riches, easy money, or a soft life. But if you can live with your own version of Coffee Bean Soup, and if you can stick it out, I guarantee that your soul will be nourished, your heart will be moved, and your corner of the world will be much better for your having made your choice. And, yes, I do hope to save you time and trouble by keeping you from making some of the mistakes I made.

Most people who start a business of any kind know only their craft. That's not enough. You've got to run a business, too, and if you run it badly, you'll fail. Other than your mom and your best friends, few people will really care. Sadly, most people do fail because, like a garden, a business is complex and challenging. It's just too much for the majority of those who try. Let's make you the exception, the one who succeeds, so that you can do what you love, earn a living at it, stay out of trouble, and have a good time.

This is a book about the business of landscaping. I'm not going to tell you how to plant roses or what kind of fertilizer to use. There are plenty of books that will help you with all that. You're going to learn how to set up your company, how to write a business plan, keep records, find and keep good employees, attract and retain clients, manage jobs, and a lot more. You're going to learn how to do things right the first time. Nuts and bolts? Yes, but don't be put off; you'll find it's as interesting as gardening. And remember what's behind it—a love of green things, of natural surroundings, of nurturing. It's all connected, all a part of the great adventure. Come on along.

01 So You Think You Want to Be a Landscaper?

Maybe you've always loved to garden and believe you could be really good at it if you had a chance to devote yourself to the craft. Then again, maybe you don't know a wisteria from a wheelbarrow, but you've been yearning to find a way to earn a living outdoors. Either way, you're motivated to get serious about gardening or landscaping and determined to go into business for yourself.

That's great. But what's it really like? What kinds of work can you find to do? Who will your clients be? How will you get work? What will your days be like? Does working out of your home make sense? And can you really get paid for having so much fun?

When Landscaping Matters

Before we get too far, it would be good to consider whether landscaping really matters. Will you be in the business of doing exterior decorating for rich people, or will there be something more meaningful about your work? The answer is, that's up to you. For instance, landscaping can have a damaging effect on the environment (toxic pesticides, water-hogging plants, destruction of native habitat), or a beneficial one (organic gardening, water-efficient plants and irrigation systems, restoration of native habitat). Similarly, landscaping can create spaces that are hospitable and safe for people, or not, all depending on the skill and intentions of the practitioner. Consider some of the many good outcomes of landscaping: trees that make oxygen and sequester carbon (helping to counteract climate change), native plants that benefit wildlife, accessible gardens for handicapped people, children's gardens that teach little ones about nature, healing gardens that offer herbal remedies and soothing space for patients at hospitals and residents of rest homes, edible gardens that provide wholesome local food, sharing gardens that engage the community in eliminating hunger among the less fortunate, watershed-friendly gardens that make use of natural rainfall to recharge groundwater and create habitat. As a landscaper, you'll be improving the environment by controlling erosion, providing climate control for houses, reducing the urban heat-island effect, producing oxygen, growing fruits and vegetables (and maybe even caring for bees, chickens or other small livestock), providing habitat for wildlife, and restoring or preserving native ecosystems. I could go on and on. These are the services that landscaping offers, and you are in charge of maximizing the benefits of the landscape you create. That's an important job, and it will become more important as time passes and people realize that a garden does more than just look pretty. Decorating for rich people? That's only a tiny part of what landscapers do these days, and the possibilities for good work are endless and deeply moving to contemplate. If you care about more than just making money, you're in the right place!

We live in the most exciting moment in the history of horticulture. We've progressed from the tradition of the purely ornamental landscape to the complex and evolving practice of *sustainable landscaping*—the idea that landscapes can benefit both nature and people when properly done, and that they can function well with a minimum of resource use and negative impacts. We're finally getting it: landscaping provides valuable services, it does stuff, good stuff that we and the planet need. That's a breakthrough idea that was far too long on coming, but it's finally here. Never before has there been such an understanding of the effects of our activities, and never before has this work been more important or more needed. We need more thoughtful, progressive people to carry on this vital mission. You can be a part of it.

Just One Little Story

You might guess that I have lots of stories to share after so many years in this business. And yes, I do. Some of them are tales of aggravation and worse, while others are the narrative of some of the best memories of my life. Someday maybe I'll write a book about these, but for now I'd like to share just one of them with you.

I was asked by an old friend to make some improvements to the landscaping at her home. I hadn't seen her in many years, and when I arrived I was surprised to find that her husband was confined to a wheelchair, the result of an accident that had left him a paraplegic. On account of the way the property was landscaped, he was also confined to the house because steps and other barriers everywhere in the garden thwarted his ability to enjoy the outdoors. I proposed an accessible path that led across the yard to a promontory overlooking the beautiful garden, thinking this would free this fellow from years of confinement. My idea was accepted with enthusiasm and we brought it into being over a period of a few weeks' time. A couple of months after we finished the job, I received this note from the client: "It was so good to get to know you. Although you are a great team, you are also great individuals sharing sensitive, kind and caring traits. Mary is very pleased with the results of your work and I am touched and most appreciative of how you sensed and were attentive to my needs. I can't remember when I have received such loving consideration. I love my pathways and place in the sun. Love Don & Mary" The client enjoyed our work for many years before he passed away. Does landscaping make a difference? You decide.

Measuring the Landscaper's Life

You'll always be learning something in this endlessly interesting business. In fact, there are so many changes coming along every day that it's a challenge to keep up with it all. And on a personal level, because you are in direct intimate contact with living systems, you'll be able to connect with the infinite reaches of nature in a powerful and moving way. In fact, doing this work is a kind of spiritual path for many people, who were drawn to it by a longing for a personal bond with the natural world. Perhaps you are one of those people, and if so, know that your desires will be more than adequately met through your work.

Then there's the day-to-day excitement of the actual physical work. Few people fail to feel the energy of a landscaping project in full swing: the tractors, the trucks arriving with plants and soil amendments and materials, the smell of freshly turned earth, the seemingly sudden beauty of a completed job. The physicality of the work itself can be equally energizing: stretching to prune a fruit tree, swinging a pick in the hot sun, combing through the soil with busted fingernails, drinking madly from a jug of cold water on a hot day, coming home tired and dirty and completely at peace.

Finally, there's the time travel—thinking ahead to the day when the flowers will be in bloom and the trees will be tall, then walking the site with your client and sharing the pleasure of having done something truly wonderful. Surely, it's one of the great experiences of life.

What Kinds of Work Are Available and Who Does What?

Many people think that landscaping is a pretty unsophisticated profession. Mention landscaping or any related field, and some folks get an image of a kind of outdoor janitor wearing old blue jeans and pulling on the starter rope of a lawn mower. Ask them what professional skills they think this person might have, and they'll likely mention weeding, fertilizing, watering, and mowing (the work of a maintenance gardener) or perhaps planting flowers and trees (the work of the landscape contractor). It's true, these jobs are all there to be done, but there's so much more to landscaping than that. The world of landscaping ranges from the small, localized work of a maintenance gardener to the bird's-eye view of a landscape architect whose tasks might include urban and regional planning, ecosystem restoration, or even global issues, such as rainforest management. The landscape industry includes both the backyard grower of a few plants for the local trade and the huge wholesale nursery with hundreds of acres of landscape plants, dozens of employees, and a constant stream of trucks shipping plants all over the country and even the world. Not all landscaping is done outdoors; the interiorscape business is a profitable and fun specialty. The part you play in this amazingly diverse world depends on your interests, your energy, and your talents.

Let's have a look at who does what and how they work together. We'll work backward, from the care of the finished product to the starting point, planning and design; then we'll cover some related fields. This approach makes sense because it's quite possible you'll get your start in maintenance, as many people do. Aside from being the easiest place to begin, maintenance gardening is also the best place for most people to start. Why? Because unless you've had to care for some of the abominable landscapes designed by landscape designers and landscape architects (most of them school-taught and with little or no real-world experience), you can't possibly understand why they don't work. If you make the long climb from gardener to landscape contractor, and then to landscape architect, as I did, you'll have a deep understanding of what you're doing from the ground up. Everyone coming up in this business should be required to take this path, but few do. And of course there is no need to take it all on, and no shame in focusing on "just" maintenance or contracting. It's up to you where you want to take your career.

The Maintenance Gardener

The gardener is the base of the pyramid, the one who is called upon to care for the landscaping after it is designed and installed. The Japanese say, "The gardener is a person who keeps things from growing." It's odd and yet very true, since the main job of the gardener is to come in on Tuesday and make everything look the same as it did last Tuesday when he or she left. Status quo is the gardener's calling, husbanding an aura of serenity by making the landscape look as though nothing ever changes. Control is part of gardening, often made necessary by bad design; one of the gardener's main tasks is to continually cut back poorly chosen plants that have become too big for their designated spaces. The gardener is also a nurturer, one who must look closely at the places under his or her care and make adjustments, often subtle, to keep things moving in the right direction. Because despite this illusion to which the gardener is an accomplice, the garden does change. Weather and seasons do their work, pests and their predators come and go, and plants have different needs at different times and at different points in their life spans. Even the soil is alive, teeming with good and bad fungi, bacteria, insects, earthworms, tunneling mammals, and dozens of other things that appear to be creatures straight from a sci-fi film. All these things and more are on the job seven days a week, and it is the gardener who must understand them, work with them, be for or against them as the situation demands. The true gardener is a wizard, a little god.

So what exactly does the gardener do? In the real world, a gardener just starting out usually puts an ad in the classified section of the local paper or on Craigslist or a local online service, puts flyers up on local bulletin boards, drives around middle-class neighborhoods searching for yards that look like they need a little help, and knocks on a few doors to pitch the services he or she has to offer. The all-important work of marketing is done on the cheap, relying on free and low-cost approaches that often work better than more costly strategies and fit better within the minimal budget of a start-up company. Eventually breaks will come, filling a once-empty schedule, and with any luck, after a while the jobs start to add up to full-time employment. What about training? Well, maybe there is none in a lot of cases, and many successful people started out knowing not much more than how to pull on the starter rope of the lawnmower, but I don't really recommend that. Show some class and learn enough about your profession to give people their money's worth, even if you're just mowing and cleaning up yards at first. When you present yourself as a professional, you're expected to know at least the rudiments of your work. (But more about that later.)

Gardening is an ideal business to operate out of your home because most of your equipment can stay on the truck at night, you need little office space, and you don't need to be open to the public—very few people bring their gardens into the shop. Your initial budget will probably not include hundreds or even thousands of dollars per month for shop and office rent, but even after you're doing well there are many reasons to keep your operation at home (and some reasons not to). We'll get into that later, too, but for now, rest assured that a home-based small operation is a prudent way to get started.

A Day in the Life of a Gardener

You may have never tried to imagine what it would be like to own your own gardening service, so here's a fictionalized but realistic account of how it might go for you. Try this on for size and decide whether you could see yourself doing this full-time.

The day starts out with a quick check of the equipment, a swipe or two with a squeegee on the dewy windshield , and a cup of coffee sloshing around in the cup holder of your truck as you head to your first job of the morning.

First stop is the Parsons place: They're retired; the old man is kind of crotchety but not a bad sort; Mrs. Parsons is pretty quiet; there's a friendly mutt dog that lollygags around in the back yard all day. You start in the front yard. The house is on a corner lot, with a higher than average number of dog deposits on the lawn, pine needles drop all over everything every week, and the old folks are particular about every needle getting picked up and hauled away instead of left as a mulch as it should be. The azaleas are always hungry and thirsty because of having to grow in the competitive environment under the greedy pine trees. You fertilize them, then mow the lawn, edge, and clean up the walks. You cut back the old spiraea where it's trying to take over the front walk, dump the clippings into your trash can, and take them out to the truck where they get deposited in the trailer you tow around behind you all day.

The Parsons' backyard is mostly paved. There's a swimming pool in the middle (the pool man takes care of that), some junipers along the back fence, a huge oak tree (the tree trimmer comes in every couple of years and does some pruning, you clean up after it the rest of the time), a stand of bamboo on the north (kind of a lame attempt at "going Japanese," from the 1950s most likely; the darn stuff's always trying to get into the flowerbeds), a beautiful view of the valley this time of the morning, a mockingbird on the telephone pole in the back corner. You do some pruning, chop at the bamboo runners to try to keep the yard from turning into a bamboo forest, you notice that the petunias are getting kind of dry and give them some water ("I sure wish these people would step outside once in a while and check on this stuff—I can't do everything!!"), pet the dog (who looks more like a tiny aging buffalo), hoe some weeds out of the beds, sweep. It's a pretty simple place and not too demanding other than that bamboo. You visit with the folks a bit, and say something tactful about the petunias, make a minor fuss over the dog in their presence (never forget showmanship), then head back to the truck. You lash down the mower and edger, tighten the cap on the gas can, and drive to the next job.

The Constantino family: Nice folks, though the kids are a bit much. (Nobody warned you about the weekly Big Wheels patrol?) Start with the back this time.

(No reason, that's just the way you like it, and who's to say different? Aah, self-employment!) The back lawn is huge, so you put in lots of mowing time here. These folks liked your idea of composting their yard waste, so you take the clippings over to the back corner behind the hedge and mix them with leaves and a layer of soil after turning the pile. You replant the bare spots in the ground cover from the flat you bought at the nursery yesterday and then water them in real well. You rotate the pots on the patio so they don't grow one-sided, then fertilize the lawn and program the sprinkler timer to come on for ten minutes to wash the fertilizer in. Next you move to the front, which is little more than a tiny strip of shrubbery, some perennials, and a brick walkway. The work is mostly cleanup here, except in the parkway, where you pull some weeds and water. The ferns have thrips again, so you spray, rinse out the sprayer, and then clean up the walks. You get out the pole saw and lop a couple of crossing branches out of the alder tree. Finally, you check on the sprinklers in the backyard, say goodbye to the client, and go to lunch.

So it goes in the afternoon, and tomorrow, and the next day. It's not a bad way to go, really. You get to smell the smells, watch the birds, get a little exercise. It's pretty bucolic and it sure beats an office job. Plus, when you're done, you get to admire your work. It feels good. Of course the specifics will be somewhat different depending on the climate where you work, but you get the general idea.

In the evenings you return phone calls, do the books, make any needed adjustments and repairs to your equipment. Saturdays you spend working on equipment, changing the oil in the truck, maybe doing a little extra work for someone. Sundays, if you're smart, are all yours. To make a living, you need to work fifty-plus hours a week, but it's a good life.

After a few years, maybe you decide you'd like to do more—get into commercial maintenance, add employees and vehicles, or perhaps build gardens instead of just maintaining them. These opportunities will come your way if you're good and if you take good care of your clients. They'll want you to do more for them, they'll tell their friends, and you'll find yourself in demand. Your success will come principally from word of mouth, the spread of your story from your happy clients to others.

You'll have to make some decisions along the way about how big you want to get, and in which direction you want to go. But whatever you do with your career, you will have made a good start by choosing to enter at the ground level. And if you stay at that level, there's no shame in that. Remember that in many cultures, the gardener is revered, because people understand the value of his or her work. To be an excellent gardener is a fine thing.

The Landscape Contractor

The landscape contractor is a builder who specializes in the construction of gardens and landscapes. The scope of the trade is very wide, from planting a few plants in Mrs. McGillicutty's backyard to heavy construction on a commercial site, such as an office building or a public park. The landscape contractor can be a one-person operation limited to small, specialty gardens or a giant corporation with hundreds of employees. At first you will probably be more interested in a small operation, but keep in mind that the typical landscape contractor will have at least two or three employees in order to be competitive.

The small landscape contracting business is easy to operate from your backyard. When your business gets bigger, you may want to move it elsewhere to avoid becoming a neighborhood nuisance, but at the start there's no problem with the simple, low-budget, home-based approach.

The work is physically and mentally difficult, much more demanding than maintenance gardening; the risks are greater (and so are the potential rewards); and a considerable amount of knowledge is required in order to be really good. Most states require that a landscape contractor be licensed. A state license is issued after a qualified applicant passes an exam, pays a fee, and posts a license bond.

Unlike the maintenance gardener, the landscape contractor moves from job to job and is always looking for work. (There are many ways to get jobs; I'll go over these in chapter 6.)

Many landscape contractors specialize in what's called "design/build," constructing gardens from their own designs. Others work from plans drawn by someone else. Each approach has its merits, and it's good to do both in the beginning.

Making the move from maintenance gardener to landscape contractor is jumping in with both feet. But unless you're very content with simplicity, you'll probably become bored with mowing and weeding at some point and yearn for the crazy life of a "real" landscaper.

Related and Supporting Fields

The complexity of landscaping has given birth to many specialties and subfields. Though most people begin with garden maintenance or general landscaping, you may have special interests. There are even specialties within specialties. For instance, the landscape contractor may specialize in water gardens or native plants or hardscape construction (walks, patios, retaining walls, and the like). Some people install and maintain food gardens. Others deal in pest management, irrigation repair, outdoor lighting, or spas. It's endless, really. Surely you'll find your own special thing to love.

To get you oriented, here's a brief introduction to some of the general categories of related fields. (Refer to chapter 8 for information on supporting trades and services, such as pathologists and civil engineers. See Appendix 1 for a list of resources.) We won't spend a lot of time on the details of these related fields, but if you find yourself drawn to one of them, there are plenty of other sources of available information. For example, your state probably has a nursery association that can help you if you want to start growing plants for a living, and an association for landscape contractors as well.

The Landscape Architect and Landscape Designer

The landscape architect is a licensed designer. Unlike the landscape contractor, who can design only private gardens that he or she then builds (called "design-build"), the landscape architect can design any type of landscaping from small gardens to large-scale urban projects, but isn't licensed to build anything. The scope of the work is broad and goes far beyond garden design.

The qualifications to become a landscape architect are stringent. If you think this is what you want to do right now rather than coming up through the ranks, look into some of the available university programs, because that's the fastest and easiest way to get the education you'll need. Look to the American Society of Landscape Architects (www.asla.org) to learn more.

There's another related profession called the *landscape designer*. The designer is usually not tested or licensed, and often takes on the work without formal training. Because of the lack of regulatory oversight, some landscape designers are very capable and others are not. In some states a landscape architect's license may not be required (to do a simple residential planting design, for example), but in others the unlicensed designer is operating illegally regardless of the scope of the work. Being a landscape designer is perfectly honorable as long as it's done with the requisite skills and professionalism and within the bounds of the law. Check with the Association of Professional Landscape Designers (www.apld.com) for detailed information on this field.

Many landscape architects and designers, even some fairly renowned ones, operate out of their homes. Because design doesn't require trucks and tools, it's easy to set up a studio/office at home. Clients visit landscape architects at times to go over plans, have meetings, and so forth; so the office needs to be accessible and attractive. It also needs to be legal, so be sure your local zoning ordinances permit visits by clients.

The Nurseryman

It seems that no one has come up with a gender-neutral term for nursery professionals, so we'll go along with "nurseryman," knowing that women are in no way excluded from this field. Nurserymen grow and sell plants. There are two basic categories of nursery operations: retail and wholesale. *Retail nurseries* you surely know about. Like any merchant, the retailer buys plants and supplies from wholesale growers (and, more rarely, grows plants on site) and sells them to the public. A *wholesale nursery*, also known as a *grower*, produces plants from seeds, cuttings, divisions, or tissue culture, grows them in containers or in the ground, and sells them to retail nurseries and to landscape contractors but usually not to the general public. Some wholesalers grow a wide variety of plants; others specialize in one thing, such as roses, perennials, trees, or ground covers.

Can you operate a nursery out of your home? Yes, as long as there are no community regulations against it. In fact many people make quite a nice little supplementary income from plants they grow in the backyard. There are a couple of strategies that could be very successful for you. If you offer planting as one of your services, a good approach is to grow the kinds of plants you commonly use on your jobs. You can usually produce them more cheaply than you can buy them, even from a wholesaler. Plus, they're always on hand when you need them. If you like to use certain plants that are hard to find or often out of stock, growing your own makes sense. Another approach is to grow specialty plants and sell them to other people at retail or wholesale prices. Most people who become involved in horticulture develop special affections for certain groups of plants. People go cuckoo over tuberous begonias or native plants or ornamental grasses or whatever. There's often a strong market for specialty plants, especially rare or choice varieties that the run-of-the-mill growers just don't handle.

If zoning laws permit it, you can sell directly to the public. Alternatively, you can wholesale your plants to retail nurseries or landscapers. The profit per square foot can be high, especially if you don't have any employees. And of course you're already paying for the land. Looking out the kitchen window and seeing rows of happy, thriving plants can make you feel rich.

The Pest Control Adviser and Operator

Managing pests and diseases is the specialty of the *pest control adviser* and the *pest control operator*, the first making recommendations for control and the second applying herbicides and pesticides and releasing beneficial insects. Progressive pest control people use biological and environmentally safe methods to minimize the application of dangerous chemicals. Pest control professionals are highly trained and licensed and often must take continuing education courses to retain their licenses.

Now, the idea of spending your days at the business end of a spray rig, squirting noxious chemicals onto rosebushes may not thrill you. But there's a whole new consciousness in pest and disease control that involves the use of beneficial insects, nontoxic and least-toxic sprays, and cultural methods that often achieve even better results than the traditional chemical approaches claim to deliver, minus the risks and negative impacts. This field, called *integrated pest management*, is really opening up, and there are opportunities to do a lot of good. It's a fascinating study of the interrelationships of plants, diseases, pests, and the environment. You'll never get bored, and you may get in on the ground floor of some exciting new research.

Operating a pest control business out of your home should be fairly easy, except that you probably won't be able to store the more toxic chemicals in a residential area. Check local regulations before you pursue this as a home-based business.

The Arborist and the Tree Trimmer

The *arborist* is a professional who is trained in the care of trees. An arborist can consult on and treat tree diseases and problems. Arborists are certified after taking an exam. If trees are your thing, look into this field. Check out the International Society of Arboriculture (www.isa-arbor.com) for career information.

Tree trimmers do just that: They prune and sometimes remove trees. The work is very physical and quite dangerous. If you love trees and are a daredevil type, consider tree work. You can start out with a couple of chainsaws, a truck, some ladders, and safety equipment. Later, you can graduate to large trucks, chippers, and other heavy equipment. For safety reasons, the crew size is usually at least two, so plan on becoming an instant employer. Licensing is required in some places, not in others. A lot of knowledge is required to do a good job in this fascinating field. You can easily operate a small tree-care business from home.

The Irrigation Contractor

Nowadays most professionally installed landscapes include irrigation systems, especially in arid climates. Many of these systems are complex, and their design, installation, and maintenance are often handled by specialists. The landscape contractor frequently handles this aspect of the job, but you may choose to focus on just this specialty. In some states, irrigation work is done under a different license than landscape contracting.

When you're getting started, consider doing irrigation repair and troubleshooting. The market is small but steady, because systems are always in need of repair. You can work for landscapers, gardeners, homeowners, or commercial or public clients. The best way to learn the trade is to go to work for someone else for at least a year. Licensing may or may not be required, and working out of your home is no problem. This is a nice business for the nuts-and-bolts type of person and is especially good if you don't want any employees right away, because you can do most things without help. Later, you may decide to move on to design and installation, which can get you into some pretty ambitious projects.

Do You Have What It Takes?

People are always saying to me, "It must be so much fun to be in your business!" Well, yes, it often is. More than fun, it's deeply satisfying in a lot of ways. But there's another side to it: Long hours, work that is sometimes brutally hard, emotional stress, enormous risks, and not necessarily a lot of money. Tiptoeing through the tulips it ain't. But still, it's good enough to have kept me and a whole lot of other people going.

So, how do you manage the stress and strain? The best way is to be the type of person to whom this lifestyle comes naturally. There are some qualities I believe you must have if you're going to be successful and happy in this business. Take this quick quiz and see if you've got what it takes.

1. *Are you emotionally stable?* If you're depressive, excitable, or unpredictable, you'd better take up something else. You're not going to hold up under fire. Inner calm will make you more effective and happier.
2. *Do you have abundant energy?* Not just the occasional burst of steam, but the ability to forge ahead hour after hour and day after day, working steadily and quickly. It takes plenty of physical, mental, and spiritual energy.
3. *Are you a self-starter?* There's no boss to watch over you, so you can get away with goofing off for a while, but it'll catch up to you. Being self-motivated is especially important when you work out of your home, because it's so much easier to snooze away the workday.
4. *Can you handle complexity?* How many things can you keep in your mind? It had better be lots, because even if you write things down all day long (which you should), you still need a good memory. Having so many balls in the air can be thrilling or terrifying. If juggling multiple responsibilities isn't your thing, you'll be in trouble.

5. *Can you think on your feet?* All day long, people will be asking you questions, making you offers, and coming to you with problems. Many's the time your success will depend on the quick right answer.
6. *Are you a good listener?* Your business depends on your ability to meet people's needs, and that means really hearing them. It also depends on the accuracy of your understanding of everything that's going on with your jobs, clients, employees, suppliers, and all the rest. You have to be able to process and store incoming information.
7. *Are you a team player?* Many misguided people approach business as though it were war. The truly successful businessperson recognizes the existence of common goals and works with the other participants (clients, employees, suppliers, subcontractors, architects, everyone) to achieve these goals.
8. *Are you independent?* An apparent paradox—team player and independent both? Yes. You'll be making your own way in the world with no one to tell you what to do. Much of what you need to know can only come from experience. You've got to be willing and able to think for yourself.
9. *Do you have a positive attitude?* Landscaping is a wonderful thing. It brings beauty and joy to so many people. That's easy to forget when you're having a bad day. Enthusiasm is contagious, and the ability to communicate it will be one of your most powerful tools.
10. *Do you like people?* You must genuinely like people and get a kick out of dealing with them. Grouches and misanthropes need not apply.
11. *Do you have a sense of humor?* Like insanity, it's not absolutely necessary, but it sure helps.
12. *Are you physically fit?* You've got to be able to lift heavy things, swing a pick, dig holes all day, maybe climb around in trees. This isn't a desk job. If you're not fit when you start, you could injure yourself.

Well, how'd you do? I think you need to have answered "yes" to most of these questions. If you're lacking in some department, consider whether you'll be able to improve yourself fairly quickly. Starting any business is a big challenge and is guaranteed to result in a lot of personal growth. You don't have to be 100 percent right away, but you've got to believe in your ability to rise to the occasion.

Why Do You Want to Run Your Own Business?

My lifelong entrepreneurial instinct arose from an apparently inborn, very strong visceral reaction to the word "boss." I can't hear it, or even think it, without cringing. The idea of having an actual boss, someone "over" me who can tell me what to do and fire me if I don't do it, or even if I do, sends a surge of adrenalin into my system, making me want to flee to a distant, very very small island. What I mean to say is, "Ask me how I really feel about having a job." Let's just say that in my opinion the conventional working world leaves a lot to be desired. I'm trying to be polite about this.

Many people who have spent years in an impersonal, dog-eat-dog corporate situation or in government or any other large organization often yearn for self-employment. They're tired of feeling insignificant, like an ant or a blade of grass. They realize that no matter how good they are, most of the recognition (and most of the money) will probably go to someone else. They're tired of being pushed around and want to follow their own star. They're willing to risk failure. They want a great adventure.

If this sounds like you, you may be ready for the world of self-employment. But don't proceed based on negative feelings—you've got to love both horticulture and business. You're not getting away from something so much as getting into something. Remember that you'll probably work harder, earn less, and risk more. But the personal rewards will almost certainly be greater. If you did pretty well on the quiz and you're still reading, congratulations. You may have found your calling. So, let's look at one last aspect of your new adventure before we move on to the details of starting your business.

Making the Transition: Amateur to Professional

Puttering around in your own backyard is fun but isn't the same as being a professional. How do you go from hobby to career? How do you learn enough to be able to really call yourself a pro? Should you begin part time or take a deep breath and quit your day job to become a full-time landscaper? It will be helpful if you learn a bit about how to prepare for your new career and to see what some of the traditional pathways into landscaping are out there for you to take.

Landscaping is a fusion of many disciplines—horticulture, engineering, the life sciences, art and design, physical work, and business management. Chances are you've got a pretty good grasp of some parts and need help with others. Fortunately, there are a number of ways for you to improve yourself to the point where you'll feel comfortable about going into business. Let's look at some.

Real-World Experience

Many of the important things about landscaping can't be learned from books. Many people never go to school, yet they become very good at their craft. I think you'll find that some type of formal education (maybe just attending seminars) will be necessary at some point. Still, there's no substitute for working in the field.

You may want to start your career by working for somebody else for a year or two. That way you can see how other people do things; you'll lose your innocence and get a wider perspective. You may even want to work for a few different companies, possibly even in different segments of the business—a retail nursery, a landscape contractor, a gardener, or an irrigation supply house. It's best if you work for someone who's really good, so you learn how to do things right. Remember, though, that employers won't be too interested in training you beyond their needs, because one of their biggest fears is that a sharp employee will eventually go into competition with them, and of course that does indeed happen all the time. Expect to learn more by observation and action than by training.

Self-Study

Begin to read voraciously. Good books abound on the subjects of horticulture, landscaping, contracting, and business management. In addition to your local bookstore or library (don't forget the library at the local college or botanical garden), check out some of the sources of professional books listed in Appendix 1. Read these books and more as you find them.

The other important source of written information is trade and professional publications, many of which also are listed and described in Appendix 1. Don't forget popular gardening magazines. And of course the vast resources of the Internet, which I'll cover later, are indispensable.

Professional Training

Attend trade shows, seminars, classes, webinars, and lectures. Join your local botanical garden or garden club. Join your trade association, and take advantage of what they have to offer. Find out what other professionals in your area do to stay informed.

Schooling

Quite a number of colleges and universities offer degrees in landscape architecture, environmental horticulture, and related fields. Many junior colleges offer certificate programs and two-year associate degrees in horticulture, either of which is enough to get you going. Some of the classes are even held in the evenings and on weekends for the convenience of those who can't yet give up their day jobs. Others are offered online so that you can complete your studies on your own schedule, choosing your school without regard to location.

Many adult education and similar programs offer short courses in various aspects of horticulture, taught by professionals or retirees. Botanical gardens and similar institutions also have informal, non-degree classes. In addition to useful course content, these classes will help you get to know other members of the professional community.

Here's what a couple of typical community college horticulture curricula might look like:

Certificate Program

This is usually a one-year program and is a good starting point if you're not ready or able to commit to a more ambitious course of study. It will give you a decent grounding in the basics, put you in touch with professionals in your community, and help prepare you for self-employment or a period of apprenticeship with an established company before you strike out on your own. A certificate program by itself won't make you an expert, but it's a great way to get started. Here's a typical array of courses included in the certificate program:

1. *Plant Identification and Culture:* How to identify and grow commonly used landscape plants. Approximately two hundred species of trees, shrubs, perennials, vines, and so on. (2 hours lecture, 3 hours lab and field study per week)
2. *Soils and Fertilizers:* Soil and plant nutrition basics. Properties of soil, kinds and uses of fertilizers, soil and nutrient requirements of landscape plants. (2 hours lecture, 3 hours lab per week)
3. *Irrigation:* Design, installation, and maintenance of drip and sprinkler irrigation systems and related topics. Kinds and uses of equipment. Basic irrigation hydraulics. System engineering and installation. Water conservation and management. (2 hours lecture, 3 hours lab and field study per week)
4. *Landscape Design:* Basic design principles, hardscape design and engineering, planting design, site evaluation. (2 hours lecture, 3 hours lab per week)
5. *Landscape Construction:* Tools and techniques for planting, hardscape installation, and irrigation. Safety. Bidding landscaping jobs. Basic carpentry, concrete, and masonry work, electrical, plumbing, and drainage. (2 hours lecture, 3 hours lab and field study per week)
6. *Landscape Maintenance:* Pruning, pest control, fertilizing, water management. Irrigation system maintenance. Equipment care. Safety. Bidding maintenance jobs. (2 hours lecture, 3 hours lab and field study per week)

7. *Greenhouse and Nursery Operations:* Introduction to wholesale and retail nursery growing operations. Techniques of plant propagation. Greenhouse and nursery structures. (2 hours lecture, 3 hours lab and field study per week)
8. *Landscape Drafting:* Measuring the site, preparing a base sheet, conceptual and working drawings, construction detail drawings. Irrigation and drainage plans. (2 hours lecture, 3 hours lab and field study per week)
9. *Work Experience:* Supervised on-the-job experience working for a private company or doing community volunteer work. Work experience is done concurrently with classroom and lab work. (225 hours during the one-year program)

Degree Program

To earn an associate in science (AS) degree, you need to complete the certificate just described and then spend a second year taking elective courses after choosing an area of emphasis. Electives include general education classes such as psychology, accounting, English, art, marketing, and management, as well as in-depth classes related directly to the selected emphasis. These areas of emphasis typically include:

1. Landscape Contracting
2. Landscape Design
3. Landscape Maintenance
4. Nursery and Greenhouse Technologies
5. Regenerative and Restoration Horticulture

Both degree and certificate programs will usually apply toward higher education at state colleges and universities. If you're interested in pursuing a bachelor's or higher degree, check with the counselor or instructors for transfer requirements.

Business Education

Don't forget that you'll also need to learn the business aspects of your career. The basics of small business are the same no matter what your chosen field. Fortunately, there are many resources for getting up to speed. Many community colleges offer night courses in small business management with classes in financial management, computers, advertising and marketing, and other general aspects of business. Adult education programs, university extension programs, private business schools, and other institutions offer similar programs.

Short courses and workshops are common in most communities. Don't forget online courses and webinars and of course books and websites that you can study on your own. Banks, insurance companies, and large accounting firms often hold seminars and produce written material that is helpful to the small business owner. The Small Business Administration (SBA; www.sba.gov), a federal agency, produces dozens of booklets and online materials for business owners and also offers free one-on-one counseling with retired businesspeople through a program called SCORE (Service Corps Of Retired Executives; www.score.org). The SBA has 900 "Small Business Development Centers" nationwide, offering free face-to-face help from business professionals as well as lots of resources. They also offer counseling online and by email, also at no charge. SBA also operates an online "classroom" that provides in-depth training courses at no charge.

There are also programs and information geared specifically to the horticultural industry or to the construction industry. Check with your trade association, local builders' groups, and the local chamber of commerce for more information.

Really, there's a ton of information out there, and it seems the more you look, the more you find. You need to avail yourself of some of it, because nobody is born knowing how to run a business, and it's not an easy thing to do. Most business failures are due to bad management, not lack of business. Probably the biggest weakness of small business owners is that they focus exclusively on their craft or profession, because they love it first and foremost, and ignore their business. That's deadly. Don't be the next fool. Learn business and learn it well.

Does It Ever End?

You'll never really "learn" this business. It's complex and it changes all the time. I still spend ten to twenty hours a week studying, reading journals and trade publications, and attending classes. Plan on being a student for the rest of your life. That's one of the greatest joys of horticulture. In twenty years or so, you'll start to get pretty good.

Part Time or Full Time?

Jumping in with both feet can be pretty scary. Maybe you're thinking about starting out part time, and that's OK. Get some Saturday gardening jobs to see if you like it; if you don't, it'll be pretty easy to back out. You can keep your investment in tools and equipment to a minimum at first, perhaps borrowing some things from the family or buying used tools at garage sales. Sometimes you can use your clients' tools, but I regard that as somewhat unprofessional. (Besides, what if you break something?)

If you do start out part time, I'd suggest you be up front with clients. Tell them you're just beginning rather than acting like an old hand. Show them you can be trusted with their valuable landscaping, but don't try to be something you're not. They'll like you that much more for your honesty.

Get two or three jobs for variety. Stick to garden maintenance at first, because the complex demands of landscaping will overwhelm you. Besides, it's pretty hard to tackle a landscaping project if you're only working Saturdays. Another strategy would be to help out a gardener with his or her route part time.

02 Getting Started

Start Up or Buy?

Compared with most businesses, getting into landscaping is a snap. There's no store to rent, no fixtures to install, no inventory, no fancy corporate offices, often not even any employees. Just borrow some money from the folks, buy an old truck, throw the family lawn mower into the back, and off you go. Because of this, most people choose to start their own business rather than buy an established business, but sometimes buying a going concern can be a wise choice.

Starting from Scratch

The advantages of starting from scratch are many. You can design everything the way you want, from the letterhead to the tool shed to the public image of your business. You don't have the sins of the previous owner to account for, or that owner's debts. You get to do things your way. I started from scratch, and I've never regretted it.

But starting from scratch isn't for everybody. You'll make a lot of mistakes, and any one of them could be fatal. It's a little like the legendary explorer John Wesley Powell canoeing down the Grand Canyon for the first time with no idea of what was ahead and only one arm with which to paddle. He made it, but what a ride! Not only will you have to build a clientele from scratch, but compared with buying a business, you'll also probably spend more on advertising and work harder to convince people your new company is as good as the one they've been dealing with for years.

Buying a Going Business

If you can afford it, buying a healthy, well-respected business might be just the thing for you, especially if your horticultural or business experience is limited. People have many reasons for selling their businesses, and not every sale comes with the rattle of skeletons in the closet. When you buy, you step quietly into the driver's seat. You take advantage of the reputation, the client list, and the momentum of a going concern. You purchase a billing system, tools and equipment, an advertising program, the whole works. And you usually get a mentor for a while, the seller, who has years of experience to pass along to you.

However, if you fail to thoroughly investigate the background of your potential business purchase, you may be buying disaster. When you buy a business, you buy the liabilities as well as the assets, and the seller may be working overtime to conceal some of these. The worst nightmare is finding out you suddenly have a few lawsuits on your hands, but there are plenty of other things that can be wrong. Has the seller cooked the books to falsify profits? Is the equipment in good shape, or does it just look that way? Are there disgruntled employees? How many of the people on the customer list are truly happy, and how many are fed up and ready to go elsewhere? Is the owner planning to open up again down the street, taking the established clients along? Are there unpaid bills? Taxes? Well, don't buy any business without a full audit from a certified public accountant ("CPA") and a darn good attorney to look everything over. Remember, too, that paying for your new business is going to cost you plenty; some up front and the rest in regular payments for many years. A good business is worth it; a bad one is not.

Maintenance routes are often for sale, sometimes at bargain prices. In some cases you buy just a list of weekly mowing or gardening clients. If the price is right, this can be a good deal, but consider the cost of developing the same dollar amount of business on your own. Make sure the jobs are bid at realistic prices, and the clients are happy. Buying a good route can be a way to get up and running fast. Often this type of sale is advertised informally—ask around at your suppliers, nurseries, and so forth. (*Tip:* Be sure the route is being sold only to you, not to six other gardeners as well. What a shock when they all show up on the job! This happened to someone I know.)

Working Out of Your Home

I've been in business for over forty-four years, and I've always worked out of my home, even when I had several crews and an office manager. I love it and hope I'll never have to have an office downtown. Now, this would sound crazy to a lot of people who, perhaps mostly for ego reasons, lust after a fancy location in a prestigious office building on Main Street. To each his own, but I like to work from home.

Consider all the good things about working from home: The best one is the short, usually peaceful commute to work. A close second is the opportunity to raid the fridge at any time. It's easier to set your own hours and maybe spend more time with your family. And it's really cheap because your overhead is so low, an especially important factor if business slows down. You can even deduct part of your house expenses as a cost of doing business, perfectly legally (more information on this later in the chapter). The idea of journeying downtown to the office every day like most poor suckers do gives me the willies. I just stumble in to the converted garage (aka World Headquarters), often wearing my funkiest clothes, usually not awake enough to drive, and I get right to work. The time savings alone adds an extra hour to my day. It's the greatest.

Disadvantages? Of course there are some. The biggest potential problem is that the zoning ordinances of your community may prohibit you from running a small business from your home or may limit the kinds of activities you are allowed to engage in. If you're planning to have twenty laborers show up every morning at 7:00, load tractors and mowers and equipment into a bunch of trucks, and then hang out in the backyard and drink coffee for half an hour before they noisily depart in a blue cloud of exhaust, you'd better think twice. That kind of activity is not only inconsiderate of the neighbors, it's probably illegal in a purely residential neighborhood. The same may be true if you're planning to open a retail nursery in the front yard.

Many communities do permit a small home office, providing you don't engage in odious behavior. (You may eventually need to rent a storage yard for your trucks and equipment and have your workers show up there, not at your house.) So before you go any further, get a copy of the local regulations from city hall or the county offices (or from their website), and be sure you can comply with them. Now's the time to find out, not later when you're kicked off your own property, maybe with the local newspaper reporter on the scene. By the way, if you're renting, check with the landlord, too.

There are some other problems with operating out of your home. One of the worst is that you can never get away from your job. Sure, go ahead and close the door; see how much good that does you. You'll still hear the phone ringing, and the stack of unfinished paperwork will cry loudly through the thin walls. You eventually grow used to this, though. If you have kids, it's not easy to make them understand that you're working. That's also true of friends who plop down in the chair next to your desk and proceed to visit, as if you had nothing better to do. After all, you're home, right? I finally made a sign that says, "WORK IN PROGRESS. PLEASE DO NOT DISTURB." It might be offensive to some of my visitors, but it usually does the job. I also suggest you keep regular office hours. It'll be easier on you and everyone else.

Some types of businesses could never operate from a home, but because gardeners and landscapers do business this way more often than not, it's seen by the public as an acceptable approach and shouldn't hurt your image. Eventually, people will figure out where you live, so you'd better landscape your place pretty nicely and keep it spotlessly maintained, at least the part everyone can see. This brings up a final point: Somewhere you've got to have a mess—trucks, equipment, soil amendments, plants that haven't made it to the job yet, leftover materials. If this mess is in your backyard, you'll have to look at it every day, even on your days off. Take a look at your yard and make sure it will accommodate your needs.

Tools and Equipment

You'll need two basic kinds of equipment: the tools of your trade and the tools of the office. Fortunately, you can start out simply and expand as needed.

One important rule for all purchases: Always buy the absolute best quality of everything: Nothing fancy, just solid good stuff that will perform well and last for a long time. I've never regretted buying a first-rate tool, but many times I've kicked myself for buying a so-called bargain. Remember that you'll be using your tools every day under severe conditions. They need to be more durable than if you were going to haul them out of the garage only once every few weeks for an hour's use in your backyard. Buy industrial-rated tools and equipment at places where the pros shop.

The standard array of tools and equipment will vary, depending on the kind of work you do and, to a minor degree, on where you live. You'll need certain basic "starter" tools right away.

Gardener's Tools

A maintenance gardener working alone or with a helper will need the following tools:

Cutting tools: Pruning shears and holster, loppers (for big branches), a folding pruning saw, a pole pruner (for trees and tall shrubs), hedge trimmers, a large pruning saw, a small chainsaw, perhaps a machete and sheath.

Cleanup tools: Leaf rakes, bow rakes, a push broom, a utility broom, a blower. (However, blowers are not popular with customers because they make noise and pollute. Get brownie points for doing without if you can.)

Lawn-care tools: A rotary mower for cool-season lawns, a reel mower for warm-season lawns (where applicable), some kind of edger (most often a string trimmer, which serves many other functions), grass shears. There's a huge and legitimate backlash against gas-powered garden machinery. Consider swearing off the power equipment and sticking to hand tools when you can. Clients will love you for having respect for the environment and for their peace and quiet.

Digging tools: Square- and round-point shovels (avoid the short-handled kind; they're too hard on the back), a spade, a scoop shovel, a cultivating fork, a trowel, a mattock (the head has a pick on one side, a digger on the other) or pulaski (an axe/digger combination), a snow shovel in cold climates.

Hauling tools: A contractor's wheelbarrow, a garden cart, a heavy-duty hand truck, a couple of trash cans or plastic tarps, a brush hook, a manure fork.

Fertilizing equipment: A drop spreader, a small hand-held crank spreader.

Pest control equipment: A tank sprayer, a backpack sprayer, a dust applicator, a couple of gopher or mole traps.

Weeding tools: You'll want various kinds of hoes (including an "action" hoe and a heavy-duty eye hoe), an asparagus knife, possibly a flame weeder, and whatever other weeding implements you like (it seems like every gardener has a personal preference).

Watering equipment: Heavy-duty 5/8-inch hoses (the rubber ones don't kink and last longer in heavy use), a pistol-type hose nozzle, a couple of soaker hoses, a hose-end sprinkler or two, a watering can.

Some special things: A soil sampler tube, a gas can, oil, a big tarp for covering loads of brush, at least 100 feet of heavy manila rope, some bungee cords, a couple of 50-foot extension cords, and a box of rags.

For climbing: An 8-foot tripod ladder; it's much steadier on uneven ground than the regular four-legged kind. A regular four-legged ladder if you work on paved surfaces.

Equipment for safety and comfort: Knee pads, leather gloves, rubber gloves, rain gear, rubber boots, steel-toed boots, goggles, a face shield, ear protection, a dust mask, spray coveralls, a respirator, a first-aid kit, a giant-sized bottle of sun block, insect repellent, poison oak/ivy protection, a safety vest, and a wide-brimmed hat.

Maintenance tools: A socket set, wrenches, screwdrivers, a grinding wheel, a sharpening stone, a couple of files, a cordless drill with accessories.

Identify your tools with a band of spray paint, by engraving your name into them, or in some other way to avoid taking home a client's favorite shovel.

Keep spare parts on hand. All it takes is the failure of some little doohinkus on your lawn mower to put you out of work and behind schedule. Carry extra doohinkuses in your truck.

Vehicles for Maintenance

Naturally, you have to put all this equipment in some kind of truck. Some gardeners use bare-bones "chassis cab" trucks outfitted with flatbeds; they're a lot more versatile than a regular pickup because they can handle more kinds of payloads and are easier to load and unload. Until recently, it was possible to order a relatively fuel-efficient mini-pickup with a custom flatbed, but manufacturers aren't doing that much anymore. Fortunately, gas mileage for all trucks has improved considerably in the past few years, so size doesn't matter as much as it used to. Lots of maintenance outfits are switching over to enclosed vans, which protect the contents better against weather and theft. You won't need anything super heavy duty for gardening, but think ahead to the day when you'll be asked to haul a load of soil or some railroad ties or tow a trailer. Your truck doesn't have to be new. Most people expect you to show up in something a little work-worn, so a used vehicle is OK as long as it doesn't look too sketchy. Just keep it in good running condition, because if it breaks down, you don't work and your clients aren't happy.

Whatever you buy, outfit it with high, solid sideboards for hauling trash and mulch, and with some sort of system for storing your tools and equipment. A row of PVC pipes strapped vertically to the backboard can accommodate the long-handled tools; you might put the smaller stuff in a couple of ready-made boxes along the sides or underneath the bed if you have a flatbed truck. There are some great ready-made tool racks available these days for very little money. For dump runs, you'll need a large, heavy tarp and about 100 feet of 3/8-inch manila rope or a couple of tie-down straps. It's also nice to have a pair of ramps for loading and unloading mowers; try a couple of Douglas-fir 2-by-12s for starters and graduate to the ready-mode steel or aluminum kind later.

Whew! That's a lot of gear. Not counting the truck, all these tools and trappings should set you back around $7,000 to $9,000 if bought new. A few weekends spent snooping around garage sales and swap meets can save you a lot of money. You could also try putting the whole purchase out to bid, assuming you have the money to buy it all at one time.

Landscaper's Tools

Landscaping work requires most of the gardener's equipment (except for the lawn-care and pest control things), plus some specialized equipment. Much of the landscaper's work involves heavy digging, grading, and planting. Now, don't go out and buy a tractor. I know you want to, but in over forty years I've never needed to own a tractor; few small companies really do. That's what rental yards are for. Why tie up so much capital in equipment you'll probably only rarely use?

The same goes for trenchers, sod-cutting machines, and even rototillers. Until you've got a bigger business and more work, just rent what you need. Don't get in over your head.

You will need a lot of hand tools, though. Here's a basic rundown:

Digging tools: A digging bar, shovels and spades, a mattock or pulaski, a railroad pick, and a hand-operated posthole digger should get you through most excavating work. For larger jobs, rent the equipment you need or hire out the tractor work, especially if you're not too good with operating heavy equipment.

Hand grading tools: A bow rake, a wide aluminum or wood grading rake, a spring rake, a flat shovel.

For moving materials: Invest in a sturdy 5-cubic-foot-capacity steel contractor's wheelbarrow. It's also great for mixing small amounts of concrete and makes a pretty comfortable easy chair at lunch. A big aluminum or plastic scoop shovel will move mulch or other lightweight materials much faster than a regular shovel. A five-tine pitchfork is great for loading mulch.

Other earth-oriented tools: You can use a lawn roller for installing sod and for compacting loose paving materials. Use a hand tamper for compacting; rent a power tamper (also known as a "jumping jack") or a vibratory plate compactor for big jobs.

For beating on things: A sledgehammer (eight to ten pounds), a single jack (fancy name for a small sledgehammer), and a stake driver for tree stakes.

Measuring: A sighting level or transit is used to measure elevations, set grades, and level things; the new laser levels are amazing and not all that expensive. You'll need two tape measures—a 100-foot fiberglass one and a 30-foot-long-by-1-inch-wide steel one. A measuring wheel is great for estimating and rough measuring.

For marking things: Invest in a marking paint applicator or a chalk wheel (to lay out beds, paving, and other proposed improvements), some pin flags in different colors (to identify the location of sprinkler heads and to flag planting locations, among many uses), and a few rolls of flagging tape (to flag plants that need to be pruned or removed).

For carpentry and other kinds of construction: You'll need (just for starters) some basic carpenter's tools—claw and framing hammers, a level, a square, a plumb bob, a chalk line, a roll of mason's twine, handsaws, a worm-drive power saw with carbide blades, masonry blades, and steel-cutting blades, a cordless circular saw, a heavy-duty half-inch drill motor and bits, and a small battery-operated drill. Don't go for lightweight power tools because they won't do the job and they won't last.

Irrigation work: Begin with pipe shears, a hacksaw, large and small groove-joint pliers, pipe wrenches (12-inch or 24-inch or one of each), a tubing cutter, a plumber's torch.

The inevitable miscellany: Tin snips, pry bars, vise-grip pliers, bolt and rebar cutters (24-inch minimum), and maybe a come-along.

The price of all this? About $8,000 to $10,000 new, much less if you buy it used.

Vehicles for Landscaping

Your first truck should be a heavy-duty one (one-ton rated), preferably a flatbed with solid plywood sideboards at least 2 feet tall. Later, you can graduate to two trucks: a little pickup for errands and estimating and a big flatbed for heavy hauling. You might even consider a small electric or hybrid car (or even a bicycle) for times when you don't need a truck. It'll save you on operating costs and clients will love your progressive attitude. Under-the-bed toolboxes are great, but you may want at least one box mounted on the bed as well. An absolute necessity is a heavy-duty overhead rack, because you'll almost always have some lumber or a couple sticks of pipe on board. A pipe vise mounted on the back is a good idea too—one clever contractor mounted his on a removable trailer hitch that could be stored out of the way when not in use. But don't get carried away with nifty truck accessories, because you'll often need the whole bed free to haul plants, soil amendments, and materials. If you can afford it, have a dumping mechanism installed; it saves you years of shoveling.

Storage Facilities

Now you know that you'll soon be the owner of a lot of cumbersome, valuable, and not very pretty (by the standards of the rest of the world) equipment. Where does it go at night? When I started, I had to park on the street, tools stashed in the back and cab of the old Ford. One Christmas night someone broke in and stole everything. I had no insurance against theft, and so it cost me $2,500 in 1973 prices just to go to work the next day. That was more money than I had, and it took a long time to recover. That's learning about security the hard way. If possible, get a shed or make some space in the garage, put some tool racks on the wall, find a place out back, do *something* to protect your equipment. It's not just security that's a consideration; the better organized you are, the easier and more productive your work will be. Plus, your tools will last longer if they're out of the weather.

Equipment Maintenance

For many years I spent evenings and Sundays in the shop sharpening mower blades, cleaning sprayers, and doing brake jobs on trucks. You probably will too, so if you're not mechanically inclined, you'll be at a disadvantage. Taking everything to the mechanic or dealer is just too costly for the average start-up company; letting it fall apart is foolish. So, learn how to keep things clean, safe and reliable and then do it. When something's too much for your abilities, take it to a pro.

Setting Up the Office

You'll be spending a lot of time out in the field, but not all of it. There's usually a good-sized heap of paperwork and phone calls awaiting you at what rightfully should be the end of the workday. You'll need a comfortable, efficient work space; nothing fancy, just good basic furniture and equipment. Working off the dining-room table is no fun.

First, locate a spot to call "The Office." The IRS wants you to put your office in a separate room or space that's used only for business. If you fail to do this, it may deny all your deductions for a home office. It also has to be your principal place of business. Check with your accountant for specifics on this important issue, because regulations change frequently.

Aside from tax implications, the home office needs to meet some other requirements. Not the least of these is peacefulness. Preparing bids, billing, and organizing jobs is mentally demanding. If there's the hubbub of kids and street noise and people running in and out, you'll risk disaster by inserting an extra zero somewhere. Peace and quiet also helps your image when you're on the phone. Did you ever try to converse with someone who sounds like they're calling from a bar or the playground of an elementary school at lunchtime? How unprofessional! So pick a quiet room. It helps if there's a door leading directly outside, especially when employees or clients need to see you. I used to march everyone through the whole house to my little office, and it was often kind of embarrassing and didn't make a good impression I'm sure. If you don't have a perfect room, how about using a corner of the garage or a shed out back?

Now to the office contents. Get a big desk. I'd say it's impossible to have a desk that's too big. Mine's a 3 ½-foot-wide hollow-core door set on two 2-drawer file cabinets. I made it in a couple of hours back in 1979 for about fifty bucks including file cabinets, and it's still going strong. When I die, they'll probably carry my body out on it ("Oh, the poor fellow, he was so devoted to his work that he died sitting at his desk . . ."). Naturally, it's always covered with stuff, except for a 2-square-foot space directly in front of me.

You'll need a phone. Phone technology has changed over the years, and today many small business people use just their cell phones so that they remain in touch all the time and save on the cost of a landline. That really makes sense, but of course you may want to invest in a conventional phone and landline to have a backup. You can have your calls forwarded to your cell phone. Virtually any modern phone has lots of features, including voice mail to take messages. Now, if they'd only invent one that *returned* the calls for you! The best phone gadget of all is a headset. You'll feel foolish wearing it at first, but boy, does it ever save your neck! Finally, you'll need a book of telephone message forms, the kind that keeps a carbon copy permanently bound in a spiral binding. Why? First, if you lose the original message, you can always look it up on the copy. Second, if there's a question you can look back and refresh your memory about who called. I do this all the time. Finally, you'll have legal documentation in case of a dispute.

Even though computers do much work that was once done by other means, some of the old-fashioned tools still make sense to have. One of those is a calculator, to be used for the many small tasks a computer would be clumsy at. A desk calculator is better than a pocket one for various reasons. Speed is one, having a printed tape is another, ease of operation is a third. Try to get one with a mark-up/mark-down key for bidding.

My desk doesn't have much on it these days. The computer has taken the place of the old fax machine, the datebook, the calendar, and assorted other things that were formerly essential. What it hasn't done is get rid of the messy heap of papers and books and other junk that I can never seem to get under control. But I suppose I have only myself to blame for that.

What about Computers?

Computers are essential in today's business world. They're great at repetitive chores; they never forget anything, and they can zoom through lots of jobs that you could never accomplish any other way. For example, suppose you were preparing a special advertising mailer and wanted to find all your clients living in a certain zip code who did more than $2,000 in business with you last year, always paid their bills on time, and have lawns larger than 5,000 square feet. If you were to rely on a manual search of your old-fashioned paper records, you could be at it for hours. With a computer, it's a simple matter of telling it what you want and waiting a few seconds for the results.

On the other hand, computers are a pain. You'll spend many hours learning to use even the most user-friendly computer and software. Then you have to enter all that data, which takes more hours, and maintain the system, which will demand at least a couple of hours a month—more if you wisely do regular backups to avoid losing everything in a crash (and personally I don't entirely trust the "cloud" and so I use on-site backups as a backup to my backup).

Still, you'll gain more than you lose, and besides, computers are more fun than paper. These days, computers can handle everything except making the coffee in the morning. Here are some of the things a computer can do for you:

- *Database:* A database of your clients, coupled with a system of forms, can automate your entire flow of paperwork, from the first contact with the client to the final bill. Your ability to respond to (and therefore please) your clients will increase markedly with this in place.
- *Bidding:* Computerized bidding is faster, easier, and more accurate. You can plug your numbers into a spreadsheet or estimating software and play "what-if" until you get the bid just right. Computer bidding can improve your competitiveness, responsiveness, and profitability.
- *Promotion and presentation:* Documents produced on the computer look worlds better than hand-written ones. Because you don't have much to impress potential clients with (no fancy store or zippy corporate image), your bids, promotional literature, and other handouts are your best chance at convincing them that you're an OK person. Put something together on the computer—perhaps using a pre-designed template that comes with the software—print it on some really classy paper, hand it to them in a nice folder, and wow! Or go paperless and send them your snazzy docs via email. For people who don't have a graphics background, it's easy to find a template in most word processing and page layout applications that you can simply fill in with your own information and get something that looks as good as if you had spent a couple thousand dollars on custom design. And today's automated print shops, making their services available online, can deliver first-class full-color brochures, business cards, and other sales materials for a fraction of what printing used to cost. (*Tip:* Don't be a spammer, sending out mass emails to recipients who have not agreed to hear from you from time to time. It will get you in trouble with your email host, and it's just rude. It may be illegal too; look up "CAN-SPAM Act" for details. What you can do is send emails to people with whom you have come into contact and who would appreciate knowing what you offer. Do this through an online service, which costs a pittance and protects you against claims of abuse from your host.)
- *Bookkeeping and taxes:* Use a spreadsheet to automate your single-entry system or, better yet, buy off-the-shelf software that will do your estimates, billing, ledgers, accounts payable and receivable, profit-and-loss

statements, and a lot more. It'll write the checks, post them, and spit out reports all day long. You'll love it at tax time because all your bookkeeping will be ready to take to your accountant. Keep in mind that your bookkeeping needs might be minimal in the first year or two of your startup, and you could probably get by with an old-fashioned paper-based system. I used the Dome system for many years until my business got too big for it and I realized that it was time to go digital. But you know, these days I can't see any reason not to start out with a computer-based bookkeeping system, since you'll need it soon enough anyway.

- *Communications:* You can send and receive documents of all kinds, communicate via email, and surf the Internet. You can keep track of the weather, the news, and the landscaping industry. Start a blog to keep clients and others informed of company news and special offers. Use social networking sites to promote your business far and wide.
- *Drafting:* Nearly all designers use CAD (Computer-Aided Design) to draw their plans. And not just bird's-eye view plot plans but astoundingly realistic 3-D images, and even mature landscapes superimposed on before-photos of the client's property, showing how it will look when the work is done. Can you imagine how compelling that can be as a sales tool for you? CAD takes time to learn how to use, but there are entry-level systems that are easy to learn, don't cost much, and are more than adequate for your needs as a small company. You don't need an expensive plotter to print your designs; just email the completed files to your local blueprint shop and they'll deliver perfect hard copies for very little money.
- *Using the Internet:* The Internet offers a galaxy of online resources for the gardener, landscaper, and small business owner that is almost overwhelming, and there are many websites of quality and value waiting for you. You can tap into the availability of plants at your favorite growers, get irrigation catalogs and design information from manufacturers, take courses on line, follow your competition by reading through their websites, network with colleagues about nearly any subject, set up a low-cost Internet-based phone network, open a merchant account for free so that you can take credit card payments, put your calendar and scheduling information on line for your staff to access, even set up a jobsite webcam and link it to a page for clients and others to monitor the progress of your work. And of course you should develop your own

company website (and a blog if you like to write) as soon as you possibly can; it's essential to most any business these days. You don't even need a web developer anymore, with the customizable templates available from several companies, many of them free if you set up shop with them as host. (That only scratches the surface. For more on the Internet, see the section below on software options and also visit Appendix 1.)

Windows or Mac . . . which computer platform should you commit to? Each has its fans and foes, and frankly either is OK. Windows machines are cheaper than Macs and there's more specialized software available. Macs are easier to use, better for graphics-based applications, and, well, sexier. (In case you're wondering, I'm a long-time Mac guy, having bought a Fat Mac in 1983 when they first came out, and I've never abandoned the Mac platform even though I have my gripes about it. And no, I don't get into a hissy fit if someone thinks Windows is better. It's just not that important. Neither is perfect, both will drive you nuts at times, and both are miracles of technology that will do a heck of a lot of your hard work for you. Just get what you like and can afford.)

Any software package that's specially tailored for a particular industry or application, such as a package just for landscape contractors, is called *vertical market software*. The idea is that everything is all set up (computer geeks call it *turnkey*), and you can do everything you need to without much training. Theoretically it's written by people who understand your business and know what you need. Vertical market software is usually more expensive than off-the-shelf software. Examples of vertical market software for our industry include landscape design and imaging software, remote time-clocking for employees, satellite-based site measuring services (imagine!), equipment maintenance tracking systems, crew routing and scheduling programs, programs that track fertilizer and pesticide applications for each of your jobs, irrigation design packages, bidding programs, and job tracking and billing applications.

Do you need a vertical market system? Probably not. First, you're starting small, with relatively simple needs that can easily be met by a good off-the-shelf software package and a few hours of tinkering. You can set it up the way you want, not the way somebody thought you wanted. In fact, the way people do things in this business is so varied that I've never seen a vertical package that truly pleased very many people, though I am no expert on the subject and I could be doing a disservice to some great products. Finally, how do you know if this fancy vertical market hot rod actually works—or for that matter, if the little company (most of them are) that produced it will even be around in a year to answer your questions? Still, if you were to get started with a vertical market package, you wouldn't have to retool your entire operation later should you decide to change over. If you do go this route, find something that's been around for a while, preferably something a few other people use and like. Many of the larger companies have booths you can visit at trade shows, where you can get a walk-through of how the system works. Before you commit to anything, insist on a free demo so you can try it out at your own speed without some salesperson breathing down your neck.

You can buy a single, relatively inexpensive software package that includes a database, word-processing function, spreadsheet, and calendar application all rolled into one. In my opinion, an *off-the-shelf integrated package* beats the knickers off any other approach for the small businessperson. Have a look at a few integrated programs, try them out if possible, and see what you think. This may be the way to go for you.

How much should you plan to spend on a computer system? Advice on the cost of computers is usually obsolete before it's written down. The great news is, prices drop constantly. Computers and software get cheaper and better the longer you wait. Also, you can buy a good used system for practically nothing.

Hardware you'll need includes the following:

- *Computer:* A good basic computer, either Windows or Macintosh, with a 15 inch display for a laptop or at least a 21 or 24 inch display for a desktop, at least eight gigabytes of RAM (random-access memory), a 500 gigabyte hard drive, and at least a 2.0 GHz processor. Consider starting with a laptop, which will save space on your desk and allow you to take the machine with you wherever you go. You can pick up a good new machine that meets these specs for around $1,000. (This advice is also usually obsolete in a hurry. Buy whatever the current technology makes available at a reasonable price and don't go overboard, because your needs are really minimal compared to those of someone who does graphics or big-time number crunching.)
- *Tablet:* In addition to your computer, consider getting a tablet for field use. You'll be able to access much if not all of your data, and you get other benefits as well. I use my tablet in client meetings to go over plant photos, design ideas, and images of hardscape details. I can access my notes, calendar, and client database. (Of course I never use it to play games or waste my time on Facebook or anything like that!)
- *Printer:* Either an ink-jet or a laser printer are fine. Get one that prints in color so that you can produce eye-catching documents. Some of the newest generation multi-use machines work great and cost practically

nothing. My newest printer is also a fax machine (how quaint!), a scanner, and a full-featured copier that's pretty much the equal of one you'd find in a copy shop; I paid around $200 for it and couldn't be happier.

- *Wi-Fi router*: There's no longer any need to hard wire into your modem to connect with the outside world. A basic Wi-Fi router is dirt cheap and gives you the freedom to move around with your equipment.
- *DSL or cable modem:* This will usually be supplied by your Internet service provider, or purchased to their specifications, and will match their needs as well as yours. Be sure to get a modem that complies with the latest technology that your ISP provides, so that you get the fastest performance available.
- *Scanner:* You don't really need a scanner, but it sure is handy at times. Use a scanner to digitize most anything that's on paper, including forms, letters, images, and notes. That keeps your paper files on the skinny side and gives you access to all your records from wherever you are. Scanners are inexpensive and easy to use.
- *UPS:* No, not the friendly brown delivery trucks. A UPS is an "uninterruptible power supply" that keeps the system in operation if there's a power failure. Built in to a UPS is a surge protector that guards your equipment against damaging voltage spikes. It's a necessity with today's complex, delicate computers.
- *Backup options:* First of all, realize the importance of backing up your data. Sooner or later your hard drive will crash, and if your data is unrecoverable, as it often is, you'll feel SO good when you can simply reload it all from a backup. Remember, these aren't kitty pictures we're talking about; your data is the lifeblood of your business. I follow my computer consultant's advice—a belt-and-suspenders approach that combines an always-on automatic and continuous cloud backup that keeps an up-to-date copy of your data on an off-site computer (for a modest annual fee) paired with an on-site backup using a dedicated second hard drive that I update . . . well, not every day like I should but as regularly as I can. I keep my on-site hard drive in a fireproof file cabinet, but you would be even wiser to store it elsewhere. Since you will be working at home, taking it home is not helpful, but perhaps you could keep it at a friend's house. I know this sounds like a pain, and it is. But hey, you'll thank me when your system eventually poops out on you and you realize the value of all this.

Now we come to the software options. The world of software is vast and confusing. Here are some of the most helpful types of programs I've found and a little bit on how to make them work for you.

- *Integrated packages:* The integrated package combines software that's otherwise sold separately: a word-processing program, a database, a spreadsheet, a calendar program, perhaps some graphics or a presentation package. The price is less than buying the programs separately, and each module is linked to the others so that the programs function as a coordinated system. The degree of integration, ease of use, and versatility vary from product to product. Integrated software is a good first software purchase; in fact, it often comes bundled with a new computer. You'll set up a database for your clients, which will generate mailing labels, invoices, and other billing records. You'll use the word-processing function for contracts, form letters, and correspondence. The spreadsheet will handle your bidding. The calendar will keep your schedule organized. You can even generate fancy presentations for selling purposes.
- *Accounting:* For a relatively small investment, you can buy a program that will create estimates, translate them into purchase orders and then into invoices, and keep track of each transaction in accounts receivable. On the payables side, it will record bills from suppliers and subcontractors, automatically write checks, and keep track of your accounts payable, reminding you when to pay bills. At the same time, all this information is going (without any help from you) into your profit-and-loss statement, balance sheet, and year-end tax returns. The program will even keep track of payroll, and remind you when to make payroll tax deposits. Some programs will even interview you when first put into service and will then set themselves up with your needs in mind. This is incredible stuff and well worth having. There are a couple of important caveats, though. First, be sure that the program meets your needs. Talk to a couple of people who are using it in a similar business—another contractor, for example. See if any professional bookkeepers are using it and ask them what problems they've encountered. Be sure there aren't any limitations in the program that would make it unsuitable for you. Second, these programs have to be set up exactly right, especially the opening entries, and you'll need to spend some billable time with your accountant before you begin to use the system. Consider hiring an expert to set things up for you; it's a wise investment for most people. Finally, bookkeeping software requires discipline to use because every-

thing has to be done just so or you'll create more problems than you solve—but that's what bookkeeping is all about anyway. The bottom line is that a good bookkeeping program is a fantastic addition to your business. It will save you many hours of work, produce superior results, and keep your business on track.

- *Calendar/scheduling:* When I got rid of the dog-eared appointment book that I'd been carrying around forever and switched to a computer-based calendar, my life got instantly easier. Now, the computer reminds me when it's time to leave for appointments, pay bills, and make phone calls. It keeps things on my to-do list until I do them and puts the list in my face every morning so I can't escape my duties. It prioritizes my work so that I'm reminded to do the most important things first. It keeps a list of active clients and dials the phone for me when I want to call them. And of course your calendar will sync with your smart phone and other devices, making sure that the details of your life follow you wherever you go.
- *Project management:* If you get into big projects, or a lot of little ones, it's helpful to master plan your workload. You can do this on a chalkboard or a piece of paper, but project management software is a much better choice. You can compare the progress of your jobs with your projections, separate jobs into discrete tasks like "install deck" or "put in sprinkler system," or allocate people and equipment to specific jobs, and handle routing to make the best use of crews and equipment and save driving time and gas, to name a few of the tasks the computer can handle with ease. When circumstances change, the computer will effortlessly reshuffle everything for you.
- *Plant selection:* People have been trying for years to come up with a computer program that will allow you to enter, for example, soil type, sun or shade, and type of plant, and get back a list of suitable species. It's a great idea that could save a lot of work and generate much richer and more accurate plant lists than the usual process of going through books and lists. Unfortunately, nobody has really succeeded at this difficult task yet, at least to my satisfaction. Investigate some of the programs on the market, but don't expect truly professional-quality results, even from very costly programs aimed at professionals. As an alternative, consider the many plant and nursery websites, where you'll find all the information you need—cultural requirements, photos, availability, and more. Or

do a search using the name of the plant you're researching. Finally, keep a master list of your favorite plants in your word processing program, and use it to select plants for each project. Another great use of a computer is to develop a library of photos of the plants you use regularly, and then paste them into a document for each of your projects. I make a digital collage of photos with a page for each area of the property. This allows me to be sure the forms and colors work, and once I have the palette fine-tuned to my liking I'm able to share the information in a visual form with the client, either digitally or in print. This is so much better than just handing over a list of names that will usually baffle the average client and which offers no indication of how the project will look in the end. I love to watch clients' eyes light up when they see all the pretty pictures and ask, "My yard could look like THIS??"

- *CAD:* CAD stands for "Computer-Aided Design." With a CAD system, you can produce plans on the screen, change them easily, and print them out on a plotter or send them to the repro shop and they will deliver paper copies to you for very little money. CAD is not a time-saver; it takes just as long to do a set of plans on a computer as it does to do them by hand. But there are enough advantages to CAD to make it worthy of consideration for even a small company. First of all, the entire profession has pretty much switched from hand-drawn plans to CAD, and it's hard to even find supplies like drafting paper anymore. Everyone is accustomed to CAD-generated plans, and if you work with other design professionals they will expect you to be CAD-equipped. If you get into big projects, CAD will be a requirement, because your plans will have to be compatible with the other layers of plans such as utility plans, grading plans, and others. And even internally, you'll appreciate being able to make changes to your plans and print out a new set in a jiffy. There are numerous CAD products out there, some of which are aimed specifically at the landscaping business. Fully featured CAD packages cost thousands of dollars, but simpler systems are priced as low as a couple hundred dollars and they will be fine for your startup. Your best bet is to read the reviews online and then go to a landscaping trade show where you'll most likely find several competing systems available for you to sit down and try before you buy. You can also download demo packages for some of the programs. Don't invest in a costly, complex system, because the jobs you'll be getting at first will be small. If money is tight, avoid the whole CAD thing and draw your designs by hand; residential clients are perfectly happy with that.

- *Image processing:* Take a digital photo of your new job and upload the photo to the computer. Play with the image, adding trees, shrubs, a lawn, a patio, a deck, whatever, until you've got the garden of your client's dreams. You can buy software that makes this a breeze. Then print it on your color printer or show it to the client on your tablet or laptop. Impress the heck out of that client. Make more money. Show the garden at one year old and at five years old when the trees have grown. Image processing is catchy stuff and is sure to win points with clients. Expensive and time consuming? Somewhat. But if you're charging for it (which you should be), it's a profit center. You can also put the images on your company website, which can be a terrific sales tool for you.
- *Internet site development software:* These days, there's no excuse for you to not have a company website, even if you're "just" in the maintenance business. You can pay a web designer thousands of dollars to craft a sexy site for you, or you can use one of the free online systems or a software package to build your own website. Use your website as a showroom to display photos of your work and information about your business. Everyone looks to the Internet first when shopping for anything, and landscaping is no exception. Visit the websites of your competitors and I think you'll find that the best of them, at least in major urban areas, are pretty darn impressive. Developing your own website from scratch is a big undertaking, though these days you don't necessarily need to be an HTML expert to make it all work right. Today's web design software is easy to use and worth considering.
- *Desktop publishing:* Use a desktop publishing (DTP) program to put together newsletters, brochures, flyers, and other advertising. It's easy to make plain text come alive. Most DTP programs come with templates to help you do all this even if you have no eye for graphic design. Throw in some clip art, pictures of your jobs, or a stock photo from a disk and you've got a good-looking layout without spending big bucks on a graphic designer. Just be sure your results are professional looking, and take a short course in graphic design if you want to improve your skills in this area.
- *Miscellaneous business management software:* There's software that writes employee manuals and performs employee performance reviews, answers legal questions, develops business plans, solves marketing problems, even provides you with prepared business letters all ready

to go except for the name and address. For a modest investment, you can save yourself a lot of time and get better results than you can on your own.

- *Utilities and system enhancements:* These are workhorse programs that help your computer operate more efficiently, prevent problems, or expand its capabilities. Some examples are virus protection programs (a must if you're online, and who isn't?), memory managers (which help you get the most out of a limited amount of RAM), security programs (to keep snoopy people out of your files), disk managers (to keep your hard drive running clean), and screen savers (to prevent damage to the screen during periods when you're not using the computer, usually by having colorful sea life or flying toasters cavort about on the screen). Most new computers come bundled with a lot of this, and more is available free, as shareware, or for very little money.
- *Odds and ends:* How about getting a Spanish-language tutorial? Or maybe a translating program that will turn your English-language versions of employee manuals, notes, and instructions into Spanish? Lastly, get a game or two to fill those awkward inactive periods during the day and prevent you from being over-productive.

Finally, here are some relevant questions and answers regarding computer use in a home-based landscaping business.

Q: I don't plan on using the computer much at first—just a database of my clients, some billing, a few letters. What kind of system should I buy?

A: Consider an inexpensive used system. People are always upgrading, and their old stuff isn't worth much even though it usually works just fine for basic needs. A second-hand computer, printer, backup drive, and UPS could run you as little as a few hundred dollars. You can always upgrade when your needs change.

Q: I'm going to use the computer for drafting, presentations, layout of a newsletter, mailing lists, and bookkeeping. How much computer do I need?

A: Invest in a new system with the minimum capacity mentioned in the section above. Get a large-screen monitor, and an ink-jet or color laser printer. This system will cost between $2,000 and $4,000. To print out full-size landscape plans, you could add a plotter for an additional $2,000 to $3,500, but frankly it's not necessary unless your community doesn't have a good reprographics shop to do the printing for you.

Q: I'm planning on having office help right away, so we'll need two or three computers. How does that work?

A: The best approach is to tie the computers together in a Wi-Fi or Ethernet network, which allows everyone to share the same data from a common hard drive and to use the same printer. You can also communicate between computers. The cost for the network will be a couple hundred dollars, possibly more, depending on hardware choices and the number of computers you're networking. Getting the computers and other equipment to talk to each other can be complex, so unless you have experience with networks, you may need expert help in getting yours up and running.

Q: I'm intimidated by the amount of time it takes to learn to use a computer. What's the fastest way to get up to speed?

A: I know people who use a word processor for all their work—billing, contracts, everything. This isn't a very efficient system, but it's lots faster than a typewriter and saves the trouble of learning five or six different kinds of software. It can be a good way to start. Many of the integrated computer software packages are pretty easy to learn, and you can start with simple things and expand as you go. There are also books, videos, online tutorials, and other training resources available. Read something besides the information that came with the software; there are books and websites explaining (often better than the manufacturer did) nearly every popular piece of software. Finally, look for adult education or other classes that can help you; many people relate better to personal instruction than to wading through a vast online software manual or endless choices on a help menu.

Q: I'm afraid I'll push the wrong key and lose everything. How likely is that?

A: That's pretty unlikely, though you could certainly lose whatever you're working on at the moment. Be happy that there's an "undo" function with most operations, allowing you to back away from a mistake. Just be sure to follow my advice above on backups so that you have recourse if things go seriously wrong.

Ways You Can Use the Internet

- Checking on the availability of plants at local and regional growers
- Advertising your business via your own website or through referral services
- Starting a blog
- Seeing what your competitors are up to by visiting their websites
- Getting information from manufacturers on the products you'll be using, such as irrigation equipment, fertilizers, building materials, etc.
- Researching pest and disease problems
- Buying and selling nursery stock and other materials

- Checking the weather forecast
- Purchasing professional books, videos, and other educational products that you won't find in your local bookstore
- Getting advice from business owners and other professionals about business or technical problems, often through online discussion groups
- Reading trade and professional magazines online
- Locating professional associations
- Buying and selling used equipment

Other Office Basics

A look past the desk reveals some other office basics. File cabinets hold client files, records, catalogs, and whatnot. (Much filing is done digitally these days, and perhaps the filing cabinet will become an obsolete technology, but most offices still need a couple of them.) A storage cabinet hides the office supplies. There are shelves for books. Designers producing drawings by hand will need a drawing board, a T-square, triangles, architect's and engineer's scales, a compass, drafting pens and pencils, and colored markers. Lighting should be bright, simple, and generous. And if you like sitting down, get a comfortable office chair. If you have a bad back, which you will after a couple of years in this business, you'll come to appreciate the more expensive, ergonomically designed chairs available now. If you'd like visitors to sit, too (a dubious approach), provide a not-too-comfortable side chair. (A clever person is said to have cut an inch off the two front legs, making guests feel vaguely uneasy and eager to leave quickly.)

Get a good, small copier for those many little daily copy jobs. Or invest in a multipurpose copier/laser printer/fax machine. There's also a lot of little stuff that's necessary or handy to have around. Some things are obvious: pens and pencils, scratch paper, a ruler, a stapler, paper clips, Scotch tape, that sort of thing. If you have kids, steal these things from them. Others are more specialized. Have a rubber stamp made with the company name and address. Get some other ready-made stamps: one that says PAID and one that says ORIGINAL and one that says CLIENT'S COPY and one that says THANK YOU! WE APPRECIATE YOUR BUSINESS. Those multipurpose date stamps with a little rubber track that says ENTERED and PAID and so forth are a great and cheap way to record your work directly onto forms and documents. Buy some postage stamps and a small postage scale (saves you hours of standing in line at the post office to get large envelopes weighed for postage). Put a bulletin board on the wall next to your desk; you'll find a use for it soon enough (it will fill up with all sorts of interesting items, preventing your office from looking too tidy). These are the basics.

In no time you'll clutter the place up with dozens of other things; the office supply store will love your first couple of years in business. (Tip: Buy some of your office stuff from other businesses that are going bankrupt. They shouldn't be too hard to find. They're desperate, and they'll sell you great things for pennies on the dollar.)

What about business forms? We'll get to those in chapter 4, but for now, know that you'll need business cards, letterheads and envelopes, invoice forms, contract forms and change orders (for landscaping work only), and a really unsettling number of other forms. Some of these are required by law, and others by good sense. Many of them are generated electronically via your various software programs, which keeps printing costs down. Remember, these are the basics. They're enough to keep you going for a long time, though, because there's never any need to outfit your office as though you were the CEO of Microsoft.

Then there are a few unclassifiable essentials. You'll need a camera for taking before and after photos of your jobs. Yes, your smart phone will do the job up to a point, but if you can afford it, invest in a good-quality digital single-lens reflex (DSLR) model with interchangeable lenses. Why? Because using a smart phone to snap photos of your jobs for promotional purposes is just not going to result in quality images that make a good impression on discerning potential clients. Get a zoom lens (I have a 28–200mm that I like a lot for its versatility) and a real wide-angle lens (I love my 20mm) that will take in a lot of landscaping and make it look great. Don't waste your money on fancy features; just get a good-quality basic camera. If you can't afford a DSLR, know that even inexpensive digital cameras, and of course modern smart phones, take great pictures and will serve most of your needs just fine. If you want photos of your best jobs, for your website and other publicity, consider hiring a professional photographer.

Also get a small pocket voice recorder or make use of the recorder on your smart phone. Why? Remember the busy life you're about to undertake? Well, when you leave a job, you can use the driving time to the next job to record your notes from the previous job. It also traps all those other brilliant thoughts you'll be sure to have while you're driving around in your truck. Soon you won't be able to live without it.

Let's talk about smart phones. They do everything and everyone has them and yes, they are indispensable. When I was a kid I used to dream about having a real "wrist radio" like Dick Tracy used in the comics. Now I have a device in my pocket that does more things than I could ever have imagined so long ago. The smart phone syncs with your other devices, making calendars, contact lists, images, proposals, and pretty much whatever else you need available to you wherever you go. It can track scheduling, routing, and bids. It reads QR codes on manufacturer's literature and can even be used in some areas to identify community trees while you're standing under them. It's a compass for when you're on site and need to know which way north is. It's a way to talk to your workers in the field, and to tell your helper when to turn on the sprinkler system at the controller while you're out on the back forty troubleshooting a leak. It can take before, during, and after photos of your jobs (get pictures of your open trenches so you remember where they are and what's in them), and even shoot videos of work in progress. You can hop online during client meetings to find answers to questions that come up or to check availability of plants at your suppliers. The only limits of a smart phone seem to be our imaginations. Oh, and it can be used as a phone, too. You probably already have a smart phone, but if you don't, then go get one right this minute.

Greening Your Operation

If you've decided to offer sustainable landscaping services to your clients, or even if you haven't, it makes sense to set up your own operation to be as environmentally benign as possible. "Going green" means swapping old-fashioned practices and materials that have a high negative environmental impact such as energy hog equipment or non-recycled paper, for newer things that are better tuned to today's need for earth-friendly operations. It's easy to do, and it doesn't necessarily cost you more. In fact, many green practices can save you money, often with little or no investment. Let's have a look at some key approaches to reducing the environmental footprint of your business.

Green opportunities exist in all aspects of your business: buildings and facilities, vehicles, equipment, the office, employee management, and even in your relations with the community.

Developing an Environmental Plan

Consider taking an orderly approach to making your operation as environmentally friendly as possible. A written Environmental Management Plan spells out practices and standards for every aspect of your operation, from office supplies to vehicles to on-the-job practices. Shared with your staff, it helps everyone to stay on track with good environmental behavior. There are some resources that will help you with this task. Have a look at www.epa.gov/osbp/pdfs/smart_steps_greening_guide_042101.pdf for a step-by-step guide to greening your business. The Small Business Administration has lots of publications at http://www.epa.gov/osbp/green-pubs.htm and a "Green Business Guide" at www.sba.gov/green-business-guide. Start work on your plan as soon as you can fit it into your schedule. Revisit it regularly, and make changes as needed. Use this as a living document that will guide your work in the right direction. Here are some specific ideas to get you started:

The Office

You're well on the way to running a green operation simply by having a home-based business. You walk to work, after all. And because your office is likely to be in a building that's already being heated and cooled, you're not putting extra energy into keeping a separate site comfortable.

If you're remodeling or making changes in the building to accommodate your new office, be sure you use green building techniques such as choosing energy efficient windows, skylights and other ways to let natural light into work areas, non-toxic low-VOC paints and finishes, FSC-certified sustainably harvested lumber, and other environmentally sound materials and practices. Take a look at the LEED standards for green building at http://www.usgbc.org/leed for ideas. Consider, too, installing a sustainable demonstration garden for your clients and prospective clients to visit; this will make a strong positive impression.

Make sure your lighting is energy-efficient, as well as your heating and cooling equipment. Buy Energy Star (www.energystar.gov) office equipment to save on electricity and lower your monthly bills. Turn equipment off at night and whenever it's not being used.

Recycling

Naturally, you'll want to recycle as much as you can: office paper, containers, etc. (Of course, the best strategy is to use less in the first place.)

Green Power

If you can buy "green" power from your utility company (that's electricity that has been generated from solar, wind, hydroelectric, or geothermal sources rather than nuclear, coal, or other dirty ones), by all means do so. Of course, if you can install solar panels on your own roof so much the better. Solar gets cheaper and more efficient all the time, and there are subsidies and tax breaks available to make it affordable for pretty much anyone.

Office Supplies

Buy recycled content paper and office supplies. Better yet, do billing and other paperwork by email to avoid both the environmental impact of paper use and the cost of printing and mailing. (That's an example of how environmentally appropriate practices can save you money.) Recycle your toner cartridges.

Vehicles

Downsize your vehicles to use the smallest, most fuel-efficient ones that will get the job done. Try not to take your truck unless you need to haul something. Can you go to appointments in a small car, by bike, or on foot? Consider purchasing electric or hybrid vehicles, using biodiesel in your trucks, and looking into other alternative fuels as they become available.

Route management is a terrific way to save fuel, time, and labor costs. Chances are that if you have multiple vehicles on the road, people are making unnecessary trips and wasting both fuel and time. Coordinate materials pickups, group appointments by geographical area, and train your employees to avoid excessive driving. A little planning every day can make a big difference in the miles (and the wear and tear) that you put on your vehicles.

Equipment

Use hand tools whenever possible; they're often more efficient when you take into account the cost of purchasing, maintaining, and fueling power tools. Newer models of power equipment are usually quieter and more efficient than old ones. Check for efficiency when you shop for gear. If you must use power equipment, keep in mind that electric tools are less polluting and quieter than gas-powered ones. If you own heavy equipment such as diesel tractors, fuel them with biodiesel (it's not perfect, but it does seem to offer a modest improvement over conventional diesel).

Employees

Train your staff to be aware of environmental issues and be sure they understand the impacts their work has. Develop enthusiasm for doing things right. Make sure all employees have read your Environmental Management Plan, and let them know that you take it seriously. Develop measurable goals and objectives, and hold weekly brief staff meetings to review them and see how you're doing. If there are training programs such as a green gardener class in your area, send your key employees. Provide incentives for employees to improve their environmental awareness on their own, such as paying for classes and course materials, as well as paying them to attend. Offer raises for achievements such as certifications and extra effort on behalf of your company's environmental goals.

Encourage your employees to bike to work, carpool, or use public transportation, perhaps even paying for part of their costs if they do so or offering other incentives. Consider the use of a flextime system under which employees can work hours that are more efficient for them and the company and keep cars off the road at rush hour.

Community Service

Get your company involved in environmental projects in your community, such as tree planting, creek restoration, or the development of public sustainable demonstration gardens. Volunteer your time and expertise to design, build, and maintain such projects, and try to get your employees involved as well. Show up at public events in your company uniforms. Make cash donations or kick in some plants or other materials if you can afford to do so. In addition to the good you'll be doing, you're going to make many valuable contacts that may lead to some of the best jobs you'll ever get.

Teach classes in organic maintenance, sustainable landscaping, or other topics that you feel comfortable presenting. Be sure you know what you're talking about, of course. You'll be educating the community and improving the visibility of your company and your services.

The Bank Account

Get a separate bank account for your business. Otherwise you'll end up with a big mess at the end of the year. Make it an interest-bearing checking account because you'll probably keep a pretty big balance on hand to cover expenses. You might as well make some money on your cash flow, even if it's only a fraction of a percent.

If you'll be operating your business as a sole proprietorship, you'll need to show the bank your *Fictitious Business Name Statement* unless your full name is used in the company name (such as Sue Wilson's Gardening Service). To get a Fictitious Business Name Statement (also known as a *"DBA"*), go to the county clerk/recorder's office, and they'll tell you what to do. If you're going to incorporate or become an LLC ("limited liability company," an easy way for a small business to incorporate), you'll need to provide them with the articles of incorporation. And if your business is a partnership, they'll need to see the partnership agreement. (*Tip:* DBAs expire after a few years. Don't forget to renew yours.)

Insurance

I know you don't want to read about insurance. But you must, just as you must have insurance. Besides, if you think insurance is a grim topic, wait until we get to bookkeeping, taxes, and lawsuits.

For a long time I said that buying tires was the least satisfying way to spend lots of money, but I now believe insurance is. The best you can hope for from insurance is that you never have to use it. Isn't that some thrill! But the law and good practice require that you carry a lot of insurance. (*Important advice:* It's impossible to generalize about insurance because laws and policies vary from state to state. Keep in mind that the rules change from one state or region to another.)

Here are the basic kinds of insurance you'll need.

Business Liability Insurance

Let's say you drive a tractor into your client's bedroom, "God forbid," as the insurance agents like to say. You'll owe for the bedroom, lodging while the bedroom is being remodeled, furnishings, medical costs if someone was injured, emotional damage, attorneys' fees, and who knows what else. No problem, because you've got $1 million of liability coverage. If you're lucky the settlement won't run any more than that, but costs mount up quickly and often a million isn't enough, especially if injury or death are part of the equation. Liability coverage also protects you against things like advertising injury, medical expenses, fire damage, equipment theft, and loss of records. Work with your agent to custom-tailor a package that's right for you.

Pay close attention to the following information:

1. The insurer will defend you only up to the limits of coverage. That means if someone sues you for $1 million and you're insured for only $500,000, you have to get your own lawyer for the uninsured portion of the suit, which will cost you plenty even if you end up winning the case. If you lose, you must pay out of your pocket any amounts over the insured amount. Got half a mil lying around?
2. Generally speaking, liability insurance will protect you if you're sued for damages resulting from work you did while the policy was in effect, even if the suit is filed several years later. But these policies can have hidden dangers, with companies exempting themselves from covering you under certain circumstances, so PLEASE read you policies carefully before accepting them and assuming they meet all your needs for protection. (There is no duller reading than an insurance policy, so do this early in the day so you stay awake through the ordeal.) The insurance company is only required to keep your files for five years after you drop the coverage, so be sure to retain your own copies of the policies. Don't ever destroy them, because damage could result from your work many years after you did it, and you'd still be responsible (laws may differ in your state, so check

with your agent or an attorney). And be sure your policy doesn't contain a *sunset clause* that releases the insurance company from liability after a couple of years.

3. If you plan to quit the business or retire, have an attorney advise you whether you'll still be exposed to liability. A nasty lawsuit popping up out of nowhere can really take the fun out of your golden years. You can purchase a *tail policy* on closure of your business that provides extended protection.
4. If you change companies, be sure there's no lapse in coverage.

Be sure you're dealing with a sound insurance company. If the company goes broke, you're not covered even if you paid your premiums in full. And keep an eye on their reputation, since companies can spoil over time like bad fruit.

Often, you need to show proof that you have liability coverage: for example, when you apply for building permits and business licenses and when you want to go to work as a subcontractor for another contractor. Proof comes in the form of a *Certificate of Insurance* that your insurer will provide at no cost on request.

The cost of business liability insurance is based partly on your payroll, even if you're a one-person operation. Rates seem to vary considerably, so shop around. You also need to be aware that your homeowner's or renter's policy probably doesn't cover things like injuries to visitors to your home office; be sure your business policy does.

Workers Compensation Insurance

This covers employees in case they're injured on the job. If you have employees, workers comp is required by law. Rates are set by the Workers Compensation Rating Bureau (it may have a different name in your region) and they usually don't vary from one company to another. They do vary for each job classification—in your case, the classification will probably be Landscape Gardening. They also vary (upwards from the base rate) with the *experience rating* of your company: An accident or injury will create an *experience modification* that will jump your rates to cover some of the costs incurred by the company for dealing with your incident. That's right, you buy insurance to pay for this sort of thing but you end up paying for it anyway, or at least part of it. Get used to being treated this way, because that's how insurers operate and it's why they're one of the highest profit sectors of the economy.

The penalties for not having workers comp are severe. In California, for example, if an employee is injured on the job and you're caught without worker's compensation insurance, you have to pay all the employee's medical expenses out of your own pocket, plus a 50 percent surcharge, plus a possible $100,000 fine and/or up to one year in jail. (*Tip:* Some contractors trade associations handle return-premium worker's compensation policies; these policies refund a portion of the premiums at the end of each year, based on the claims costs. They can save you big bucks.)

Group Health Insurance

If you have employees, you may want to or be compelled to provide them with health insurance or to cover part of their premiums. This is a complex and rapidly changing issue, especially with the advent of the Affordable Care Act ("Obamacare"), so check with your agent.

Vehicle Insurance

You have to have vehicle insurance on every truck and car you have on the road. Be sure your policy covers multiple drivers if you have employees. Also be certain employees are covered in their own autos if you have them run errands for you; this important coverage costs very little to add.

One of the most important liabilities you'll be exposed to is vehicle-related mishaps. It's unbelievable how many employees lie to the boss about their suspended licenses, drunk driving convictions, and other offenses. Remember, these people are driving your vehicles, which are often large, heavily loaded trucks pulling trailers. You simply must check the driving records of all employees and prospective employees and keep current about the status of their driving records. The Department of Motor Vehicles will supply a prospective or current employee's driving record (with a signed release from the employee), and may also, for a modest fee, keep an employer informed of any changes in the driving record of employees.

Bonds

A bond is a special type of coverage that protects third parties (in this case, your clients and the public) against damages arising from your screw-ups. If you're a landscape contractor, you'll probably need a license bond, the annual cost of which is minimal. The license bond pays an injured party if, for example, you leave a job unfinished or do it improperly. In some cases it can also protect your employees in case you fail to pay benefits owed them.

If you end up bidding big jobs someday, you'll need to know about other kinds of bonds, such as completion bonds, which guarantee that you'll finish the job. If you don't, the bonding company brings in, at their expense, another contractor to finish it. This type of bonding is a few years down the line for you, though, and you'll have plenty of opportunity to learn about it when the time comes.

(TIP: A bond is not an insurance policy, and the bonding company can come after you for reimbursement for any payments they make. Even though you're the one who has to pay for it, a bond is for the public, not for you.)

The Cost of Insurance

Unfortunately, it's impossible to give you an estimate of what you'll have to spend on insurance. There are several reasons for this. First, the types of coverage and the limits of liability you choose are highly variable; therefore, so are the resulting premiums. Second, rates for all types of insurance vary by state, region, and even neighborhood in some cases. Legal requirements vary, too. Rates also vary from company to company and change over time like any expense. Finally, rates are partially set by your claims record, the driving records of you and your staff, the kind of vehicles you own, and the age and value of the equipment you're covering.

Still, it's fair to say you'll spend quite a bit of money on insurance each year—at least a couple thousand dollars just to start out. The best advice? Seek out a good independent insurance agent and plan a reasonable package for your business. Many years ago, I was lucky to find a good, honest agent who spent a lot of time educating me about the ins and outs of the insurance game. If you can do the same, you'll be in good shape.

Insurance Agents

There are two kinds of insurance agents: the *independent agent*, who can shop around for you and seek quotes from different companies, and the *company agent*, who works for only one company. You may get a better deal from an independent agent, but don't rule out a company agent with a good reputation and the right stuff for your needs. Also be sure to choose someone who specializes in business insurance, not consumer insurance (such as homeowner's coverage), which is a completely different ball game. In fact, try to find an agent who understands gardening or contracting or whatever field you plan to go into. Why? Because there are always special quirks in any type of business, and landscaping is no exception. Here's a case in point: My agent discovered that a local equipment rental yard was offering an optional extra charge for what they called a "damage waiver," which allegedly protected the renter against liability for damage to the equipment. After one of his clients had a problem with this, the agent got a copy of the waiver and discovered it offered no protection at all. He then alerted all his contractor clients, telling them not to pay for the useless add-on. That's service that only an experienced person can offer.

Insurance Tips

Check your homeowner's policy to see to what extent it covers office equipment in the home. Make sure your policy covers loss of structures used for business, as there is sometimes an exclusion for business use. Note any *exclusions* on your policy, that may not cover certain lines of work you might do, such as retaining walls and ponds; you'll be on your own for those unless you pay for an extra *rider* to cover them. Look into special deals offered as part of membership in a business or trade organization. Shop around a lot, because rates on all types of insurance except worker's compensation can vary a great deal. Also, review policies at least annually to be sure you've got the kind of coverage that lets you feel comfortable, and get two or three quotes every year even if you love your current agent and carrier.

Legal Considerations

The Legal Form of Your Business

Typically, a small one-person or family-run business is operated as a sole proprietorship, at least at first. That is to say, it is not a partnership (which is where you share ownership and responsibilities with one or more people) or a corporation (where the business itself becomes a "person," protecting you to some degree from the liabilities of the business operations). The sole proprietorship is easy to set up and gives you the most control over your operation with the least hassle. But a proprietorship also exposes you to having your personal assets seized as a result of a judgment against your business, and that is no small thing to consider.

I strongly advise you think twice about beginning your business with a partner, even though my own experience with partnerships has been mostly positive. The partnership has been aptly described as a marriage without the sex. Many partnerships don't work, and because they're often entered into by friends, the common result is the failure of both the business and the friendship. What happens? Perhaps one person works harder than the other and eventually gets fed up. Or one person spends all the money, enters into questionable deals without the other partner's knowledge or consent, or otherwise jeopardizes the business. You probably don't need a partner. If you do form a partnership, have an attorney draw up a formal legal agreement, and be sure to plan for its graceful termination when you prepare the agreement. It'll save a lot of grief later.

You also probably don't need to incorporate. Traditionally, the small corporation has been considered a way of protecting the business owner from personal liability for business problems, such as lawsuits and debts. Unfortunately, you can't count on that protection as much as in the past. There also may be tax advantages to incorporating, but again, they ain't what they used to be. A full corporation has to have a board of directors, hold regular meetings, keep elaborate and detailed records, and jump through a million hoops set up by the government. One false move and you lose many of the advantages of the corporate structure. Many people set up an *S Corporation* or a *limited liability corporation*, ("LLC,") which are special types of corporations better suited to small business owners than a traditional full corporation. The LLC, where available, is a particularly easy way to get more protection than a proprietorship affords, so do look into this one for your startup. This can get complicated, so be sure to talk to an accountant and an attorney about this if you're just dying to see "Inc." or "LLC" after your company name.

Licenses

You'll need a city and/or county *business license*, possibly a *permit* for each vehicle you operate, and maybe a special permit to operate out of your house. You'll need to register your company name using a *Fictitious Business Name Statement* that's on file with the county and is also published in a legal ad in a local newspaper in some jurisdictions. You'll have to get a *seller's permit* (also known as a *resale number*) from an outfit called the State Board of Equalization (or something similar) in order to collect and remit sales taxes (note that some states don't have sales taxes). If you have employees, you'll need a federal *Employer Identification Number* ("EIN") that's obtained by filing a form you can get from the IRS website (www1.ein-gov.us). If you do landscaping work (as opposed to maintenance), you'll probably need a *contractor's license*. More about that in just a minute. There's no use grousing about the burden of obtaining and maintaining all these licenses. Everyone has to have them, and you're no exception. Just grit your teeth and do it. Obtaining most of these is easy—fill out a form or two, give them some money, and off you go.

The *contractor's license* is different. Not just anyone can become a licensed contractor. You'll need to have several years of experience or some schooling, meet certain financial requirements, get letters of recommendation from other professionals, and take a rather detailed exam. If you pass, then you pay more money and walk out with your license.

Why bother? Because the law says that to do landscaping work (not garden maintenance in most cases) beyond a certain low dollar limit, you must have a contractor's license. Yes, I know a lot of people get away without having a license, but they're risking fines, possibly jail time, bad publicity, and perhaps the loss of their businesses. They can't bid on big jobs or get building permits. And their clients don't have to pay them. That's right—imagine doing a $20,000 job and having the owner refuse to pay because she knows you're unlicensed. Take her to court? Forget it! You might as well call the cops because you got burned in a drug deal. You're an outlaw. (*Tip:* Don't believe those people who confidently tell you that you don't need a contractor's license as long as you bill people on a time-and-materials basis. That's not true anywhere that I know about.)

So, how hard is it to get a contractor's license? Probably a lot easier than you imagine. Requirements vary from state to state, but here is a typical experience: Work for four years for another licensed contractor, or complete an accredited college-level program to reduce the experience requirement. Have $1,000 in the bank. Don't have a felony on your record. Get a couple of friends in the business to fill out letters of recommendation. Apply for the test. Take it (about four to six hours of questions and work problems that won't be all that difficult if you have a basic level of competence). Pass (you hope), or take it again the following year. Get a contractor's license bond. Pay your annual license fee.

That's it. It's not all that bad, and you'll immediately feel better, get more respect, and be free to pursue the kind of quality career you dream of having. No more looking over your shoulder all the time. It's a great feeling. Contact your state *Contractor's License Board* for more information. If you've never worked for a licensed landscape contractor, you may still be able to qualify to take the exam by virtue of several years of experience as a self-employed person.

There are schools and online courses that will help you study for the exam, but you could very well be just as successful on your own. You'll be tested on many things in addition to landscaping, among them safety requirements, mechanics lien laws, employer laws, business laws, and building codes. The license board might be able to provide you with a reading list, which will be a big help. I used a correspondence course that was inexpensive and quite good. It provided copies of tests from previous years, which took away a lot of the fear of the unknown. After devouring book after book for months, I completed the test in just over two hours, out of eight allowed. Lest you think I'm some kind of genius, quite a few people had already left when I handed in my test booklet.

The contractor's license usually permits you to do any type of landscaping work, including grading, planting, irrigation, building decks and retaining walls, and installing low-voltage lighting systems. Sometimes you have to get a separate license classification to do irrigation and possibly other aspects of your work. You can also usually do landscape design under your contractor's license, as long as you also install what you design. (To do only design work for others to install, you'd need to be a landscape architect or landscape designer, as described in chapter 1.) What you *can't* do is construct habitable buildings, or do the work of any other trades such as high-voltage electrical work, house plumbing, roofing, that sort of thing. In other words, the license allows you to do landscaping and nothing more. Rules vary from state to state.

Home improvement contracting (under which residential landscaping falls) is one of the most regulated kinds of business, on account of the fact that so many flakey people have contaminated the industry over the decades, leading to laws and regulations that protect the public. Thanks to generations of creepy crooks, the form of your contract with the client, the terms of payment, the conduct of any salespeople you hire, your relationship with your employees and subcontractors, lien law filings, and a whole lot more are rigidly controlled by state law. One misstep and you could be penalized or even lose your license. Still, once you get the rhythm of it, it's just like any other job, so don't suffer too much anxiety over the prospect of your responsibilities. Anyway, it's worth it.

Business Taxes

Employee Taxes

You need to deposit the taxes you deduct from employees' paychecks and pay them to taxing agencies such as the IRS through a special kind of deposit at your bank. (More on this in chapter 5.)

Sales Taxes

Regulations and tax rates vary, and some states have no sales tax at all, but in general, if you sell a product, either as a retail sale or by incorporating materials into your jobs, you will need to collect and pay sales tax on the value of the goods. The sales tax laws were written primarily with merchants in mind, and they apply very clumsily to contractors. The mechanics of figuring your sales taxes can be baffling, even to the bureaucrats who run the system. Check with your *State Board of Equalization* (it may have a different name in your state) for a resale number and instructions on how to file your returns. Good luck on this one.

Defining Your Niche

What Kind of Work Will You Do?

We've discussed the diversity of opportunities in the business. Have you decided where you fit in? With so many possibilities it's not an easy choice. That's especially true if you haven't had any direct experience of the various branches of the horticulture tree, so do consider going to work for one or more companies before you make your final decision on what business you'll go into. It also helps to ask yourself some questions about your own skills and preferences. To that end, here are some issues that you may want to examine:

- Do you want to do landscaping, maintenance, or both?
- Do you want to offer one or more specialties, such as tree care, low-voltage lighting, irrigation troubleshooting, water management, organic maintenance or lawn care, yard cleanups, hauling, etc.?
- If you'll be doing landscaping, do you want to offer design/build services or do only the installations?
- What class of work do you want to do: high-end residential, middle-class residential, budget residential, large or small commercial, public works?
- Do you want to eventually go after large, complex projects or stick with smaller backyard jobs?

Let me give you some advice about how to proceed. Unless you've had considerable experience working for another company, start with small residential work. It takes years to get good enough (and for your company to be substantial enough) to go after the big jobs. Give yourself time.

Include maintenance in your mix of services, even if you don't want to do it forever. That way you'll learn how things *really* work, because you'll have to care for the finished product.

If you're not sure what you'd like to end up doing, try a bit of everything. Be sure you're qualified to do the work, of course, but don't limit yourself. Be a generalist. You'll learn a lot, and you won't be limiting your clients to just those who want one kind of thing.

At first, avoid complex design/build jobs unless you have training in landscape design. It's easy to get in over your head and design something that doesn't work. Move gradually from the simple projects to the complex ones, one step at a time.

Stay on the high road with respect to the environment. More and more clients are requesting, even demanding, that landscape services be done in an environmentally conscious way. That means reducing or eliminating the use of chemicals, using organic methods, choosing low-impact construction materials, and developing landscapes that make minimal demands on the environment. Sustainable landscaping, as these practices are called, is the hottest, most lucrative aspect of the landscaping business today. And it's not just a fad; as our culture changes, sustainable landscaping is becoming the norm. (See "Business Opportunities in Sustainable Landscaping and Gardening" in chapter 6 for more on this subject.)

Whom Do You Want as Clients?

All sorts of property owners purchase landscaping services. You may sometimes have to take what you can get in order to stay busy, but you will be able to choose which sectors you want to market to, based on your skills and interests, and also on what market segments are strong in your area. Each of the following potential job sources has its own personality. Use the information below to help you understand the nature of each market segment; then decide what mix of clients works best for you.

Homeowners

Most likely, this is where you'll start. Homeowners can be some of your best clients. They tend to be honest and usually won't take advantage of you the way some commercial clients often do.

A sprinkler contractor I once met had a rule about clients: He would only work for homeowners improving their own homes for their own enjoyment; no landlords, spec house builders, developers, commercial jobs, or anything else where someone was trying to make a buck off his work. He had done very well by this rule, and I think he has a point. In my experience, a profit motive on the part of the client contaminates the business relationship and increases the risk of not getting paid or of being asked to do things that aren't right. (The following discussion reflects some of my own observations and prejudices about various kinds of residential clients, developed over decades of good and bad situations with all kinds of people and projects. I admit that I'm cynical about clients, because I know how difficult some of them can be and I want you to see the pitfalls as well as the rosy side of the business. Not everyone is nice and you need to know more about that before you go any further. Most people are fine, and there are plenty of exceptions to my generalizations below, but there is much truth in them nonetheless. You'll understand my crankiness after you've been in business for a while.)

Some of the best clients in the world are middle- and upper-middle class homeowners who work for a living and understand that you do, too. They're accustomed to paying their bills on time. They respect you. They're more or less your peers, so you can relate to them pretty easily. They don't look down on you. They usually want to do things right and can probably afford quality services.

Rich clients can be great, mainly because they have a lot of money. A good rich client is a real find, a source of lots of top-quality work. But the rich are different, and it is not always pleasant to do business with them. They can be haughty and not a lot of fun to be around. Some people got rich by cheating other people, often in clever and devious ways; they'll eat you for a snack. Watch out for them. Others got their money the old-fashioned way: They inherited it. They've never worked and may not understand why you need to get paid on time. This trait can be exasperating and costly. To top it all off, many of them are tightwads who despite being able to pay full price will try to bleed you for discounts and special treatment. And finally, rich people can afford better lawyers than you can, and they know that. (You may think I'm a bigot, but what I'm telling you is true, and you might as well hear it now as learn the hard way. I've got nothing against any group, but after over forty years in this business, I know trouble when I see it coming.)

On the other end of the spectrum are homeowners who have just enough money to pay for a little bit of budget-quality landscaping or maintenance work. Some of these folks are OK, especially when you're getting started, but be aware of the fact that such people will often persuade you to lower your quality standards. Don't do it. Doing a poor-quality job reflects badly on you. Besides, once such clients see the job you did, they may suddenly become perfectionists, demanding first-rate work even though they only paid you for junk. It's a trap that many beginners fall into quite easily. Still, an honest client of modest means, with a small but decent project, can be a wonderful addition to your clientele.

There are some subsets of the homeowner trade that can be particularly rewarding to pursue. One is the two-income family. Some of these folks have plenty of discretionary income (especially if they don't have children—these folks are sometimes called "DINKs"... double income, no kids), they like to spend it, and they often have no time to work in their yards. They need you. Another good group is affluent seniors. They have money, taste, and needs, and they can be really nice. One strong market is people in their fifties whose parents are dying and leaving them with large inheritances. Among my clientele, some of these are people I started with when they were in their thirties and struggling, and later in life they found themselves spending inherited money like crazy; this is another reason to stick with your established clients. (*Tip:* Never work for renters. They have no right to contract with you for improvements to the landlord's property and neither they nor the actual property owner are under any obligation to pay you. Furthermore, landlords may go after you when they find out you've been messing around with their property. If you get an inquiry from a renter, whether residential or commercial, tell them you need to get a written approval from the property owner, or better yet that you need to work directly with the owner.)

Income Property Owners (aka Landlords)

Landlords are usually looking for a maximum return on their investment, and that means spending as little money as possible. And some of them are cheap and often don't pay their bills on time. Check them out thoroughly before you get involved with their projects. Do a credit check and ask around about them to see how they treat other contractors. The other thing about landlords is that they often don't care about quality work, so unless you like to do things badly for some reason, you'll be frustrated. Naturally, there are exceptions, and a good income property owner can be the source of a lot of work for you.

Condominium and Homeowners' Associations

More and more people are moving into condos and planned unit developments with common public spaces and shared landscaping. Operations are run by a *Homeowner's Association* ("HOA") that represents the owners in matters like hiring and firing, safety, rules and regulations, and so forth. There's usually a landscape committee, made up of owners, that oversees maintenance and changes in the landscaping, and deals with the gardeners and landscape contractors who work there. There's a lot of work, especially maintenance, in these places. One of these jobs can require one or more people full-time, and if you land one you will have steady work and earnings. Naturally, you have to bid against others and so your profit margins will be low, but an efficient operation can make you some money. These properties usually re-bid maintenance contracts every year, and most often go with the lowest bid, even if it means giving the boot to the previous year's contractor regardless of whether the service has been satisfactory. So don't expect faithfulness or even decency, and don't be surprised or hurt when you get a Dear John letter at the end of your contract; it's not about you, it's about the almighty dollar. In the meantime, do good work and hope for the best.

Warning: A huge percentage of condo and similar developments are involved in lawsuits with the builder, subcontractors, suppliers, and, yes, landscapers. People seem to go kind of crazy when they get on landscape committees, and it can be a nightmare to work with them. Quite a few business-people simply refuse to deal with associations, and some insurers refuse to cover work for HOAs as part of their business liability policies. Be aware of the risks and frustrations.

New Housing Developments

There's a lot of work landscaping new housing tracts, and there are two ways to get some of it. One is to get in with the builder or developer and do the landscaping in common areas, front yards, and model homes. Sometimes, you can do this by the back door and not have to go up against every other hungry person in the county with a pickup truck. In other words, if the builder is your buddy, he or she may let you do the job without bidding against others. More often, you bid the job just like any other.

Warning: Many, many builders and developers are sharks, and when they see a fresh-faced newcomer like you, they'll count on bleeding you for all you've got. They'll give you the business, all right, but not the money, and they've got a million well-tested schemes for cheating you. If you don't understand how the development game works, stay away from these situations. Not to tar everyone with the same brush, but this is often rough territory and no place for a beginner.

The other approach is to wait until homeowners move in and then go to work directly for them. This is a good source of jobs. They have to do something with their raw yards, so they're automatically in the market for your services. Some of the projects may be modest because they just spent all their money on the new house, but there is work there. (*Tip:* Be careful on new tracts because the soil is often compacted and/or of poor quality, and you can lose a lot of plants. Builders frequently skim over poor soil with a couple inches of good topsoil to make things look OK, and various tradespeople have often cleaned out paintbrushes, tubs of mortar, and other toxic materials directly into the soil that you will be planting in. Have a clause in your contract that exempts you from liability for these situations.)

Commercial Property Owners

Many shopping centers, office complexes, and other high-visibility properties are landscaped and maintained beautifully. The owners care a lot about their image and are willing to do things right. Usually, they put everything out to bid, so you'll have to work for a slim profit margin, much less than what you can get doing residential work. Still, if you're efficient, you can earn decent money on this kind of work, and you may even get to put up a sign with your company name somewhere on the property, to be viewed by hundreds of people every day.

Public Properties

Some of the projects in the public sector (parks, municipal buildings, school campuses, etc.) are done in-house by staff workers. But this isn't true of everything, particularly new construction, which often has to be put out to bid according to law. Many municipalities and other public bodies contract out their maintenance work. Some communities also have annual lot-clearing work that you can bid on.

Working for a public agency, whether it's the federal, state, or local government, involves a lot of paperwork and the ability to deal with bureaucrats who are sometimes incompetent or hostile, obscure regulations, and interminable delays. Many public projects also require that you pay the *prevailing wage*. (See chapter 5 for an explanation.) Still, it's good work, and the government virtually always pays its bills. In most cases, you'll have to work from a landscape architect's plans rather than your own. Most public jobs must go to the lowest qualified bidder. Bidding is often cutthroat, and profit margins are low. Don't get into public work until you've had plenty of experience in the private sector.

Conclusion

Congratulations on making it this far. I know this chapter has been a little heavy, and you may feel as though going into business is a lot more trouble than it's worth. Remember, you have to do some of these things only once. Anyway, you'll adjust to it all in time, learn to make peace with the situation, and even enjoy the process. If you're careful and honest, you'll probably never have a serious problem. I haven't, and I've been at this for a long time. Despite the burdens, it's still fun to go to work every day.

03 Writing a Business Plan

Chances are, you've never had to write a business plan until now. Maybe you've never even heard of such a thing. So let's begin at the beginning: What's a business plan? What kind of information does it include? What's it for?

A *business plan* is a detailed description of your proposed business: What kind of business will it be? Who will own it? Where will it be located? Who will your clients be? What geographical areas will your business serve? What kinds of products or services will it offer? Who's the competition? How will your business be better than or different from the competition? How will your services be advertised to the potential clients? What kinds of equipment will you need to start up? What are your other start-up costs? What will the total costs be to start the business? What will the overhead be? When will your business begin to show a profit? What are the seasonal variations in sales? Will there be employees? How many? What kind—laborers, supervisors, office help? What will the cash flow be for the first few years? How much money do you need in order to make a living and put something away for your retirement? These are some of the important issues that the business plan addresses.

Though you can find plenty of books that provide ready-made business plan formats, there's no universally accepted way to prepare one. In fact, the way your business plan is organized will depend to some extent on how you'll be using it. First, decide if you'll be using the plan to attract capital: a bank loan, money from Uncle Harry, Small Business Administration financing, or whatever. You'll tailor the business plan to the source of funds. For example, a bank is interested in how you're going to pay off the loan. They'll be justifiably cautious in loaning money to something as risky as a landscaping business. They'll want to see lots of *financial projections:* five years' *pro forma* (projected) *income statements* and *balance sheets,* and other evidence of your good financial planning. On the other hand, Uncle Harry might be more interested in the personal or philosophical aspects of his descendant's proposed business, perhaps even assuming he will never get a significant return on his investment.

If you won't need start-up capital, then the plan is mostly for you and possibly for key employees when you expand someday. It'll be a road map to guide you as you develop your business. Though you still have to do the financial projections (trust me, you do), you can format the plan more to your own liking.

Either way, there are some essential elements the business plan must contain, and there's a systematic approach to preparing it that will make it pretty easy for you to get the job done well. I'm going to give you my version of what a business plan for a small gardening or landscaping business should look like and how to go about writing it. That's what we'll spend most of this chapter on; but first, let's deal with the obvious question.

Why Do a Business Plan, Anyway?

Thinking about actually preparing a business plan may give you a bad case of anxiety. "Hey," you may ask, "isn't this all a waste of time? After all, I'm not starting Wal-Mart! Why not just get some jobs and start making money?"

The answer is, this is not just a job, it's a business. It has to function smoothly over the long haul. It's complex, and your success depends on your understanding, in depth, what you'll be doing and why—understanding it now, before you begin. You wouldn't build a garden by going out and buying any old plants and throwing them into the ground any old way. That would lead to a mess, not a garden. You plan first, then plant. Similarly, your business needs guidance and form right from the beginning, and that's what a business plan is all about. It's a plan for success.

Let's hope you'll do really well and attract a lot of business. That would be great, but if you don't have management systems in place first, you'll soon be overwhelmed and your initial success will be compromised by your struggles to get organized in the midst of lots of activity rather than in advance as it should have been. Your business plan forces you to develop, in nitty-gritty detail, a strategy for exactly how you'll do things—marketing, hiring, financing, and a lot more. That way, you can create a business that really works. As your business grows, your business plan will continue to guide your development and help you prosper.

Speaking of financing, you may very well need some money for your start-up business. Remember how costly those tools and equipment are? Well, if you go to the bank and tell them you want to start a landscaping business and you'd like, say, $50,000, what's the first thing they're going to do? That's right! They're going to say, "Let's see your business plan." You don't want to be caught short at this important moment. Even good old Uncle Harry, if he's got anything on the ball, will ask for a business plan before he empties part of his bank account into yours.

Putting together a business plan, while certainly not as much fun as a week at the seashore, isn't all that bad. Parts of the job are even enjoyable. It'll give you a lot of clarity about your new business. When you're done, you'll have new confidence and enthusiasm, knowing that you're well prepared for your adventure.

Finally, a business plan doesn't have to be fancy. There are certain tasks you want your business plan to accomplish. Accomplish them and stop. No glossy printing, no vast acreage of numbers, no frills. A business plan is like a shovel; it's a tool, nothing more.

When do you prepare a business plan? Easy: before you commit any significant time or money to the business. Don't put this off as you would cleaning behind the fridge. Get it done. Remember: business plan first, business second. (*Tip:* Visit the website of the Service Corps of Retired Executives ["SCORE"] at www.score.org to find some cool business plan templates, helpful advice, and even a hot line you can use for personal assistance. It's free!)

Preparing the Business Plan, Step-by-Step

OK, this isn't going to be all that difficult. Just follow the steps below, answering questions as you go. Take the time to develop realistic numbers and projections rather than just making up a number to get the job over with. Do a good job on this and you'll have a tool that will serve you and your new business well.

Step One: A Statement of Purpose

Can you describe in thirty-five words or less what your new business is all about? If not, maybe you're not too sure yourself. Hammering out a *Statement of Purpose*, though it may seem silly, is a terrific way to focus your mind on what you're doing and boil it down to one pithy definition that you can use to remind yourself (and everyone else) what your business is about. Try it. To help you get the idea, here's a statement a friend of mine developed (with the help of his employees) for his landscaping business:

> Boulder Creek Landscaping Company is a quality-oriented organization specializing in ecological enhancement of the environment for the benefit of the entire community.

So, ask yourself . . . will you just be doing landscaping? Not really. You'll also be serving the needs of your clients, your employees, your suppliers, the community, and the environment. You'll be a business manager, an employer, a public relations person, and more. Each task and each role you play takes a place within the ecology of your little business. Which ones are the most important to you? Use your statement of purpose to define the basic character of your business. Then frame it and hang it right in the middle of your bulletin board, or put it on your desk where you'll see it every day.

Step Two: General Information about Your Business

This is the place for some very basic facts about your proposed business. What general classes of service will you offer (maintenance, new landscaping, etc.)? Where will your business be located (your spare bedroom)? Who will own it (just you, you and your spouse, two or more partners)? What will the form of the business be (sole proprietorship, partnership, LLC, corporation)? When do you plan to start doing business? What will the name of your business be?

Choosing a company name can be difficult. After all, your company name will be with you for a long time. Select something that sounds solid, not frivolous. Make sure it'll appeal to a wide range of people. Avoid trendy names that'll sound dated in a few years (imagine if your company name was Frieda's Far-Out Garden Service). Make sure the name conveys what you do. Finally, be sure you choose something that makes sense. Many years ago there was a company in my town called Inner-Plant-A-Terrarium. Seriously. I never did figure out why they chose such a goofy moniker, but it didn't matter because they weren't around for very long.

Step Three: Your Background

One of the goals of the business plan is to try to convince potential investors of your management and technical skills. Here's where you sell yourself.

Write a couple of paragraphs telling how you came to be interested in landscaping and why you've decided to go into business. Describe any applicable training or degrees you have, your employment experience, volunteer work, and anything that demonstrates your dedication to your profession. If you don't have any professional experience but have always had a beautiful backyard, put that down; it counts, too. (Naturally, the background description applies to partners and any other key employees whom you propose to have on board when you start up.) The bank will need to see this information, just as a prospective employer needs to see a résumé. It'll be good for you, too, giving you a clear perspective on where you've come from and why you're qualified to follow this dream of business ownership. Remember, keep it brief and to the point. Finally, mention any licenses you will need for the services you offer and indicate whether you have them yet.

Step Four: Services Offered

In detail, tell what you plan to offer your clients. Do you want to specialize in water gardens, organic lawn care, or commercial landscaping? Do you want to do design/build landscape installation? Irrigation troubleshooting? Pest control? Are you interested in selling any products in addition to services? What are they? The chart that follows lists some of the services typically offered by small gardening and landscaping companies.

Consider, too, what you'll do in the off-season. Many companies offer snow removal service or holiday light installation, for example, to keep crews busy and produce income.

Your decisions should be based in part on what you like to do, of course, but also on what services the community needs and will purchase from you. You may want to do water gardens, but if nobody's interested in having one you'll have a hard time making a go of it. It might be easier to mow lawns or do irrigation work or whatever else is in demand. And trust me, the smart money is not with snow removal services in south Florida.

Remember, too, that most successful businesses offer a range of services. I've always done well because I tried to do whatever people wanted, as long as I had the necessary skills, and it made sense in other ways. There are limits, of course, but the point is to try to serve people's needs. (An old business adage, one worth following, is to "find a need and fill it.") Try to never say no. If you're not capable of doing a job, find someone who is and use that person as a subcontractor (then learn by watching him or her). So, prepare your business plan with a wide spectrum of services in mind. After due consideration, you may want to narrow your focus somewhat (some people are successful because they pursue a small niche), but start with the broad view.

Is there something different about your business? Will you offer all-organic lawn care, landscaping with native plants, or construction using recycled materials? Do you plan to include a year's free monthly inspections with each landscape? Say so. Investors often equate innovation with potential for success. If your ideas are good, they'll make a favorable impression.

Step Five: Markets

Who will your clients be? Homeowners? Contractors? Property managers? Developers? Architects? Landscape architects? Realtors? Apartment house owners? Owners of commercial property? Federal, state, or local governments? Will you focus on young families, middle-aged homeowners, or retired people? What will their income level be? (Do you see how a business plan forces you to answer all kinds of pointed questions?)

Now, how many of these people are out there? Ten? Ten thousand? Ten million? How many will you need to attract? How do you find this stuff out? For some categories, it's easy. For instance, if you're interested in working with Realtors, get a head count from the websites of local realty companies. Others are more difficult, such as apartment house owners, because they don't advertise anywhere. But I bet there's an association of apartment house managers or something similar in your community. Ask around. Your local library probably has a reference desk that's staffed with nice people who can help you research the most obscure things, and they are usually better at it than an inexperienced person surfing the web without knowing what to look for or how to find it (they have access to special search engines, too). Give them a call or stop by.

Next, where are these potential clients located? That is, how far afield are you willing to go to look for business? (For starters you'll probably want to stick to your local community. It's too much to try to become Statewide Landscaping Company right away; long-distance projects are harder to manage, and the travel time and vehicle expenses make your services too costly to be competitive with those of local companies.)

How many potential clients live in your community? How many people move into your community each year? What percentage of these people do you intend to grab away from the competition in the first year, two years, five years? The marketing people call this *market penetration*. It's an important question because you need to know not only what the potential for your company is but also how much business you'll need to do to be successful. This also relates to the financial projections we'll be getting to soon. (*Tip:* Find all sorts of useful and interesting facts about your community at www.city-data.com.)

Finally, take a look at overall industry growth trends to see whether your strategy is really viable. In other words, is the work actually out there? For example, if you choose to only landscape new homes, working for builders and developers, make sure there's going to be a sufficient volume of new construction in your area over the next couple of decades. If not, you're kidding yourself about your potential success. (*Tip:* Do an Internet search for "landscape industry growth" to access articles on this subject.)

Step Six: Competition

You won't be the only one out there. Searching on the Internet for "landscaping [your community name]" is the best way to size up the competition. You'll quickly see who's in the business and what kind of services they provide, whether they give free initial consultations, give discounts to seniors, or offer things that you may not have

Gardening Jobs versus Landscaping Jobs

GARDENING

Lawn care (mowing and edging, fertilizing, pest control, weeding, aerating, renovating, overseeding)

Plant care (pruning and hedge trimming, fertilizing, pest control, weeding, replanting, mulching)

Tree care (pruning, fertilizing, pest control, cabling and bracing, usually for smaller trees only)

General cleanup and refuse management (sweeping, washing down walks, trash hauling, composting)

Irrigation maintenance (replacing sprinkler heads, repairing valves, etc.)

Water management (watering, programming automatic controllers)

LANDSCAPING

Lawn installation (sod and seeded lawns)

Plant installation (annuals, perennials, shrubs, trees, food gardens, etc.)

Tree planting and transplanting, guying and staking

Hardscape construction (walks, retaining walls, fences, patios, planters, decks, arbors, etc.) and lighting installation (low-voltage walkway and landscape lights)

Irrigation installation (sprinklers and drip systems, water mains, backflow devices, automatic controllers, etc.)

Drainage system installation (grading, drainpipes, catch basins, etc.)

Water features (ponds, fountains, streams, etc.)

thought of. Websites are also a good indication of the quality of your competition; if they have a hokey website they may be a hokey operation all around, and vice-versa.

In my community there's a pretty consistent 50 percent turnover of landscape companies every year. Scary? You bet, but don't be discouraged. Most of those people didn't take an orderly approach to business management like you're doing. They crippled themselves with ignorance and lack of professionalism right from the get-go. And they probably had one or more serious flaws in their service, leading clients to quickly abandon them and even spread word of their crummy service to their friends and via Yelp, Angie's List, and other online review sites. You'll do better. (By the way, somebody needs to step in to service the clients who are abandoned by these failures. Why not you?)

Because most gardening and landscaping companies are privately owned, it's pretty much impossible to find out what their sales volume is, how many employees they have, or how profitable they are. Even if you've seen a company's shiny new trucks running around town, it doesn't mean they're profitable. It also doesn't mean their clients are satisfied with the services they offer. Remember, to be successful you need to be better than the competition at keeping clients happy, not necessarily flashier or bigger.

One good way to learn about competing companies is to ask a few questions of their suppliers, such as nurseries, irrigation supply houses, and other vendors. Ask them who's busy, what kinds of work are available, and who's doing what. Find out who's hiring. You might even learn who's behind in their bills.

Another approach is to apply for work with a few companies, even though you're not looking for a job. This is a little underhanded, but business isn't always pretty. During an interview, you can probe for information about the company and get a good inside look at their operation. You can even bring up the subject of other companies and get some interesting dirt. Remember, of course, that not everything you hear will be true. You'll need to read between the lines. (Who knows, maybe you'll end up working for one of these companies for a while.)

Once you've gathered information, you need to write a short summary and evaluation of the results. How many companies are there? How many are large, how many small? What's the sales volume? How many people are employed locally? What are the major services being offered? To whom? Who's booming and who's just hanging on?

Finally, how will you fit in? Which competitors are the most important to you and why? How will you draw business away from them? (*Tip:* Maybe you could offer your competitors some kind of service that they aren't set up for or interested in doing. Some examples would be irrigation work, backflow preventer testing, leak detection, pest management, or small equipment repair.) Why will your business be better? Be brief, but be specific.

Step Seven: Marketing

How are you planning to attract business? That's what marketing is all about. Read chapter 6 and then choose strategies that are right for the type of business you're after, the clients you're interested in, and the economic conditions in your area.

Pricing

Describe your price strategy in detail. Are you planning to appeal to small clients by offering low prices and discounts for seniors, or will you be trying to attract top-end work where prices are high? Will you offer specials or coupons to get new clients? An hour's free consultation? Special prices on the first month's garden service? Internet-only discounts to track your website traffic?

Warning: One of the most annoying and potentially deadly problems in this business is "low-balling" competitors—cut-rate operators who somehow get by charging less than the actual cost of the job for their work. There are many variations on the basic theme (see chapter 7), but for now be aware that low-ballers exist. They drive prices below the profit level for everyone, and they may affect you, especially if you plan to enter into the cutthroat world of competitively bid maintenance or landscaping jobs.

Low-ballers never go away (a new crop sprouts every year like crabgrass), but they really come out of the woodwork during difficult economic times or when there's very little work around. So, before you get too far, check out the situation in your area. You can still do fine even with a heavy population of low-ballers, but you'll need to avoid going head-to-head with them. Stick to custom work, provide top-quality service, and retain your clients. Don't waste your time and resources getting into bidding wars because even if you get some jobs you'll make little or no money on them.

Advertising

How will people find out about you? Will you go door-to-door? Send out direct-mail pieces? Join the chamber of commerce and network with influential businesspeople? Advertise on radio or in the local newspaper? Market through your own website? Develop a Facebook page? Stand on the corner in a gorilla suit? What? Tell it.

Show it, too. Do a mock-up of your proposed advertising in print and on your website. Lay out any brochures and handouts you plan to use. You'll force yourself to see whether you actually like your ideas once they're on paper.

If you plan on working with an advertising agency, a web designer, or a graphics company, describe the work they'll be doing for you.

Next, describe the results you expect to get from your marketing program. That is, X dollars invested in marketing should produce Y dollars in sales. Be realistic. For example, direct-mail campaigns usually produce a 2 or 3 percent response. Believe it or not, that's considered a success. If you project a 50 percent response, you'll look like a rube to investors. Plus, you'll be in for a shock when you put your plan into action.

Remember to think about both short-term and long-term strategies. That is, you'll probably do one set of things to get started and then switch to a different set once you're rolling. What's different about them? Why? Justify your choices.

Step Eight: Company Organization

In years one through five, how many employees will you have and what are their duties? Who answers to whom?

Let's have a quick look at big versus small. The first year, your organizational chart may look like this:

Yes, that looks pretty silly, but still, there's no shame in being a one-person operation. By year five, it may look like this flowchart:

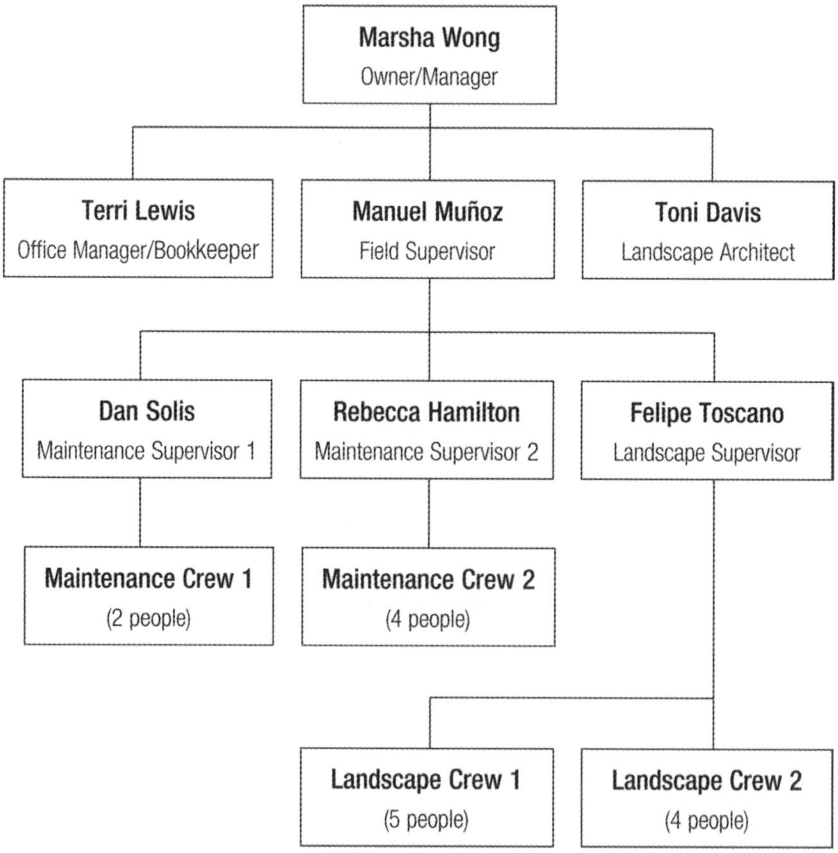

Now you've got twenty-two mouths to feed (plus their families), plus casual labor brought in as conditions warrant, subcontractors, consultants, and who knows what else. You've got a big, consumptive company on your hands, and you'd better know how to run it. Here's where lack of management skills can do you in quickly.

Big versus Small

Though "big" looks a lot like "successful" to most people who haven't been there, "big" is actually a whole lot riskier, more stressful, and more unstable than "small." Here's why: If you're little Joe Gardener working out of the spare bedroom, your overhead is practically nonexistent, the volume of work you need to do in order to get by is minimal, your exposure to risk is small, and you can easily keep a lot of things in your head without losing control. (Does working out of your home start to make sense now?)

Get big, and you've got a lot of potential problems. First, you have people (including yourself) who are part of the overhead of the business—in the previous example, the office manager, the field supervisor, and possibly the landscape architect. You can't bill for their time like you can for the laborers, but they cost you lots of money nonetheless (maybe more than the laborers whose work pays *all* the bills, including overhead). They're probably on salary, which means you have to pay them even if business is slow. That can drain you dry in no time.

Similarly, you've suddenly got an office, a storage yard, equipment loans, upkeep on everything, and lots more insurance. All this is overhead, it's all expensive, and it can't be shut off. So the rules of the game change. Suddenly, you've got to sell jobs like crazy because you need so much more cash every month. Your overhead has gone from literally a few dollars per day in the good old spare bedroom days to many thousands per month with the big fancy outfit. Naturally, doing all that work exposes you to more liability—defects, accidents, lawsuits. And, of course, sooner or later those employees will start to give you problems, such as injuries, theft, substance abuse, and personal conflicts.

How do you control this huge organism? When do you find time to stop by all your many jobs that may be scattered over two or three counties? How do you know if you're making any money? When do you have any time for yourself?

Most companies that start to grow hit the "in between" stage of 2 to 15 or so employees that is one of the most challenging periods in the life of a small business. A company that size is too small to have the resources or the earnings potential of a larger operation, but too big to enjoy the simplicity of a one-person show. That's not to say you can't make money with an outfit that size, but it takes special effort and a bit of luck to make it.

The point is, now is a good time to think hard about whether your goals include eventually getting big. Let's hope that you understand that there's a world of difference between the small home-based business with maybe one or two employees and the big company downtown. What about that fifth year? Unless you're up for the challenge of running a business in addition to doing landscaping, maybe you'll be a lot happier if you're still working by yourself or with a helper out of your spare bedroom.

You might have guessed that I favor staying small. I got bigger for a while, with 5 trucks and a bunch of employees and an office manager, but I soon decided that even though I could probably learn to handle it as well as the next person, I didn't want to do so. I like running a really small business because it's safer, more fun, and just as profitable if you play your cards right. Most people think getting big is an inevitable aspect of business success, but that's folly. If you just want to earn a living, you can do that just as well with a tiny operation as with a big one. Ask yourself whether you are trying to build an empire or do landscaping work, because those are two really different things. Always run your business with your head, not your ego. If you decide to get big, be sure that it makes business sense, that you can handle it, and that you want that kind of life.

Now, all this drives your sales and staffing projections. Once you've decided how big to be, it's easy to figure out how many people you'll need. (Refer to chapter 5 for a rundown on the wonderful world of employees, and use the information to calculate your staffing needs year-by-year for the first five years.)

Briefly describe what employees will do, whether they'll be full or part time, permanent or temporary, and whether they'll be part of overhead or of cost of sales. Tell how much you'll pay them. Indicate what the *labor burden* will be (worker's compensation insurance, social security taxes, fringe benefits, and so forth). Describe vacation and sick-leave policies, paid holidays, and so forth.

Also describe how you'll use subcontractors and outside services. Justify all staffing that's not part of the cost of sales (that is, any employees that don't generate a profit through billable hours and are therefore a drag on profits)—do you really need an office manager, for example, or is that something you can handle yourself in the early stages of your company?

Step Nine: Facilities and Equipment

Based on the sales volume for each year, describe the kinds of equipment you'll need to own, lease, or rent (tools, vehicles, heavy equipment, office furnishings, etc.) and the kind, location, and size of facilities you'll need (office space, storage yard, employee facilities, etc.).

For instance, if you plan to have two gardening crews in year three, that means you'll need two trucks (plus a truck or other vehicle for yourself unless you're part of one crew), two sets of tools and equipment, and a place to store it all. You may or may not need a bigger office; this is still a reasonable-sized company to run from home, provided the employees don't create a nuisance for the neighbors.

Add up what all this will cost, item-by-item and year-by-year. Don't forget to allow for inflation in the cost of future purchases. (*Tip:* It's not easy to calculate future costs. Doing a web search on "how to predict inflation" will produce a bunch of numbers-heavy articles and calculators that take more math chops than I have to understand them, and that may or may not prove to be accurate. I wish I had an easy answer for you on this one. Try looking up the *Consumer Price Index* ("CPI") and extrapolating forward based on past increases. One thing's for sure: your costs will change over time and that needs to be taken into account in your projections.)

Step Ten: Financial Projections

OK, we've put this off long enough. Now that you know what you're planning to do for the next five years, you need to get down to the details of how much money this is going to cost and how much you're going to make. Here are some questions your number crunching is going to answer:

1. What are my start-up costs?
2. How do I plan to meet those costs?
3. What's my cost of doing business (years 1–5)?
4. What are my projected sales (years 1–5)?
5. What are my projected profits (years 1–5)?
6. What's my equity (years 1–5)?
7. What's my cash flow (years 1–5)?
8. What accounting and control systems will I have?

How will you answer all these questions in an orderly way that others will understand? Well, there are several standard formats for presenting this information that are universally accepted and are required in any business plan. These include the following:

1. Profit-and-Loss Statement (also called the Income Statement)
2. The Cash-Flow Statement
3. The Balance Sheet

Add a form for start-up costs and a description of your accounting system, and you've got it. Yes, this is going to hurt, but not that much. You may even find it interesting. But just in case you're tempted to skip this part, here's a *BIG WARNING:*

If you're not the numbers type, then get a job. You haven't got what it takes to run a business. Running numbers regularly is how you keep track of whether your business is making money or not, and it's how you predict your cash flow, which is critical in a seasonal business like landscaping.

Nobody cares whether you make money or go broke. The only way you'll make money is to keep track of everything via the income statement and the balance sheet. Do this now, and do it regularly after you're actually in business. Skip it, and you'll probably go broke. It's that simple and that cruel. The successful business owner manages money well, no matter what type of business he or she has. Now let's get to work.

Start-up Costs

Make a list of all the things you'll need on your first day in business. It should look something like the "Estimated Start-up Costs" form (see later in chapter).

The total is the amount of money you'll need to set up your business. (*Note:* The figures shown are examples only. Don't use them for your own start-up costs.) Most of these are pretty easy to figure out. Be realistic about the cost of things, and allow enough to cover actual costs. For example, don't figure you'll spend $1,000 for a truck, because you know you can't get a reliable one for that price. Even if you could find one at such a low price, it would certainly soon break down, and the repairs could possibly cost more than the purchase price. Some costs, such as advertising, you simply carry forward from your work in previous sections of the business plan. Others require a little homework.

A couple of items need to be explained. *Operating Cash* is the money you'll need to run the business until it becomes profitable. (*Warning:* The chief cause of failure for start-up businesses is insufficient start-up cash. Be sure you have enough.) Ever optimistic, new business owners assume all they have to do is hang their sign out and in no time they'll be driving around in a fancy European sedan, and flying their private jet to Paris for lunch. Sorry, but there's just no way that's going to happen no matter how talented or optimistic you are. If you have debts, you'll have to service them. That's a fancy banker's way of saying that you have to pay off your loans, and that money has to come from whatever work you manage to find. Also, you may not have a lot of business at first but your overhead costs will still need to be paid. Finally, it'll take you a while to figure out how to make a profit, especially if you just quit your job at the burger stand, so even though business may be brisk you could lose money for a while. The bottom line? You have to have funds to cover yourself while you're getting started. (You'll get an exact amount for this item after you've done your cash-flow projections in a little bit. For now, leave it blank.)

Owner's Draw Prior to Start-Up is grocery money, shoes for the kids, and that sort of thing. Allow for it.

Finally, something with which you'll soon be familiar: *Contingency* is the money you've allowed to cover your very human tendency to underestimate the cost of nearly everything and your understandable but probably unrealistic belief that everything will go just the way you planned it.

Now that you have some solid numbers, you can go to the bank and say, "Here's what I need, so how 'bout letting me have it?" But hold on. Did you think they'd finance you 100 percent? Sorry, but investors (banks or anybody else with half a brain) are going to expect you to risk your own money first, up to reasonable limits. That's called *owner's equity*. If you were to work entirely off other people's money, you could just walk away if things started going bad, couldn't you? Investors know that. They want *your* neck on the block along with theirs; otherwise they won't play. So that means you'll have to put up at least some of this money. You don't need to sell the house, but you may be asked if you'd be willing to take out a second mortgage on it or pull some money out of savings.

So now you need to look at your own financial picture and ask yourself how much you can come up with on your own. If your startup costs are modest, then maybe you don't need investors after all. If you do, how much money are you going to ask of them? That's the bottom line.

If you're buying a business, you need to look at the price of the business plus the carrying costs and contingency. Other than that, the same rules apply.

Sales Projections

Let's think a minute about your sales projections in general terms. Are you going to remain a one-person operation forever? That's fine. Are you planning to employ several people after the first year? That's fine, too. To achieve your goals, you have to know how much you'll need in sales in order to cover your overhead and profit. In other words, it takes a lot more business to keep ten people working than just one.

What's the dollar volume of your sales expectations over the first five years? For the one-person maintenance operation, you might be satisfied with $50,000 in sales the first year, operating part time, and $100,000 every year thereafter. This would be a modest goal, and your expectation would be to make a basic living for yourself. These sales figures are the total amount you take in. They include the big four: labor, materials, overhead, and profit. You don't get to keep the whole $100,000. Sorry.

On the other hand, you might need $350,000 per year to keep a three-person landscaping outfit in business. (*Note:* Sales per person in landscaping are higher partly because there are a lot more materials used.) Can you realistically expect to achieve that in the first year, or should you make that your third-year goal? In the financial section, you'll fully justify these projections; for now you need to simply state them.

One more thing about sales: They'll vary seasonally. In cold climates, winter is the slow season. In hot climates, it may be the opposite. For me, fall is busier than spring because people procrastinate, then panic at the last minute. Summer's slow because everyone's on vacation. Ask around and find out what the seasonal sales curve is for your area. You won't be able to get straight answers from your local competition unless you resort to some very sneaky spy tactics. But guess what? People who are in the business a couple of counties distant from you might tell you a lot because you're not a potential competitor. Try going to a state gathering of your trade association and buying drinks for a few successful people. Oh, and your vendors can tell you about seasonal sales volumes, too.

Profit-and-Loss Projections

Also known as an *income and expense statement*, a *profit-and-loss statement* ("P&L") is a list of all your income and expenses for a given period, usually a month or a year. When you're actually in business, you'll do these at the end of every month. For now, you're going to project the same information, on a monthly basis, for the first five years. Simplified just a bit for now, a typical landscaper's P&L looks like the one later in the chapter.

Let's look first at the general structure of the P&L. *Income* is pretty self-explanatory: Whatever checks you get from clients for work you did for them go here, sorted out by whatever categories you choose. In this case, we're segregating *Income* into *Landscaping, Maintenance,* and *Other. Cost of Sales* is sometimes called *Cost of Goods Sold* or *Variable Expense* or *Controllable Expense*. It's the stuff—labor and materials—that goes into the actual work you do for your clients, as opposed to overhead. The more work you have, the higher your Cost of Sales. When you buy a bag of fertilizer, or pay a laborer to dig a trench, it gets entered into *Cost of Sales* under *Materials & Supplies.*

Now look at what happens: In July, you take in $1 million (let's dream) of *Total Income*. Your *Total Cost of Sales* is $750,000, due to the unpleasant fact that you have to pay your employees, vendors, and a bunch of other people. The quarter-mil you have left over is your *Gross Profit*. "Gross, indeed," you might say. "I had a lot of money there for a little while. I could've gone to Brazil and lived like a king." Now you're getting the idea. Still, you're an honorable person, so you pay everybody.

Estimated Start-up Costs

Fixtures and Equipment (tools, trucks, etc.)	$9,750.00
Materials and Supplies (parts, etc.)	$600.00
Office Supplies	$750.00
Decorating and Remodeling	$800.00
Legal and Professional Fees	$450.00
Licenses and Permits	$375.00
Initial Advertising	$1,200.00
Operating Cash	$1,000.00
Owner's Draw Prior to Start-Up	$1,200.00
Contingency	$600.00
TOTAL	$16,725.00

Next, there's the *General Overhead*. Buy a box of pencils for the office, and it gets entered into *General Overhead* (aka *Fixed Expenses*) under *Supplies, Office*. Simple, right? All the costs of operating your business, the ones that continue even if there's no work, go here. Let's say they add up to $200,000. Deduct that from your $250,000 *Gross Profit,* and you're left with a *Net Profit* of $50,000. Not bad for a month's work. But wait—that's only a 5 percent profit, which is not considered a great return on your investment and effort. You should feel rotten! To justify your existence, you might want to make at least 10 percent. Next month, you'll just have to try harder.

Besides, what if your *Total General Overhead* was $270,000? You would have *lost* $20,000! Yikes! Time to start looking for a job! (Seriously, you WILL lose money some months. That's because of the differences between the income cycle and the expense cycle, and it's not necessarily a sign of problems. Quarterly and annual numbers are more important than monthly ones in determining the success of your operation.)

Well, naturally this is a bit fanciful, because you'll probably never take in a million bucks in one month, even your best month. Still, I hope you get the idea of how profit and loss works, because understanding this concept thoroughly is important to your success.

Now, let's suppose you do these projected P&Ls for the first five years. Things look good to you on paper, but any banker can see you're nuts to put in such optimistic figures. For example, if you project that *Cost of Sales* will run 10 percent of *Total Income,* and *General Overhead* will run another 10 percent, leaving 80 percent for you, you'll look stupid or conniving or both. There goes your credibility and your loan. So, how do you know what to put in all those little blank spaces? Let's take it step by step. (See chapter 4 for a discussion of cash versus accrual accounting, another important aspect of financial control. The following examples use a cash basis for the accounting.)

Income. How much work can you realistically do each month and each year? That depends on a lot of factors. Among them are crew size (think of each person as a profit center, capable of generating a certain amount of work per day), productivity, quantity of work available, and selling prices in your area at any given time.

First, consider exactly what kind of work you'll be doing. Mowing lawns? Great. What's the going rate in your area? (*Hint:* Call a couple of competitors and ask them what they charge.) Let's say that mowing is priced by the square foot. Now, given a certain mower type (ask the manufacturer about the performance of their equipment) and allowing for travel time and nonproductive time like loading up in the morning, how many square feet can you mow in a week? A little arithmetic, and there's your income.

Some kinds of work are a little harder to figure. For example, suppose you'll be doing custom landscape carpentry—fences and arbors and decks. Let's say you and your helper are working a forty-hour week. You figure you'll bill yourself out at $32 per hour and the helper at $25. Your total labor billings would be $2,280 per week or about $9,500 per month, assuming you could work every week ($2,280 times 50 weeks divided by 12 months. No, there aren't exactly four weeks in a month, and you're allowing for two weeks off during the year).

Now, let's say you'll sell your materials for an amount equal to your labor. Conveniently, the cost of labor and materials are often about equal for many kinds of construction work. For projections like these, it might be safe to go with this assumption. Better yet, call the lumberyard, get some prices, and figure out how much lumber you can use up in a week. Experience with the work really helps you in estimating these costs.

Remember that you should be marking up most materials at least a little bit—10 percent, minimum. You have a right to make money on materials as well as labor. Some items, such as plants, are quite profitable—you can usually increase the wholesale price (the price you pay the supplier) by 50 to 100 percent and still remain competitive. Others, such as the lumber in this example, are sold to you at maybe a 10 to 20 percent "contractor's discount" off retail, so there's not as much

Sample Profit-and-Loss Projection Sheet

JUNE 2015

INCOME	
Sales, Landscaping	$8,400.00
Sales, Maintenance	$ 3,500.00
Sales, Other	$ 500.00
TOTAL INCOME	$12,400.00
COST OF SALES	
Dump Fees	$150.00
Equipment Rental	$350.00
Labor	$3,200.00
Materials & Supplies	$2,840.00
Miscellaneous	$100.00
Outside Services	$800.00
TOTAL COST OF SALES	$7,440.00
GROSS PROFIT (income minus cost of sales)	$4,960.00
GENERAL OVERHEAD	
Accounting	$20.00
Advertising	$200.00
Bank Charges	$15.00
Car & Truck Expense	$250.00
Depreciation	$800.00
Dues & Subscriptions	$30.00
Entertainment & Meals	$25.00
Insurance	$200.00
Interest Expense	$525.00
Legal Expense	$0.00
Licenses & Permits	$20.00
Meetings & Seminars	$25.00
Miscellaneous	$75.00
Postage	$20.00
Professional Fees	$90.00
Rent/Real Estate	$175.00

Sample Profit-and-Loss Projection Sheet (Continued)

Repairs & Maintenance	$100.00
Supplies, Office	$40.00
Taxes, Other	$0.00
Taxes, Sales	$100.00
Telephone	$25.00
Tools	$80.00
Travel & Lodging	$0.00
Uniforms	$0.00
Utilities	$20.00
Wages	$265.00
TOTAL GENERAL OVERHEAD	$3,100.00
NET PROFIT (LOSS) (gross profit minus overhead)	$1,860.00

profit to be had. How you express these prices depends on whether you're working on a time-and-materials basis or a lump-sum bid, but either way the markup is still there. Often, the markup on materials is what makes the difference between profit and loss on the job. (Read about bidding in chapter 7.)

You'll have some other expenses, too, such as equipment rental and maybe subcontractor costs. You'll need to at least recover these costs, and you should make a 20 percent profit on them. So, after figuring out what those costs will be (do some test bids, call subs, etc.), you might decide to add another $2,200 a month to cover them (this is just an example; actual costs will be different for each job you do). Your *Total Income* would then be $21,200: $9,500 for labor, $9,500 for materials, and $2,200 for equipment and subcontractors plus your markup on those items.

Of course, in the slow season your income will probably drop. That's why you do P&Ls for each month, then add them up to get the year's income.

Remember, projecting this stuff is part science and part fine art. Do all your homework, figure things as best you can. Project, don't just guess. Spend time, examine your assumptions, take it to your accountant, run your numbers by that landscaper you met at the state convention. It's important that you do this right, because if your assumptions are wrong, you'll be in for a shock after a year in business. (*Tip:* Some professional and trade associations offer for sale "time-and-motion studies" that purport to offer realistic information on how long it takes for a typical worker to perform various tasks like planting and mowing. This data can be quite helpful in understanding your costs, since labor is much harder to estimate than materials. But of course take these studies with a grain of salt, because as the car manufacturers say, your mileage may differ.)

Cost of Sales. Next, deduct your anticipated variable costs one-by-one to arrive at a total cost of sales. Remember that these expenses vary directly with the amount and kinds of work you do.

Here's where you put the actual amounts you pay for labor, materials, and incidental expenses. For instance, the cost of your lumber goes into the *Materials & Supplies* category. Money you pay employees goes into Labor. Money you pay to subcontractors gets entered into *Outside Services.*

General Overhead. Under normal business conditions, overhead figures don't change with the ups and downs of sales. Utility bills, license fees, insurance, and other overhead items are going to be there whether you have a lot of work or none at all. Enter them month-by-month, remembering that some of them will only occur at certain times of the year or will vary throughout the year. For example, your accounting costs will increase markedly at tax time. It's important that you enter expenses in the months when they actually get paid, because they'll affect your cash flow then. Figure your advertising budget based on the marketing strategy you developed earlier in the business plan. Depreciation is based on the cost and age of your equipment; ask your accountant for help on this one. Continue the process, entering an amount in each category, for each month. Add it all up, and there's your *General Overhead.*

Net Profit (Loss). Let's hope you'll show a 10 or 20 percent net profit. Why? Well, recently someone asked me why businesses should show a profit, as if it was some kind of crime against the people. First of all, without a profit, you're just making wages, and if you're going to settle for that, well, why not get a job and save yourself all this effort? Second, without profit, there's no reserve to pay for problems, to cover the replacement of expensive equipment as it wears out, to fund research and development, or to make improvements in service. Profit is also your reward for taking all the risks associated with starting and operating a business. Finally, profit is the earnings you hope to make on the money you and your investors put up to start and carry the business. That seems reasonable, doesn't it? So, don't be afraid of honest profit. You're taking the chances, making the investment, doing the hard work. You've got a right to that profit.

By the way, if you're sharp, you're wondering where *your* salary comes from. Good question. The answer is, that depends. When you start, your income will come out of *Cost of Sales* ("above the line," businesspeople sometimes say), because you'll be helping to do the jobs and you should be paying yourself an hourly wage just as if you were an employee. Later, you may abandon the fieldwork and become a full-time manager. Now you've moved "below the line" and become a part of overhead. Now your income must come out of *owner's draw* or out of profits. Many, many people get to this point and don't understand that they've just added $30,000 or more to their overhead. Fail to account for that money in your bids, and you'll go broke. Remember to check on this in a few years when you think things are going just swell.

The easiest way to grind through five years of monthly P&Ls is with a computer. Any spreadsheet program can make this task much easier. If you don't have a computer and can't borrow one, do it manually, but just do it. (Many public libraries have computers available for public use. Or, you might be able to use the computer lab at a local community college.)

Don't forget to increase sales by a realistic amount each year to account for anticipated improvements in your business and also to take care of inflation. Naturally, when sales go up, so do expenses. Overhead probably goes up, too, especially if you're planning to grow. Every time you add a new element to your business, such as an office manager, more insurance, or a storage lot, your overhead takes a sudden large jump. This may cause you to lose money for a few months until the increase in business begins to pay for the added expenses. On the other hand, if you continue to work out of your home and keep your crew size small, maybe your overhead won't increase much at all.

Play around with the figures, make test assumptions, and see what happens. When you're satisfied that everything is as accurate and believable as possible and you're comfortable with the scenario, put it all together in a neat form. Include a brief written explanation for your projections—what your reasoning was behind the major assumptions you've made.

The Cash Forecast

The *cash forecast* (aka the *cash-flow projection*) is a tool for predicting how much actual cash you'll have at any given time in the future. It's a simple way to tally up cash on hand, anticipated income, and anticipated expenses.

Why bother? Because you might be making a great profit on paper but have no money on hand, leading to what business people call a *cash-flow crisis*. How does this happen? Well, there are many possible scenarios, but often it's a simple matter of having too much month left over at the end of the money. If you get a big job and have to pay cash up front for materials, and if perhaps the progress payments weren't structured right, you'll suddenly be paying out more than you're taking in. The cash forecast is a way to avoid this unpleasant surprise. It's a tool you'll use to operate your business in the black, but you'll also include it in your business plan. Look at the sample *Cash Forecast Sheet* on the following page. (Remember, the figures are only for illustrative purposes—don't use them!)

You can see this isn't too complicated, but there are a couple of tips that will help you do it right. Where do you get the *Cash in Bank* figure? The first month, it's whatever you put into the account. For subsequent months, you simply carry forward the *Cash Balance* from the previous month. *Petty Cash* is money set aside in the desk drawer or your pocket for incidental purchases. *Anticipated Cash Sales* are any amounts you may receive in cash or checks from clients. *Anticipated Collections* is money received for bills you sent to clients. *All Disbursements* refers to your total monthly cash outlay—payroll, materials purchased for cash, amounts paid on your charge accounts, office supplies, everything you expect to spend that month. Notice that some of the overhead items, such as *Accounting* and *Insurance*, represent a portion of lump sum payments made on an annual or other non-monthly basis; although you may not have to write a check for these items in the month of your *Cash Forecast*, you should be setting aside the funds from your income every

Cash Forecast Sheet

	JAN	FEB	MAR	APR	MAY	JUN	JUL	AUG	SEP	OCT	NOV	DEC
1. Cash in Bank (start of month)	2,100	3,800	5,500	6,300	8,700	11,400	15,400	18,300	23,900	28,000	31,900	35,400
2. Petty Cash (start of month)	200	200	300	300	300	400	400	400	500	400	300	200
3. Total Cash (add 1 and 2)	2,300	4,000	5,800	6,600	9,000	11,800	15,800	18,700	24,400	28,400	32,200	35,600
4. Anticipated Cash Sales	500	700	1,500	5,000	6,840	7,600	9,500	8,500	8,000	7,000	4,000	1,500
5. Anticipated Collections	3,000	2,300	2,900	4,400	4,260	4,700	5,600	8,200	9,100	9,200	6,000	4,200
6. Other Anticipated Income	—	—	100	200	300	300	400	500	500	300	200	—
7. Total Receipts (add 4, 5, and 6)	3,500	3,000	4,500	9,600	11,400	12,600	15,500	17,200	17,600	16,500	10,200	5,700
8. Total Cash Receipts (add 3 and 7)	5,800	7,000	10,300	16,200	20,400	24,400	31,300	35,900	42,000	44,900	42,400	41,300
9. All Disbursements	2,000	1,500	4,000	7,500	9,000	9,000	13,000	12,000	14,000	13,000	7,000	3,000
10. Cash Balance (subtract 9 from 8)	3,800	5,500	6,300	8,700	11,400	15,400	18,300	23,900	28,000	31,900	35,400	38,300

month so that you'll have the money later when the time finally comes to make the payment.

What if your *Cash Balance* is a negative number at the end of a month? Well, that means you're going to run out of money. It's a signal that you had better make some arrangements for a *cash infusion* from some source during that time period. As a part of the business plan, those negative numbers prove that you'll need start-up money and tell you approximately how much. Naturally, your forecast is based on educated guesswork, but attention to detail can get you pretty close. You should know by now what your overhead will be, so that's easy to include in *All Disbursements. Cost of Sales* is, of course, a little trickier, as is *Income* (in your P&L projection), but if you remember that your figures represent goals, and if you're willing to work hard to achieve those goals, you should be fairly accurate.

The Balance Sheet

The *balance sheet* shows your *assets*, your *liabilities*, and the difference between the two, called *net worth*. There's nothing mysterious about it. Unlike the Profit-and-Loss Projection, the balance sheet looks at the big picture: What's the final judgment on how you're doing? The sample *Balance Sheet* shows what it looks like.

As you can see, this *Balance Sheet* is simply a list. Fill in the blanks, and you're done. *Current Assets* are your liquid assets, ones you'll normally use within a year. If you have any doubtful *Accounts Receivable* (ones from deadbeat clients that you think you'll never get paid for), use *Less Allowance for Bad Debts* to exclude them. Use *Prepaid Expenses* for things like insurance that you've paid in advance. *Inventory* for a service business is usually small—maybe just a few bags of fertilizer in the toolshed, but they're still assets. *Fixed Assets* are ones you normally don't liquidate within the year, such as your truck or your lawn mower. *Liabilities* are similarly separated into *Current Liabilities* and *Long-Term Liabilities*. Now, the reason this is called a *Balance Sheet* is that the *Total Assets* have to equal *Liabilities & Net Worth*—that is, the two figures must "balance." The difference between *Assets and Liabilities* is *Net Worth*.

Balance Sheet

12-31-15

ASSETS	
Current Assets	
Cash:	
Cash in Bank	$12,510
Cash on Hand	$400
Petty Cash	$200
Accounts Receivable	$4,200
Less Allowance for Bad Debts	$<–200>
Adjusted Accounts Receivable	$4,000
Prepaid Expenses	$700
Inventory	$350
TOTAL CURRENT ASSETS	$18,160
FIXED ASSETS	
Land	$ —
Buildings	$ —
Equipment & Fixtures	$5,700
Vehicles	$11,500
Less Allowance for Depreciation	$<-6,500>
TOTAL FIXED ASSETS	$10,700
TOTAL ASSETS	$28,860
LIABILITIES	
CURRENT LIABILITIES	
Accounts Payable	$3,400
Notes Payable (due w/in one year)	$2,000
Payroll Taxes, Current	$1,400
Sales Taxes, Current	$300
TOTAL CURRENT LIABILITIES	$7,100
LONG-TERM LIABILITIES	
Notes Payable (due after one year)	$5,600

TOTAL LIABILITIES	$12,700
NET WORTH (Owner's Equity)	$16,160
LIABILITIES & NET WORTH	$28,860

These few simple forms have answered all the questions you or an investor might have about your financial projections for the first five years of your operations. True, the actual numbers will be different once you're in business, but if you're careful, you won't be in for any rude surprises.

Description of Accounting Systems

The final step in preparing your financial information is to describe your proposed accounting and bookkeeping systems. (Study chapter 4, then write a simple description of how you'll handle record keeping.)

Some Tips on Raising Money

What if your projections show a net loss for the first year or two? That's not improbable, because you'll be paying for your start-up costs and maybe not having such great sales. That's when you know you've got to find some money to carry you through.

Conveniently, you now have an impressive document. Potential investors can see what your goals are, how much capital you'll need, and when and how you plan to pay it back.

Alternative Sources of Financing

Banks will probably be happy to lend you money for a piece of new major equipment because they can repossess it pretty easily if you get behind in your payments. They'll be less likely to give you a loan for general operating expenses. If you can't get a bank loan for general funds, what do you do to cover your needs?

Well, there are two basic classes of financing: *debt* and *equity*. A loan is an example of debt financing: You borrow money and then pay off principal and interest over a period of time. Remember that you have to pay loans back in full and on time. Failing to do so will ruin your credit rating, a major mistake when you're in business. Guard your good credit with your life, just like your mom and dad told you.

Equity financing is different: In exchange for money, you give up part of the ownership of your company. Generally, you don't have to pay this money back, but your investor will expect to receive a percentage of the income on a permanent basis. Because you'll be starting out small, you'll probably want to use debt financing, but you should know about both. Here are the commonly used alternatives.

Vendor Credit and Progress Payments (Debt)

Fortunately, there are a couple of important methods of financing built right into standard business procedure. One is *vendor credit*; another is *progress payments*.

They're linked in an important way. (See chapter 8 to learn more about these topics.) These are the everyday sources of money for your business. Here's the idea: You buy materials from your vendor on credit, collect progress payments of money that your clients owe you for the work you did, and use it to pay your vendor's bills. There's no interest charge if you pay on time. (Related to this is *accounts receivable financing,* which is sometimes used as a short-term solution to a cash crunch. A bank or other lender advances you a percentage of the value of your good receivables. It'll cost you, so don't use this method unless you get into trouble.)

Vehicle Loans (Debt)

If you choose to buy a new truck, you'll have no problem financing it as long as your personal credit is OK. Using a loan to purchase the vehicle is the most common and least costly way to do this, but you can also lease a vehicle. A lease costs more than a loan and has some other disadvantages, but unlike a purchase, you can usually take possession with very little money out of pocket. (*Tip:* Buy if you can; lease if you must. And be sure you look carefully at the terms of the lease, particularly what happens at the end of the lease period when you have to turn the vehicle in or buy it.)

Turning Fixed Assets into Cash (Debt)

Take out a second mortgage on your house if you have to. If you have an old high-interest loan, you might consider refinancing, which could lower your monthly payments, freeing up cash that you can put into the business. You may even be able to pull some cash out of your equity. Talk to your lender or to a reputable mortgage broker to find out what your options are. (*Tip:* Watch out for loans with unrealistic payment requirements; many people have lost their homes because they accumulated too much debt against them.)

Personal Loan (Debt)

If you have good credit and a good relationship with your bank, maybe you can get an *unsecured personal loan,* which is a loan without any collateral such as a vehicle to back it up. Then there's the loan (gift?) from Mom and Dad or good old Uncle Harry. As for loans from your boyfriend, girlfriend, best friend, or whatever, do what you want, but you might want to ask a few people who have been there whether that's such a good idea. It can be a great way to end a relationship. Be careful about drawing your personal associates into your business.

Partnerships (Equity)

You could go into business with a partner, either one who shares in the work or a "silent" partner who is part owner of your business on account of a financial interest but who does not take part in the day-to-day activities of the business. Partners share ownership, investment, and risks. Not all partnerships are 50/50; they can be structured any way you want. Read the section on partnerships and decide whether you really need a partner.

Nonprofessional Investors (Equity)

Mom and Dad, Uncle Harry, a co-worker, a friend, possibly a supplier, or even a client—all could potentially be equity investors in your company. Do you want to share ownership with them? Remember, they'll be looking over your shoulder all the time. Maybe this is a good idea, maybe not. Before you do this, talk to an accountant, an attorney, and yourself.

Small Business Investment Companies (SBICs) and Similar Investors (Equity)

The government operates or sponsors numerous kinds of small business investment organizations. Call the Small Business Administration for current information or use the Internet: www.sba.gov.

Selling Assets

Do you have idle personal assets such as an extra vehicle, a piece of property, or a coveted antique hubcap collection that you could liquidate, either now or later, if you need them? Look at your entire financial picture, not just your proposed new business.

04 Learning to Live with Record Keeping

If I have you figured right, you're probably not a records type of person. You love the outdoors, physical work, action. You hate bean counting, writing little things in little boxes on little pieces of paper, keeping track of numbers. "My momma didn't raise me to be a clerk!" is your motto. OK. Fine. But listen carefully to what I believe is some of the best advice in this book:

Records, believe it or not, make life easier. Just ask anybody who's been audited by the IRS, who's been sued, or who ended up losing a million-dollar job because they lost track of an important piece of information. *Records are your friends. They are life itself.*

Here's something your momma may have told you. I know mine did, over and over, and she was right. "You'll just have to learn to like certain things. That's life." If you hate record keeping, learn to like it. I can help.

Let's get you set up with a good basic record-keeping system so you avoid all the stupid and unnecessary hassles that other beginning business owners go through. It's another step in doing things right the first time, in being a true professional. It's not hard. It's a lot easier than the alternative. Let's go.

Bookkeeping

Bookkeeping is the recording and management of financial information relating to your business as a whole, including the checking account, income ledger, expense ledger, income and expense statements, balance sheets, and cash-flow projections.

For some reason, bookkeeping terrifies most people. In reality, the worst thing that can be said about bookkeeping is that it's tedious. There's nothing mysterious or all that complicated about it, and it can be mastered easily by anyone. But, of course, there are things you need to know.

Why do I need to keep books? First, the Internal Revenue Service requires that you keep records of where the money went. They have certain well-defined minimum standards, and if you don't adhere to them, they take your house. A pizza box stuffed with a mishmash of crumpled receipts and invoices and miscellaneous bits of paper doesn't meet minimum standards.

Next, *you* need to know where the money went, too, because it may be going down the toilet and taking your business with it. That's where bookkeeping comes in; it's a record of income and expenses, money owed to you, money you owe to others, and money in your bank account. Period.

Is this going to get real complicated? No. You're going to learn how to set up a simple set of books that will serve you well in the early years of your business. Later, you can get real complicated if you need to. But even if you do, the basics are still the same.

How much time will I have to spend doing bookkeeping? For now, probably under half an hour a day, every working day, to keep everything current, then three or four hours every month to reconcile everything. Less if you use a computer.

What if I just hire somebody else to do it? No. Not at first. Hire someone and you'll never pay any attention to the matter again until you're in bankruptcy court. The bookkeeper will hand you things, and you won't have the slightest idea what you're looking at. And if the bookkeeper is a larcenous type, he or she will soon figure out how to rip you off. Keep your books yourself.

But what about an accountant? An accountant is another matter. First, let's talk about the difference between a bookkeeper and an accountant. The *bookkeeper* enters the day's activities—income and expenses—into the books. The *accountant* periodically takes that information and uses it to generate profit-and-loss statements, balance sheets, and other tracking data. An accountant also advises you on the direction in which your business is going and can keep you out of financial trouble. And most importantly, the accountant will prepare or help you to prepare your tax returns. Yes, you probably do need an accountant. Good ones, though expensive, will pay for themselves in tax savings alone. Tax laws, always complex, have become truly Byzantine, impossible for the layperson to understand. Understanding them is the accountant's job. Budget $400 to $500 per year to pay for the accountant.

Can a computer help me? Yes and no. No computer program can replace an accountant. That's like letting a robot do brain surgery. But a good *accounting software package* can help you with routine bookkeeping chores, remind you of payables on their due dates, write checks for you, and produce an impressive and useful set of financial records at the click of a mouse button—income-and-expense statements, balance sheets, and others. A computer can make bookkeeping easier to do, and it can save you lots of time.

Finally, accounting software for the small business is cheap. You still need to understand the principles, though, so we're going to look at bookkeeping in more traditional terms. If you decide to computerize, it'll be easier because you learned the old-fashioned way.

Rules about Record Keeping

1. You can't remember everything.
2. The thing you don't write down is the thing you'll need.
3. Ten seconds spent recording a bit of information will save you an hour of time trying to remember it later.
4. The longer you work at keeping good records, the easier it gets.
5. A record is no good if you can't find it later.
6. A record is no good if other people can't understand it.
7. It's better to keep too many records than too few.
8. The longer you're in business, the more kinds of records you'll develop.

Forms of Bookkeeping

Single-Entry versus Double-Entry

With a *single-entry system*, you record each transaction only once. For example, when you write a check to the nursery, you record it in the expense ledger as check number 1234, Wilsonville Nursery, May 8, $416.50. You do the same with income in the income ledger, recording, for instance, a check in the amount of $705.00 that you received from Mr. and Mrs. Hickenlooper for planting a hedge. At the end of the month, you total them up, subtract expenses from income, and hopefully end up with a positive number. It's a simple system that's adequate for many small businesses. The drawback is that there's no way to know if you've made a mistake. Because it's easy to transpose numbers or add wrong when doing the entries, this is a significant risk.

In a *double-entry system*, each transaction is recorded twice—once as a *debit* and once as a *credit*. The check to Wilsonville Nursery would be entered in two categories: once in Merchandise & Materials as a debit (increasing the amount) and once in Cash in Bank as a credit (decreasing the amount). The debits and credits must balance, which is how you check for errors; if the books don't balance, it's time to go looking for the problem. The drawback here is that a double-entry system takes more time to use than a single-entry one. It's also a little harder to understand.

I suggest you begin with either a manual single-entry system or a computerized double-entry system. Either is easy to learn and adequate for your needs. I began with a ready-made single-entry system from the office supply store. I learned to use the system in about an hour, and it served me well for many years until I finally got a computer. Then I went to a computerized double-entry system that I'm still using.

Cash versus Accrual

Using the *cash method*, you enter income when it's received and expenses when they're paid. Even though it's called a "cash" system, checks and credit card sales are treated the same as cash. If you deposit a check from Mrs. Jones, you enter it into the income ledger as of that date. Likewise, you enter the check you wrote to Wilsonville Nursery as of the date you wrote it.

Using the *accrual method*, you record income as of the date the transaction occurs. For instance, when you send Mrs. Jones a bill for last month's gardening work, you enter the amount as a sale in your income ledger even though you haven't received the money yet. When you charge something at the nursery, you enter that as an expense, even though you haven't paid the bill. Accrual accounting, like double-entry bookkeeping, is more complex and requires more work. Either cash or accrual bookkeeping can be a single- or double-entry system.

So why would anyone want to use the accrual method? Because it gives a more accurate picture of your financial condition. Do you *need* to use the accrual method? No. In fact, because yours is a service business with no inventory, the cash method is preferred. (*Tip:* The IRS needs to know which method you're using. You can change from cash to accrual without asking permission, as long as you do it at the beginning of a fiscal year and tell them about it. Ask your accountant for more information.)

The key to using a cash system successfully is collecting from your clients as soon as the jobs are finished and paying your bills as soon as they're due (that's not just the key to success with your accounting; it's the key to your success in general).

Fiscal Year versus Calendar Year Accounting Period

Large businesses often use a *fiscal year* as the basis for their bookkeeping: a twelve-month period beginning at some time other than January 1. If you'll be operating as a sole proprietor or a partnership, you're required to use a standard *calendar year*—January 1 through December 31.

A Simple Bookkeeping System, Step-by-Step

Here's a basic set of books and instructions on how to use them. It's a single-entry, cash-basis system that operates on a regular calendar year. You can set it up in less than an hour, using a few dollars' worth of ledger paper and a box of file folders.

The Chart of Accounts

The heart of the system is a list of all your income and expense categories, called a *chart of accounts*. Accountants will include other items in the chart of accounts, such as asset and liability categories that are used to produce the balance sheet, but for now all you need is the income and expense portions. Every transaction—income and expenditures—is then entered into one of these categories, using the *income and expense ledgers*. Numbering the accounts is optional, and not used as often as in the old days, but it's still handy if you choose a paper-based system. Each category is given a four-digit *account number*. To conform with standard accounting practice, numbers for income accounts are in the 4000 range and expense accounts in the 5000 range. Numbering is done in steps of 10, which allows you to enter new categories later without disrupting the system; you just insert the category as 5055, in between 5050 and 5060. (Note that a computerized set of books often doesn't use account numbers.) A typical landscaper's chart of accounts looks like the one that follows.

Naturally, many of these categories require a little explanation. First of all, notice the layout: first income, then expenses, with the expenses divided into variable and fixed so that you can separate the job-related costs (variable) from general overhead (fixed). Notice, too, that the numbering jumps from the 5000s in variable expenses to the 5500s in the fixed expenses. That keeps them both in the 5000 range but gives them a little breathing room from each other. Now, let's look at specifics.

Income

You can divide your income up any which way. If you have multiple crews, you might want to put each one into its own income category, or subdivide maintenance into commercial and residential, or add categories for other kinds of work you specialize in, such as sprinkler repair or tree work. All the IRS will want to see on your profit-and-loss statement is income, period. The special categories are for you, so set them up however you want.

Expenses, Variable

Remember, these are all your job-related costs. I've shown some of the common ones, but you may wish to add or delete. *Dump Fees* and *Equipment Rental* are self-explanatory categories that are typical in the landscaping business.

Chart of Accounts

Joe's Landscaping & Gardening Co.

Income

4000	Sales, Landscaping
4010	Sales, Maintenance
4020	Sales, Other
5000	Expenses, Variable (Cost of Sales)
5000	Dump Fees
5010	Equipment Rental
5020	Labor
5030	Materials & Supplies
5040	Miscellaneous
5050	Outside Services

Expenses, Fixed (General Overhead)

5500	Accounting
5510	Advertising
5520	Bank Charges
5530	Car & Truck Expense
5540	Depreciation
5550	Dues & Subscriptions
5560	Entertainment & Meals
5570	Insurance
5580	Interest Expense
5590	Legal Expense
5600	Licenses & Permits
5610	Meetings & Seminars
5620	Miscellaneous
5630	Postage
5640	Rent/Real Estate
5650	Repairs & Maintenance
5660	Supplies, Office
5670	Taxes, Other
5680	Taxes, Sales
5690	Telephone
5700	Tools
5710	Travel & Lodging
5720	Uniforms
5730	Utilities
5740	Wages

Labor is *payroll* and its related *labor burden* (taxes, worker's compensation insurance, etc.), but you might wish to divvy this up to show labor burden as one or more separate categories; it's up to you. Don't put the office help or other employees who aren't doing the actual landscaping work here. They'll have their own category, which you'll learn about in a minute.

What the Heck is "Labor Burden?"

Suppose you pay an employee $15 per hour. As you well know if you have ever been an employee yourself, a whole lot of money gets withheld from that hourly amount when the time comes to write paychecks. What you may not know is that in addition to the taxes that are withheld from the employee's pay, the employer also has to pay for certain costs, based on the amount paid to the employee. Some of these payments are required by law, and others cover benefits that employers have the option of offering to their workers. So as an employer, you have to take into account all of the out-of-pocket costs you will be paying on top of the hourly wage, and you have to factor them into the hourly rate that you charge for that employee's time. Those extra charges are called *labor burden.*

Mandated employer-paid costs include a share of the social security taxes, and all of the unemployment benefit taxes (called "FUTA"), worker's compensation insurance costs, disability insurance payments, and possibly state-required benefits as well. Optional labor burden costs could include the employer's share of health insurance, paid vacations and holidays, paid sick time, retirement benefits, bonuses and gifts, profit sharing, and paid uniforms and laundry. You also need to take into account other expenses that are necessary to keep that employee working, such as liability insurance, vehicle expense, cell phone costs, the cost of managing payroll and general employee administration, small tools that so often disappear for one reason or another, and the cost of initial and ongoing training. Depending on tax rates, state requirements, your experience rate for workers compensation insurance, and your ability to offer optional benefits, the total labor burden could run anywhere from 30 to 150 percent of the base pay. Wow, huh?

Now, when you decide how much to charge clients for that employee's work, you need to add both the base pay of $15 per hour and the labor burden, to get your actual costs. Next, you add on whatever markup you need to make in order to cover your overhead and profit. You can see that the price you charge clients will be well over the $15 per hour that you are paying the employee. When I was an employer,

I always wanted to laugh when an employee would gripe about how much more I charged for their time than I was paying them. But rather than laugh, I had to try to explain the concept of labor burden as best I could. Usually, the employee would be unconvinced and would simply go on assuming that I was pocketing tons of cash off their hard work. Of course you do have a right, and a need, to profit from the work of your employees (why have them otherwise?), but the share of the money you get to take home is usually the smallest portion of all, with the employee taking most of the money and the various cost centers taking the rest.

Use *Materials & Supplies* only for things that actually get incorporated into your jobs, not for mower parts or building materials for your shed—those go into fixed expenses because they're not job related. But suppose you bought a tool and wore it out on one job. Should you call it a material for that job and therefore a variable expense? You could argue the point either way, but I would think its cost should be included in the cost of the job, therefore it's a job-related expense. (By the way, did you remember to charge the client for that tool? You should have.)

Miscellaneous is a good friend—it'll accept stuff you can't figure out where to put. But if you keep putting the same kind of stuff into this category, set up a new category for it instead.

Outside Services is for *subcontractors* you bring onto your jobs, such as the electrician who puts in an outlet for your sprinkler controller or the arborist who diagnoses and treats a diseased tree. (*Tip:* Not all states allow you to hire subcontractors; check your contractor's license board regulations to find out whether it's OK in your area.)

Expenses, Fixed

Accounting includes the fees you pay to an accountant for annual tax-return preparation and other services throughout the year.

Advertising could include a number of things other than ad space that you buy in the local paper. For instance, you could put the cost of business cards here (or in Supplies, Office if you prefer). Hiring a pro to take photos of your jobs could be posted to Advertising. So could "Joe's Landscaping & Gardening Co." T-shirts. Or the hosting costs for your website.

Bank Charges are monthly charges for your checking account, overdraft charges (shame!), and the like. However, interest you have paid on your credit card purchases (shame again!) might preferably be put into the *Interest Expense* category. (Do you see that there aren't such rigid rules here? Figure out how you want things, ask your accountant if it's OK, then do it.) Those bank charges are an exception to the rule that every expense must be represented by a check, because they're simply deducted from your account balance by the bank. So remember to *post* (that's accountant language for writing something into a ledger) them here even though you didn't write a check for them (the amounts you were charged will be listed on your monthly bank statement).

Car & Truck Expense is any money you spend on maintaining your vehicles: oil changes, repairs, and so forth. You can put your vehicle insurance here or in the *Insurance* category. *Note:* These categories (all of them) are for *expenses*, not capital expenditures, such as the purchase of a truck or major improvements to assets (like remodeling your office). Major purchases are called fixed assets and are depreciated in the next category, *Depreciation*.

Any *asset* (truck, mower, office remodel) that you expect to last longer than one year must be *depreciated*, that is, written off over the anticipated life of the asset. Let's say you buy a mower for $800. The IRS has rules about how fast you can depreciate various things, and maybe they say you have to depreciate your new machine over a four-year period. That means you can *write off* only $200 this year, $200 next year, and so on. (That's really oversimplified; you need to visit the IRS web page on depreciation or talk to your accountant. Please do it.) So if you want, you can enter 1/12 of $200, or $16.67, into this category each month. If you prefer, you can just wait until the end of the year and enter the whole thing, but posting it every month will give you a more accurate picture of your financial condition. (Like *Bank Charges*, this isn't going to be represented by a check, of course.) Remember that depreciation is a big expense, even when you're small, so whatever you do, don't forget to account for it.

Dues & Subscriptions can be used for trade association dues, membership in the botanical garden, business magazine subscriptions, and the like.

Entertainment & Meals might puzzle you. "Who am I going to be entertaining?" you may ask. Well, maybe you'll take a prospective client to lunch, or a general contractor whom you're trying to impress. You also use this category to account for any meals you have while out of town on business, at a trade show or a seminar, for example.

Insurance can cover all your insurance, or you could break this up into several categories, such as liability insurance, vehicle insurance, bonds, and so forth.

Interest Expense is a catch-all category for any kind of interest you pay, such as interest on vehicle loans, business loans, credit card purchases, or mortgage interest. *Warning:* If you work out of a home you own, you can deduct a percentage of the mortgage interest, but not the entire mortgage payment. The IRS won't let you get away with having the business pay for the principal on your house; they consider that going too far. So, if you use, for example, 20 percent of the total square footage of your house and land for business purposes (office, storage yard, sheds, etc.), then you deduct 20 percent of the interest you pay to the mortgage company each month. You can find a breakdown of interest and principal on each monthly mortgage statement (remember that the proportion of interest and principal you pay each month will usually change over time, so don't keep using the same figure year in and year out).

Legal Expense is for attorney fees. You'd better hope this category stays real empty, except for an annual legal checkup with your friendly attorney. (Some law schools offer free or low-cost legal advice to low-income people including those hoping to start a business. Of course the advice comes from students, so it's a bit like getting your hair cut at the barber school only the stakes are higher. You decide whether such advice is worth taking.)

Licenses & Permits covers fees for business licenses, contractor's license, and related expenses. Not your personal driver's license or your fishing license, though.

Meetings & Seminars is for fees you pay to attend professional educational events. (No, not that Saturday golf clinic. Sorry.)

Then there's *Miscellaneous* again for whatever didn't fit elsewhere. These Miscellaneous categories had better not get too full of questionable expenses or the IRS will raise an official eyebrow.

Postage is for stamps, overnight package services, courier services, and similar items.

If you rent your house rather than own it, or if you rent a storage yard, use the *Rent/Real Estate* category to account for these costs. You have the option of paying yourself monthly rent for business use of your home; talk to your accountant about the wisdom of doing this.

Repairs & Maintenance is for repairs to anything, though you may want to use it only for tools of the trade, not office equipment, which could be charged to its own category.

Supplies, Office is used for letterhead, copier paper, pens and pencils, books, and other such stuff.

Taxes, Other is for business property tax, real estate property tax (a percentage of your home's property taxes goes here), and any other business taxes. (*Tip:* You can't enter your personal income taxes here as an expense. They're not an expense, and the IRS knows that just as well as you do. People who pull that one get a little room at Leavenworth. Don't try.)

Taxes, Sales is used when and if you pay sales taxes (see "Tax Planning" in chapter 9).

Telephone ought to be simple because you'll have a separate business phone line not used for personal purposes. If your cell phone is partly for business use and partly for personal use, charge an appropriate percentage to your business. Sometimes the phone company bills you for Yellow Pages advertising, and that really should be separated out of the total amount of the payment and posted to Advertising.

Tools is for small tools like rakes, pruning shears, gas cans, and whatnot. Remember, any big items that last over a year have to be depreciated, not posted here. *Exception:* You can "expense" (write off in one year) a certain dollar amount of tools and equipment if you like. A reasonable maximum is $200 per purchase; there's also a limit to the annual total. Ask your accountant first, because there are rules and also important tax consequences.

Travel & Lodging is for hotels, airfares, taxis, anything related to a business trip. A business trip? That's travel for business purposes, like meeting with a client, attending a seminar or convention, researching new developments in your field. (Not golf, even if you *are* a turf expert.) By the way, you can take a trip that's only part business and still write off that portion. There are, of course, rules, so ask first.

Naturally, you'll want to look professional, so you'll set up a *Uniforms* category for the cost of purchasing, maintaining, and replacing uniforms.

You'll write off a percentage of your gas, water, and electric bills and post them under *Utilities*.

Payroll for any non-job-related employees goes under *Wages*. This employee could be a part-time office helper, a salaried estimator, a salesperson, or a mechanic. Admittedly, you may not use this category at first, but it's a good idea to have it in there, if only to remind you of the bright future ahead of you as a landscaping big shot.

> Keep in mind the important fact that you don't have to pay taxes on expenses. In other words, every expense reduces your taxable income by the amount of the expense (or sometimes less, for certain expense categories). So be sure to keep track of ALL legitimate expenses so that the taxable income you report to the IRS is realistic and you don't end up paying too much in taxes.

The Bank Account

For cash-basis accounting, the *bank account* is the beginning of all transactions. First, get a separate checking account for the business. (See chapter 2 for information on how to do this.) You'll deposit all business income into this checking account and pay all your business bills from it. No exceptions. That way, things are simple and orderly. If you somehow end up paying for something any other way, such as out of your personal checking account (a pox on you!), pay yourself back by writing a check from the business account. If you pay for something with cash (sometimes necessary), reimburse yourself by check. (See "Petty Cash" under "Accounts Payable" later in this chapter.) If you want to take some money out for yourself, write a check to yourself and label it "Owner's Draw."

Just as you don't pay business expenses from your personal checking account, never pay personal expenses from your business account. It's just too difficult to separate things later.

Finally, when you write a check, always record the *payee* (the person or company to whom you're writing the check). Never write a check to "cash" because you won't be able to post it to a specific expense account later. Regarding deposits, need I warn you to deposit all business income into this same checking account? No cashing client's checks to get beer money; they all have to go through the account first. (*Tip:* When you open your account, request *end-of-the-month cutoff* so that your statement will be issued at the end of each month rather than at mid-month or some other arbitrary point of the bank's choosing. It makes reconciling your bank statement easier.)

Balance the account every month, as soon as you get the statement in the mail. It's easy and quick, and it keeps you from running out of money without knowing about it in advance. Balance just to the end of the month even if you've written checks into the next month. Retain your bank account statements for at least five years in case you're audited. Use business-style checks, not small personal-style checks. If possible, don't carry your checkbook around with you, and never leave it unattended in your truck while you're in the doughnut shop. Theft is just too common nowadays, and having your checkbook stolen can cause you unimaginable disruption and agony. I know this from grim personal experience. Better yet, leave your checks in the office and pay for everything with a credit card.

Be sure to identify each transaction completely. For payments, write the *payee*, the *job name* (if appropriate), the date, and the payee's *invoice number* in the check register. (Some checks, such as one used to pay off your monthly credit card statement, cover multiple transactions. Remember that for those checks, you'll be posting them to several expense categories.) For income, enter the details into the *income ledger*, which we'll get to in a minute, and the total amount into the *check register*, using a date or a deposit number to cross-reference the two.

An Option: The One-Write System

With the *one-write system*, each time you make a deposit or write a check, you're automatically posting the information to the ledger by writing through a carbon-backed form that copies your work onto the ledger, which is located underneath the check or deposit slip. For a small business, this can be a great way to go. It's cheaper than a computerized system and easier than a manual system.

How to Balance a Checking Account

It's amazing how many people don't balance their checking accounts just because it's intimidating to them. Really, there's not much to it, and it's something you've just got to do when you're in business. Here are some tips on how to make the process easier and less scary. (*Tip:* Using a computerized system makes balancing the checking account a snap, almost a pleasure, and could be reason enough to go that direction.)

- *Keeping your checkbook organized:* First of all, be sure you make a note of the amount of each check you write, and the payee, at the moment you write it. Also, keep your balance updated in the check register as you go along. Be careful with your arithmetic, especially transposition errors, which occur when you write "3,012.44" when you meant to write "3,102.44." Keep all receipts for things you purchase, so that you can check back on the amounts if you lose track.
- *Balancing basics:* When you get your statement at the end of the month, go through the check register and put a mark in red pencil by each check that has cleared (the ones that are listed on the bank statement). As you do so, make sure that the amount in the register agrees with the amount written on the check; this is the amount the bank has deducted from your account for that check. Next, tick off any other charges, service charges, check charges, ATM withdrawals, and so forth, and enter them into your register if you

haven't already done so. Finally, tick off deposits, comparing them with the ones listed on the statement. Now you're done comparing the statement and checks to your register.

On the back of your bank statement is a form that you can use to finish reconciling the account. First, put the amount listed as the "statement balance" (it's printed on the front of the statement) at the top of the form. Then, list all deposits you've made recently that haven't shown up on the statement yet. Add them to the statement balance to get the adjusted statement balance. Next, list all the outstanding checks (the ones you haven't received back yet) and total them. Subtract the total from the adjusted statement balance. The amount you get should be the same as what's shown in your check register after you've made adjustments for interest, and so forth.

- *Troubleshooting:* What if it doesn't work? Bank statements are rarely wrong, so the first person to suspect is you. Check all your addition for the past month because this is where you'll most often find the problem. Make sure you adjusted for any differences in balancing last month's statement. Look for old checks that haven't come back yet—ones from previous months that you may have forgotten about. Double-check that you've entered bank charges, interest the bank paid you, and so forth correctly (it's common to mistakenly deduct interest instead of adding it, for example). If you're very methodical, the error will always show up sooner or later. (Tip: If your balance is off by a number that's divisible by three, you've probably made a transposition error. I don't understand how this mysterious phenomenon works, but a former bank teller assures me that it's a reliable way to narrow down the search for your error.)

  If you have a stubborn error, don't give up. You will find the problem if you stay after it. Putting it off until next month only makes it worse. The worst thing is to let the account go unbalanced for months until you have no idea how much money you have. That can bring your business to a halt when you run out of money unexpectedly and have to transfer funds, pay bank charges, and apologize to a lot of people who are holding your bounced checks. Besides, by that time, you'll never be able to unscramble the mess you've gotten yourself into, and your only recourse may be to go humbly to the bank and ask them to open another account. It's not a good showing. If you're really stumped, ask the bank to help you balance your statement.

Accounts Receivable and the Income Ledger

Accounts receivable are simply the amounts owed to you by clients. You need to keep track of what's coming to you but hasn't arrived yet. The *income ledger* is the place to post all income.

The Invoice

Always prepare a written *invoice* for each sale. It could be a simple handwritten form from a preprinted invoice book that you got at the office supply store. Use a rubber stamp with your company name and address to identify your business. Alternatively, you could have invoices printed with your company name or use a computer to generate invoices.

Sequentially numbered invoices provide you with a way to track each invoice through your system. If you make a mistake on an invoice, mark it void and keep it in your book. When you prepare an invoice, be sure to write in the date, the amount of the sale, a description of the work that was done or the materials that were used, and whether it has been paid or not. If you're doing a time-and-materials job, be sure to enter the sales tax as a separate line item, because you'll need this later to do your sales tax return. Your client gets the original; you keep the carbon copy. Consider keeping a third copy in the client's file, so you'll have a record of all their transactions over the years. That way, if a question comes up, you can go directly to the individual file rather than having to search through your master invoice file.

Accounts Receivable

Until the client pays you, the invoice is part of your *Accounts Receivable*—the amounts owed you.

Here's a simple, reliable way to keep track of your receivables: Put a copy of each invoice into a file folder titled "Accounts Receivable" and keep it there until it's paid. Then move it to another file titled "Accounts Paid." That's it. Periodically, add up the totals on the invoices in the Accounts Receivable ("A/R") file—that's how much money people owe you. If an invoice sits in the A/R file for more than thirty days, send the client a reminder. If it's still there after another thirty days, give them a call and ask when you can pick up the payment. (See chapter 8 for more information on getting paid.)

Keeping Track of the Accounts Receivable Balance

One of the things you need to do every week or two is reconcile the total value of your unpaid invoices with the reality of how much money people owe you; the two should be equal. Here's how you do it: First, you'll need to keep a running total of your receivables, called an *accounts receivable balance*. It's the sum of the previous A/R balance plus the invoices you've written since then, minus the money you've been paid. Once you get that total, it becomes the new A/R balance. Compare it with the total value of all the invoices in your A/R file; they should be equal. If they're not, you know there's a mistake somewhere—a lost invoice, an incorrect entry, an arithmetic error. Here's how it looks on paper:

Accounts Receivable Balance

Previous A/R Balance	$1,756.49
New Invoices	914.16
Subtotal	$2,670.65
Bank Deposits	$<–1,122.03>
Checks on Hand, Not Deposited	0.00
New A/R Balance	$1,548.62
Total, Current Invoices Due	$1,548.62
Difference	$0.00

Income Ledger

When a check comes in, you'll deposit it into your checking account. But first, you need to enter it into the *income ledger*, a record of all your deposits. Look at the "Sample Income Ledger" that follows.

Although somewhat simplified, this format will probably work fine for quite a while. (*Tip:* You might consider adding a column for *Sales Tax Collected*, where you separate out the amount of sales tax on time-and-materials jobs. This makes doing your sales tax return easier and also reminds you that you owe this money to the government.) Let's look at some of the features of the income ledger.

The *Date* column will reflect the date of your deposit—the day you put the checks into your bank account. You'll notice that each deposit includes several checks and that each check has its own separate row of information. The *Job Name/Description* column tells what portion of the job this payment covers. *Code* helps you remember whether this was a deposit (D), a progress payment (PP), a final payment (FP), or a payment on account (OA).

(*Note:* A *payment on account* ("OA") differs from a *progress payment* ("PP") in an important way. Any payment made during the time you're doing the work is usually a progress payment. Any payment made after you've finished the work, but not a final payment, is called a payment on account. This doesn't come up too often, because you'll try to get a final payment as soon as you're done and not let people pay you off in stages. Still, now and then you have to make deals with people because they need more time to pay the final bill and because you regard them as credit-worthy based on their past payment history, so the indication OA helps you.)

Cash and *Check* columns are partners: They're for entering the total amount of the payment. The next three columns separate that payment out into the different income categories. Notice the Gillon deposit on 3/12: Part of the check they wrote was for maintenance ($675.00) and that was payment in full; the rest ($1,000.00) was a deposit for the landscaping work that's going to start soon.

The *Totals* column on the right adds up the total amount that each client paid you. Note that if someone paid you part cash and part check, this column would reflect the sum of both of these. Finally, there are lines for totals for each column at the end of each deposit and grand totals for the month. With this simple system, you can easily see who paid you what, how much income you have in the different sales categories, and your total sales. Whenever you make a bank deposit, spend a couple of minutes recording this information into the *income ledger* (which you keep with your checkbook) and you'll always be current and there'll be no end-of-the-month bookkeeping nightmare. (*Warning:* Post the information to the ledger first, then fill out your deposit slip and enter the deposit total into the check register. That way you won't forget. It's a pain to have to reconstruct the information from invoices.)

Accounts Payable and the Expense Ledger

It would be nice if your business was all income and no expenses. Unfortunately, you do have to pay people and companies for the things they provide you. To keep things simple, you make all these payments by check or credit card, all from the same business checking account (monthly credit card statements are paid from this account, the same as a check you write directly to a vendor at the time of purchase). Then, to keep track of where the money went, you maintain an *expense ledger*, which is simply a list of expenses, segregated into categories and totaled up. Here's my simple system that has served me well for many years.

Accounts Payable

The job of your *Accounts Payable* system is to keep track of bills you haven't yet paid. Like Accounts Receivable, there's a simple system I've used since time immemorial.

Sample Income Ledger

DATE	JOB NAME/ DESCRIPTION	CODE	CASH	CHECK	4010 SALES, LANDSCAPING	4020 SALES, MAINTENANCE	4030 SALES, OTHER	TOTALS
3/4	Koenig/Front Slope Planting	FP		1,430.00	1,430.00			1,430.00
	Bowman/Maintenance Feb.	FP		240.00		240.00		240.00
	Northside Plaza/Construction	FP		350.00			350.00	350.00
	TOTAL DEPOSIT			2,020.00	1,430.00	240.00	350.00	2,020.00
3/12	Gillon/Landscape & Maint.	D/FP		1,675.00	1,000.00	675.00		1,675.00
	SWX Corp./Soil Test	OA		100.00			100.00	100.00
	TOTAL DEPOSIT			1,775.00	1,000.00	675.00	100.00	1,775.00
3/27	Mullins/Maintenance Feb.	FP	165.00			165.00		165.00
	Lee/Back Yard	PP		10,000.00	10,000.00			10,000.00
	TOTAL DEPOSIT		165.00	10,000.00	10,000.00	165.00	10,165.00	
	TOTAL FOR MONTH		165.00	13,795.00	12,430.00	1,080.00	450.00	13,960.00

First of all, you need to understand that there are two kinds of purchases. One is *cash purchases*. An example is when you go to the mower shop and write check number 1416 for mower blades. The other is *charge purchases*, of which there are several kinds. The most common is when you buy plants at the nursery and sign an invoice but don't write a check. The invoice goes into your file at the nursery, and at the end of the month they bill you for all the invoices you've signed for that month. When you get the bill (known as a *statement*), you write a check and send it to the nursery. Another kind of charge purchase is a *credit card purchase*. For instance, you use your business credit card to charge a repair for your truck. At the end of the month, you receive a statement, which you pay.

There are also *recurring expenses*, such as rent and utilities. These are paid every month, usually at the same time of the month.

First, you need a file folder in which you stick all the invoices you get from your charge purchases. You call this folder *Unpaid Invoices* . Second, you need a folder within which to keep your current *Accounts Payable*. In it you put statements from suppliers (note that these statements are related to the unpaid invoices in the previous folder), credit card statements, utility bills, phone bills, anything else that you'll need to pay soon. To make this even better, I use three folders marked *Accounts Payable 1*, *Accounts Payable 8*, and *Accounts Payable 20*. I pay my bills three times a month—on the 1st, 8th, and 20th—and it's a snap to just pull out the appropriate folder on those dates and pay whatever's in it. That way, I don't have to sort through a messy stack of bills and figure out which ones are due and which ones aren't. It helps me to be a lot more prompt, which is important in keeping the goodwill of my creditors.

Why those dates, you ask? Well, the mortgage payment is due on the 1st. Many suppliers offer a 2 percent discount if you pay your bills by the 10th of the month, so I pay on the 8th to take advantage of that. Finally, I pay the rest of the suppliers on the 20th; they can wait since they don't offer me any incentive to pay earlier, and I get interest on the money I keep in my checking account.

You should also create a temporary resting place (another set of folders) for all your paid bills, all sorted out by expense category. They'll sit there until you post them to the expense ledger, after which they'll get stamped paid. You'll write the date and check number on them, and then they go into an identical set of folders called the *Posted Expense* files. That's the final resting place, at least until the end of the year when you pull them out and put them in the archives to make room for the next year's bills.

Petty Cash

What about items you paid for by cash, not check? The receipts for these go into yet another folder marked *Petty Cash*. At the end of each month (or week if you prefer), you sort them out into the standard expense categories and make a simple ledger sheet listing them by category, with subtotals for each category and a grand total. You write yourself a check for the total, make as many copies of the *petty cash ledger* as there are expense categories, staple the invoices for each category onto a copy of the ledger, and put them into the *Unposted Expense* files in their appropriate categories. Then later when you post the expense ledger, they show up along with other related expenses. See the following example of a *Petty Cash Ledger*.

PETTY CASH,	CHECK NO. 3452, 4/8/15	
DATE	**ITEM**	**AMOUNT**
	ENTERTAINMENT & MEALS	
3/4	Doug's Deli (Ashville Job)	$ 11.33
3/15	Harborview Restaurant (Boland Job)	26.55
3/22	Taste of Thailand (Optimist Club Meeting)	12.14
	Subtotal	50.02
	POSTAGE	
3/7	Postmaster (stamps)	4.90
3/19	Postmaster (mail bid to Wallace)	2.16
	Subtotal	7.06
	SUPPLIES, OFFICE	
3/12	Office World (pencils)	3.45
3/27	Northside Bookshop (marketing book)	20.59
	Subtotal	24.04
	Grand Total	81.12

Expense Ledger

There are a couple of ways to do the *Expense Ledger*. However it's arranged, the information you need to include is the same: check number, date paid, to whom paid, amount, and expense category.

If you had just a few expense categories, it would be a simple matter to line them up across the page as shown in the Sample Single-Sheet Expense Ledger that follows.

Unfortunately, you've got so many categories that your spreadsheet would spread all the way across your desk and onto the floor. So, what to do? The cleanest approach I've seen uses two separate sheets, one for all the checks and one for the categories. It looks like the Sample Double-Sheet Expense Ledger that follows.

Of course, a real system would include all the categories in the chart of accounts, but this shortened version will give you the idea. As you can see, it provides a running total of your expenses to date, which makes it easy to prepare a profit-and-loss statement.

Profit-and-Loss Statement

Go back to chapter 3 and look at the Sample Profit-and-Loss Projection Sheet. You'll see that it's an easy matter to transfer the numbers from your income and expense ledgers to the appropriate categories and get yourself an instant P&L. You should do this at the end of each month so you stay informed on the condition of your business. Remember that with a cash bookkeeping system you won't get an exact picture of what's going on, because there may be outstanding income or expenses not shown in the current entries. To avoid the problems that may cause, adjust your figures to account for these anticipated changes.

Fixed Assets

You need to track the depreciation of your *fixed assets*, things like vehicles, equipment, computers, and other durable business property. Discuss depreciation with your accountant or get the current regulations from the IRS or from a tax book. The rules change all the time, so stay current.

Balance Sheet

Reread "The Balance Sheet" in chapter 3 to refresh your memory about how this works. Note the connection between the *profit-and-loss statement* and the *balance sheet*: Your net worth will change in relation to the profit (or loss) you make. Therefore, you should do a balance sheet every month along with your P&L.

Tax Returns

At the end of the year, you or (preferably) your accountant uses the year-end profit-and-loss statement and balance sheet to prepare your taxes. (See "Tax Planning" in chapter 9 for tips on avoiding nasty surprises at tax time.)

Sample Single-Sheet Expense Ledger

CK. NO.	DATE	TO WHOM PAID	AMOUNT	5020 LABOR	5030 MATLS. & SUPPLIES	5510 ADVERTISING	5530 CAR & TRUCK EXP.	5660 SUPPLIES, OFFICE	5960 TELEPHONE
217	5/14	Coast Nursery	314.22		314.22				
218	5/16	Mary Cook	280.12	280.12					
219	5/16	Shell Oil Co.	56.10				56.10		
220	5/20	Bell South	221.50			195.00			26.50
221	5/20	Office Depot	12.70					12.70	
222	5/20	Farm Supply	201.88		201.88				
223	5/20	Auto World	83.14				83.14		
		TOTALS	1,169.66	280.12	516.10	195.00	139.24	12.70	26.50

Sample Double-Sheet Expense Ledger

Payments				
CK. NO.	DATE	TO WHOM PAID	AMOUNT	ACCT.NO
217	5/14	Coast Nursery	314.22	5030
218	5/16	Mary Cook	280.12	5020
219	5/16	Shell Oil Co.	56.10	5530
220	5/20	Bell South	195.00	5510
220	5/20	Bell South	26.50	5690
221	5/20	Office Depot	12.70	5660
222	5/20	Farm Supply	201.88	5030
223	5/20	Auto World	83.14	5530
		TOTAL	1,169.66	

Expense Ledger				
ACCT. NO.	**ACCOUNT**	**TOTAL THIS WEEK**	**TOTAL TO LAST WEEK**	**TOTAL, YEAR TO DATE**
5020	Labor	280.12	6,715.22	6,995.34
5030	Materials & Supplies	516.10	7,783.65	8,299.75
5510	Advertising	195.00	817.14	1,012.14
5530	Car & Truck Expense	139.24	2,502.67	2,641.91
5660	Supplies, Office	12.70	224.60	237.30
5690	Telephone	26.50	107.13	133.63
	TOTALS	1,169.66	18,150.41	19,320.07

Summary

Here's a flowchart of how all this works together. Let's hope it makes sense to you right away. If not, study it until you understand it, because it's important.

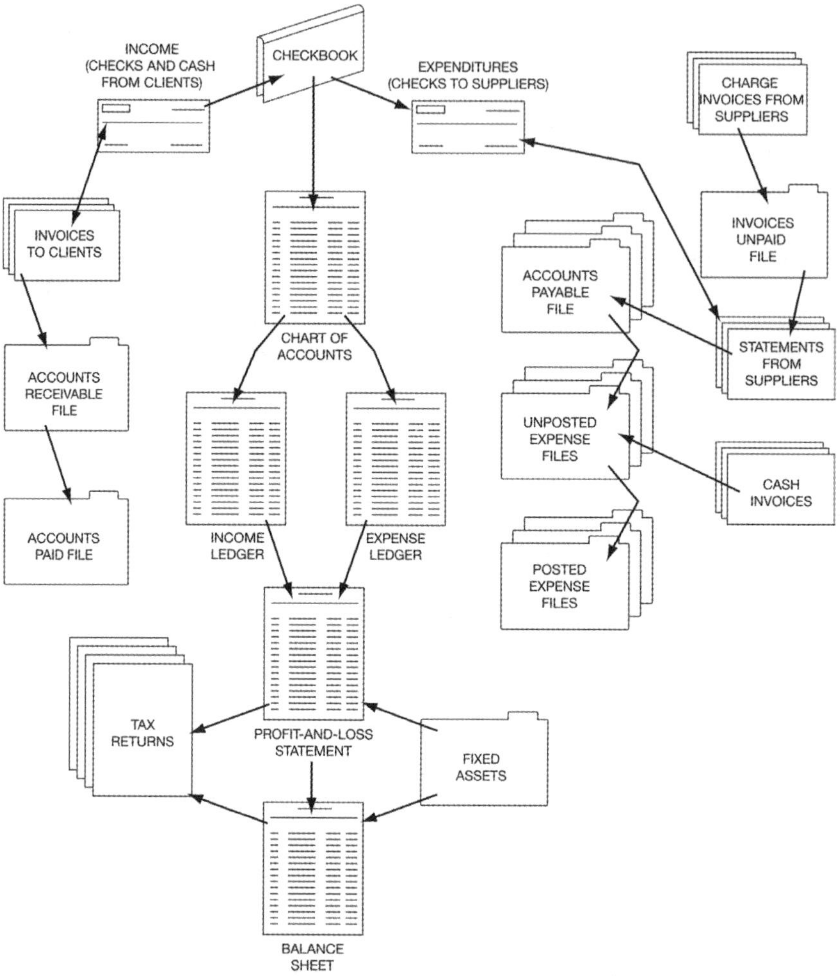

General Business Records

You need to keep more records than just those required for taxes. Records accomplish several important tasks that just aren't possible any other way. There are two purposes to communications: to provide information to others ("Here's the price of the work." "Please be ready to pour the walkways on Friday." "You're fired.") and to get information back ("How much will the lighting system cost?" "Can you supply the junipers by early next week?" "If I do this job, will you be able to pay me?"). Good communication achieves one or more of several important goals: It informs ("We'll be there Tuesday."), it clarifies ("Although the drawing doesn't specify, please use 3/8-inch machine bolts on the gate."), it verifies ("Your price for the elm trees is OK."), it documents ("The lawn was sprayed on February 19."), and it protects ("You are hereby given a third and final warning about showing up late for work."). The best way to accomplish these goals is to put everything in writing and provide copies to all interested parties.

Remember that it's your job as a businessperson to make sure all parties (employees, suppliers, clients, etc.) are informed of what the others are doing. It will be one of your most constant and demanding tasks. If something goes wrong, it will automatically be assumed to be your fault, because you are at the center of the action, the hub on which all activities turn. You will answer for everything everybody else does, both good and bad. Without your active management of the communications process, people will make incorrect and potentially damaging assumptions ("He's going to do the additional work for free."). Bad communication is the stuff of which lawsuits are made.

The following information will provide you with some effective ways to keep yourself and your projects organized and to keep you out of trouble. Some are pretty standard; I've developed others over the years. They work for me, so they'll probably help you, too.

Client Files

Before you start developing a lot of forms, you'll need a place to put them and a system for their organization. The heart of the business record system is the *client files*. The simplest way to keep things orderly is to have a separate file folder for each client. Stapled to the inside is a sheet of paper with basic information about the client and the job: name, address, email address, phone number, type of client, type of work, etc. If you use a computer, you'll keep client files in a computer database, but you'll still want a physical file for all the bits of paperwork that inevitably accumulate on even the smallest job. If you start with a manual system, just use the same information in any format you choose.

Filing Blueprints and Plans

Whether you do your own designs or bid from other people's plans, you'll accumulate a lot of *blueprints* (this old-fashioned term hangs on from the days when blueprints were actually blue). They can be a nuisance to store and keep track of. First, always fold up one copy and put it in the client's file. That's where you'll need to find it, after all, not in some dusty pile of rolls out in the garage. For originals (always keep the originals of any plans you draw) and additional copies, there are two ways to go. Rolled-up plans are space wasters, but easy to throw together in a box and call it a system. The problem is, how do you tell one from the other? Use special labels that you can order from drafting places or tie hang-tags onto rubber bands and loop them around the end of the roll. The other approach is to use a special flat or vertical filing system made just for large drawings, but they cost a lot of money. Whatever you do, keep forever all plans for all jobs you've ever done. You may need them again. (With the transition to digital drafting, more plans are on hard drives and fewer are on paper. You can even have your hand-done plans scanned by a reprographics shop and store those instead of paper versions. But you'll still have the paper plans you used on the job, often dirty, tattered, and covered with notes. Although these aren't too pretty, keep them for at least 10 years after completion of the job because you may need to refer to them in the event of a question about how things were done, or because you got sued and need evidence to back up your side of the story.)

A Basic Set of Forms

As your business grows and becomes more complex, you'll develop many kinds of forms. There are infinite ways to design forms. In upcoming chapters you'll find many examples of forms, both ready-made ones you can buy from a catalog and specialized forms that other people in the business have developed.

Some forms are required by law, others by good sense. For really small jobs, you may not need or want to use all these forms. Check your state law for minimum legal requirements and then decide how far beyond these you want to go. *Remember* that legal requirements vary from state to state, so don't just copy these forms without knowing if they'll be OK for you. Unless noted, these forms are useful for either maintenance or landscaping work.

Here are a few helpful general forms and other ideas for management of your records that you'll want to know about.

Emails

If you're like most of us, and assuming you use email (who doesn't?), you'll find yourself sending a lot of emails to clients, subs, vendors, and others connected with your projects. In fact, I encourage you to send LOTS of emails, because they document everything for everyone. Follow up phone calls and face-to-face conversations and meetings with an email to all parties memorializing the key points of the conversation. Send an email when you want to advise a client of a change in your schedule. Email orders to vendors rather than calling them in. Email, email, email. I sometimes have several THOUSAND emails for one large project, and even a modest residential job can generate several hundred emails. I save them all for at least 10 years after completion of the job (that's because the statute of limitations for latent (that is, hidden) defects is usually 10 years, and I don't want to lack documentation in the event that I get sued). Emails are at the core of my business communications system, and they should be at yours too. File emails by client, or by project, and be sure to make a backup.

Appointment Book

You cannot live without some kind of calendar or appointment book. In the old days I used two calendars. One was a big calendar pad that sat on my desk, used for scheduling jobs. The other was my appointment book. These days I have a calendar program in my computer (see chapter 2). You may want to have one on your smartphone too, synced with the one in the office. If you have office help or supervisors in the field, be sure everyone's calendars are linked and synced every few minutes. Get used to entering every appointment, note, and scheduled event. Every one. Two reasons: (1) You can't remember it all, and you don't dare forget. (2) You might need to prove that you were somewhere or did something at a certain time. I refer to past entries every day; you will, too.

Meeting Notes

I've been using this form (see following sample) for years. It contains spaces for all kinds of salient information and is versatile enough to be used in many situations.

Equipment Maintenance Log

Soon you'll have a collection of vehicles and equipment that need regular, timely servicing so that they remain reliable and last as long as possible. At the end of this chapter are some forms that will help you keep track of this. (*If you use a computer:* These forms could also be set up on the computer, perhaps in a spreadsheet. You can also use your calendar or scheduling program to automatically remind you of service dates.)

To-Do Lists

I keep a list with the names, addresses, and other vital statistics of all my current clients. Below the listing for each client, I note all the unfinished things that need to be done for that client. Nothing leaves the list until it's done. This is a great way to one-up the competition because one of the biggest complaints about service people is how they forget about little details on every job, leaving clients unhappy. Put the form on the computer and you won't have to retype it each time; just eliminate completed items and add new ones. The calendar program on your computer may also double as a to-do list.

Contact List

You'll be in the field most of the time. You'll need to call subs, suppliers, and others. You'll need their phone numbers and other information. Carry a *contact list* around in your truck and/or on your portable devices.

Window Envelopes

If you set up your forms so they all fit in standard window envelopes, you won't have so much addressing to do if you need to mail things to people (less common in these relentlessly digital days, but it does still happen). It'll be pretty easy to do if you're creating custom forms. Many ready-made forms already come this way.

COUNTY
LANDSCAPE
& DESIGN

MEETING NOTES

LOCATION

[ ] on site
[ ] office
[ ] client's office
[ ] telephone
[ ] fax
[ ] email
[ ] other:

TYPE OF MEETING

[ ] initial
[ ] estimate
[ ] estimate review
[ ] measure
[ ] bid
[ ] bid review
[ ] consultation
[ ] design
[ ] design review
[ ] layout
[ ] progress
[ ] completion
[ ] punchlist
[ ] follow-up
[ ] warranty
[ ] other:

[ ] BILLABLE

PROJECT: ____________________

CLIENT: ____________________

ADDRESS: ____________________

JOBSITE PHONE: ____________________

WORK PHONE: ____________________

EMAIL ADDRESS: ____________________

OTHER CONTACT INFO: ____________________

PRESENT: ____________________

DISCUSSION: ____________________

BY: [ ] OD [ ] other: [ ] over

DATE: **TIME IN:** **TIME OUT:**

(BACK)

Scale: __________ North: __________

Pressure: ________ psi Static: ________ psi @: ________ GPM: ________ Meter size/type: ________

Vehicle Maintenance Card

Vehicle No.: ______________________ Week of: ______________________

DAILY SERVICE & LOG:

DAY	OPERATOR	GASOLINE	OIL	MILEAGE IN	MILEAGE OUT
Mon.		gal.	qts.		
Tues.		gal.	qts.		
Wed.		gal.	qts.		
Thurs.		gal.	qts.		
Fri.		gal.	qts.		
Sat.		gal.	qts.		

Total miles driven for week: __________

WEEKLY SERVICE: Tire pressure checked by ______________________________ Date: ____________________

Repairs needed: ____

Equipment Use and Service Card

Equipment No.: Equipment Type:

DATE	OPERATOR	JOB NO. EQUIP. USED ON	CHECK SERVICE PERFORMED							HRS. USED ON JOB	REPAIRS NEEDED/ REMARKS
			LUB.	ENG. OIL		TRANS. OIL		FILTER			
				CHECKED	CHANGED	CHECKED	CHANGED	CHECKED	CHANGED		

Truck Record

Foreman: ______________________________

Date: ______________________________

Truck: ______________________________

Mileage: P.M. ______________________________

A.M. ______________________________

TOTAL: ______________________________

Gas purchases: ______________ # Gals.: ______________

Oil purchases: ______________ # Gals.: ______________

Greased (mileage): ______________

Other work done: ______________________________

____

What work needed? ______________________________

____

Tires: ______________________________

Trips to: ______________________________

05 Employees: A Joy and a Nuisance

If you're planning to do only maintenance, you can do quite well working by yourself. Forty hours of fieldwork, plus another ten in the office and shop, can make you quite a nice little living if you're efficient and energetic and you price your services right. Eventually you may want to get a helper or two.

Landscaping requires much more labor. Unless you plan to do very small jobs, you'll soon need someone to help you. So even if you're going to go it alone for the first year, read this chapter carefully because you'll soon be an employer.

As you add employees, you gradually move from being a worker to being a manager of workers and then finally to being a manager of managers. There comes a time pretty early in this progression when it just doesn't make sense for you to be out there digging holes because it means you're neglecting your other more important duties. (*Tip:* There's an old adage that still makes sense: "When you can find someone to do the work cheaper or more efficiently than you can, hire them." Save yourself for the most important work, such as client contact, sales, administration, etc.)

How Many People Will You Need?

Workloads vary so much that determining your personnel needs is a continual process. A good manager looks ahead to the coming few weeks to determine how many people she or he will need each day. Routine residential maintenance is best done by one or two people in most cases (more just get in the way), but installing 10,000 square feet of sod lawn requires a crew of five or six because the work has to get done promptly or the sod will die.

Key Employees

Your *key employees*, the ones you plan to keep for a long time, should be full time. They should be paid well, given good benefits, and kept happy. They're the heart of your business; without them you're in big trouble. One of your main jobs is to get enough work to keep these people busy. Laying off key employees and then starting over is a disaster.

Second-String Employees

Second-string employees are full time or part time, depending on the workload. These employees come and go as the workload changes. Sometimes you'll need people for only a day or two, sometimes for a few months. Seasonal layoffs are common. Clearly, it's better for everyone if you can keep people busy with off-season tasks, but there are limits.

The reality is that many, perhaps most, employees in this business are more or less temporary, and you should make that explicit when you hire people. Don't feel that this is cruel or unfair—it's a commonly accepted reality of the construction industry. The people you hire will understand it if they have any previous experience.

The disadvantage of this high turnover of employees is that you're always dealing with new people—hiring them, getting to know them, training them, and weeding out the bad ones. The advantage is that you have a flexible workforce that can vary with your needs. The other advantage is that you don't have to keep giving people raises that will eventually make them unprofitable to you.

Subcontractors

In addition to your regular employees, you may use the services of other contractors, called *subcontractors* because they work under you, to do portions of the project that you aren't skilled or licensed to handle with your own forces. (This is not allowed in some states; check with your state contractors license board to learn about regulations in your state.) In this relationship, they're working for you (not the client), and you are acting as the *prime contractor*. Over time, you'll build up a team of subs you can count on and with whom you enjoy working. You'll move them on and off jobs as you need them, with no obligation to keep them employed full time. Using subs is a great way to expand the services you offer without having to learn new skills and invest in new equipment.

Like employees, subcontractors are a source of profit for your business. Normally, you'll ask a sub for a bid and then mark it up (you customarily take 10 to 20 percent of the bid price). When you submit your bid to the client, it includes the subcontractor costs and your markup; you can show this as an itemized part of the work (the *total* price, not your markup!) or as part of a lump-sum bid. When the work is done, the sub bills you, and you bill the client.

(*Tip:* Subcontractors have to carry their own liability and worker's compensation insurance, with limits of coverage at least equal to your own. You must get *certificates of insurance* from all your subs and keep them current and in your files. If your insurance company audits you—which they often do annually—and you can't produce certificates, they'll charge you for subs as if they were your employees. This can get expensive. *Never* do business with a subcontractor unless you have current certificates on file.)

A good subcontractor can be a valuable asset; a bad one can drag your business down the hole. Remember, you're responsible for the work of your subs, and if it's not right, you'll have to fix it. That means you have to be able to evaluate and control the quality of the sub's work. When you get a bid from a subcontractor, go over it in exquisite detail, looking for errors and omissions. During the course of the sub's work, visit the job frequently, looking carefully at every detail of the work to be sure it's getting done correctly, just as you would with your own employees. If you're working from plans drawn by a landscape architect, the *specifications* included with the plans will dictate the details of how the job is to be done. If you're working from your own design, you supply the specifications. Problems can occur if you don't give enough detail or don't say the right thing. For help with this critical item, study the specifications that the landscape architects supply with their designs or get a book on the subject.

Employee or Independent Contractor?

Often, employers treat employees as if they were independent contractors, paying them without taking any payroll deductions, offering no benefits or job security, and not paying worker's compensation or liability insurance for them. The advantages are obvious: more profit, less hassle.

The catch is that if the IRS decides your workers are actually employees, you'll be stuck with back taxes, interest, and stiff penalties that could bankrupt you. Since this kind of abuse is so common, especially in the construction industry, they'll be watching you. Fortunately there are pretty clear differences between employees and independent contractors, and if you're careful, you'll stay out of trouble. The chart that follows shows some of these differences. You should also visit irs.gov for an up-to-date set of rules.

There's no simple test of whether someone is an employee or an independent contractor; it's a matter of how many of the conditions he or she has met, and that's pretty much up to the IRS, which can be as arbitrary as it wants to be. The burden of proof is on you. (Warning: You cannot make someone an independent contractor simply by getting a signed agreement saying she or he is. The requirements still have to be met. Sorry.)

It's vital that your subs be the best you can find. Approach the job of finding subs just as you would if you were looking for someone to work on your own house. Ask suppliers and others whom they'd recommend. If you see a beautifully done job, ask the owner who did it. Keep an eye out for jobs in progress and see who's doing them. Notice the bad jobs as well as the good ones. Get to know the ins and outs of everyone in all the trades you might need.

Have the prospective sub show you some of his or her work. Check with the contractor's license board to make sure the person's license is current, and ask if there are any complaints against him or her. Talk to people for whom the sub has worked. (See chapter 8 for more information on working with subcontractors.)

Temps

Some employers solve their short-term employee problems by hiring people through *temporary help agencies* or *labor contractors*. The employee works for the agency or contractor, not you, and the agency or contractor handles all the paperwork and taxes and takes responsibility for the performance of the employee. Although this costs more per hour, it can be cheaper if you factor in the time you'd normally spend on employee bookkeeping. It's a good way to get a few people quickly for that big sod job.

Job Categories (Field)

Different people do different kinds of work filling the various niches in your staff. Here are the common categories of employees.

The Laborer

The *laborer* is the base of the pyramid. It is these least-paid, first-laid-off, and generally under-appreciated people who will make you most of your money. They'll earn you far more than markups on materials ever will and more than their

Employee or Independent Contractor?

Factor	Employee	Independent Contractor
Control over methods	Methods of doing the work and the sequence in which it is done are controlled by the employer	Responsible only for results
Availability for work	Work is done only for the employer	Services are offered to the general public
Training	Training is done by the employer	No training is necessary to do the job
Tools and materials	Supplied by the employer	Furnishes own tools and materials
Profit or loss	No risk of loss	Risks profit or loss
Contractor's license	No license required	Has own license
Insurance	No insurance required	Has own insurance
Relation to business	Part of employer's regular business	Not part of regular business
Personal rendition of service	Must do the work personally	May hire others to do the work
Hours of work	Working hours set by the employer	Can set own hours
Full or part time	Full time	Free to choose
Investment	No investment	Significant investment
Right to discharge	Employer has right to discharge, employee has right to quit	Cannot be discharged, must complete work or face liability
Hiring, supervising, and payment	Done by the employer	Hires, supervises, and pays workers
Works under boss	Works under supervision of a boss	Works under own supervision
Title or position	Has a specific title or position	Operates an independent business
Premises	Works on employer's premises	Right to choose location of work
Reports required	Employer may require reports	Reports not required
Expense account	Expenses paid by employer	Pays own expenses
Payment	Paid salary or by the hour	Paid by the job

supervisors, whose contribution to profit is often indirect, based on their ability to increase the efficiency of the laborers and the overall productivity of the project. Ultimately, your financial success will be borne on the backs of your laborers.

The laborer is a follower of instructions. Laborers dig and move earth, plant, install irrigation systems, help construct hardscape features, and do whatever other skilled or semiskilled tasks are needed to complete the project. They help your *skilled trades people*, who handle the more exacting and knowledge-intensive aspects of the work. Some laborers will have specialized skills; others may come to you ignorant about which end of the shovel is which. Some will have the potential for advancement; others are satisfied (or doomed) to dig and dig forever.

A good laborer is physically fit and strong enough to do heavy work, aware of good safety practices, reliable, cooperative, and a good team player.

Some employers and their foremen treat laborers like dirt. Laborers are often considered disposable—get rid of one and there'll be six to take his or her place. This is a mighty poor approach. First of all, it's just morally wrong. Laborers have the same needs that you do, and the same rights, too. Like any of us, they respond to attention, warmth, and encouragement. Many of them, though they might be uneducated, are intelligent and willing to learn. Treat them like winners, and a certain percentage of them will rise to the occasion and may become your most loyal and valuable employees.

The Skilled Worker

A *skilled worker* has the experience and knowledge to tackle complex construction projects. Your skilled workers will understand the details of how to construct a retaining wall, build a fence, or install an irrigation system. You will count on them to do the job right even if you're not there. A skilled worker has to have at least a few years of broad experience in landscaping or in their specialized field (such as masonry, concrete finishing, or irrigation) and preferably some formal training. Skilled workers must understand construction techniques and standards and know how to read blueprints and specifications. They must know how to run equipment and be able to teach others. They must be aware of safety practices and know first aid. Their driving records must be excellent. Skilled people get paid more than laborers, of course, and you want to keep the best ones around for a long time if you can. The skilled worker is key to the quality and successful outcome of the work, and therefore to the satisfaction of your clients and to your success. Each skilled worker will have one or more particular areas of expertise, such as being good at building patios or stone walls or lighting systems. When you hire skilled people, look at examples of their work to be sure they know what they're doing, and ask them pointed questions during the interview that will confirm their knowledge of details such as how far apart to space the rebar in a block wall or how to put a broom finish on a concrete patio.

The Foreman

The foreman (who can be a woman, too) has multiple responsibilities. The foreman leads the laborers and skilled workers, instructing them in what to do, and watches them to be sure they do it right. He maintains quality standards and safe conditions on the job. He keeps track of tools, equipment, and materials. He often handles picking up materials and supplies for the job. He keeps track of paperwork: purchase orders and invoices, employee time cards, daily job reports, and equipment logs. He coordinates the work with the property owner, general contractor, landscape architect, their agents, delivery people, subcontractors, and others who show up on the job. He makes sure tools and equipment are in good condition. He starts up the job in the morning and shuts it down at night. He handles employees' problems and reports to management on their performance. He is the key on-site contact person for your clients, ready to discuss project details and concerns at any time. Sometimes he even pitches in and helps with the physical work.

In addition to having all the qualifications of a skilled worker, the foreman has to be able to direct workers efficiently and get the best out of people. The foreman needs to understand project management and have at least a rudimentary grasp of business principles. The foreman needs to have a keen eye for quality and for safety as well, and guard the project every minute of the working day. The foreman's communication skills, both verbal and written, have to be excellent and it's a good idea if he or she is fluent in Spanish as well as English. Finally, people have to like the foreman; this is no job for a grouch.

The first people you hire will be laborers, and you'll be the skilled worker and foreman. As your business grows you'll probably promote your most promising laborers to skilled workers, and, eventually, your best skilled worker to foreman. Be sure you train people in the skills needed to become deserving of promotion and a reliable part of your expanded team. (See the section on training later in this chapter.) Don't ever just put someone in charge without teaching him or her what to do—that kind of blind faith has been the downfall of more than one promising company.

Finding Good Employees

It's easy to whine about the poor quality of the workforce, yet there are lots of good, enthusiastic people out there. You just have to find them. You're lucky because at first you won't need highly trained workers. Most of the people you hire will be young, relatively uneducated, and malleable. Spend some time with them and you can turn them into real pros, people who don't know any way to do things but yours—the right way. If you wind up with poor-quality employees, you'll have to ask yourself who hired and trained them.

Where to Look

Here are some ways to look for employees, presented in approximate order of importance (my subjective opinion, anyway).

- *Promote your company to impressive people.* Now and then we all encounter a clerk or a gas station attendant who has been doing an exceptional job, someone whose spirit really shines. Take the opportunity to sell this person on the benefits of working for your company.
- *Promote from within.* Move your good people up. You already know their strengths and weaknesses. An opportunity for advancement is the best thing you can offer them. They already know how the company operates, which means you'll have to do less training.
- *Seek referrals from your present employees.* This is one of the best sources of new people. Spread the word, then reward anyone who produces a good new employee: Give them a bonus, a paid day off, tickets to the ball game.
- *Rehire former employees.* Sometimes good people leave for one reason or another. If you'd like them back, give them a call. Maybe their circumstances have changed.
- *Approach trade associations.* Many landscape contractors associations operate very progressive testing and certification programs for field personnel. They may also have a placement service.
- *Check out schools.* Contact high schools and community colleges that have landscape or horticulture departments. Keep in touch with instructors; sometimes they'll point out an exceptional student. Also check with school counselors; they may also have exceptional people they can recommend. Sometimes a student that you take on for the summer will become your best employee.
- *Advertise the job.* Put a listing in the classified section of the local paper, or put it up on craigslist or other Internet service. A lot of people, many of them unsuitable, will call. Don't sign up for a weeklong ad—you'll get way too many calls. You can show the company name or not, depending on whether you want your current employees to know you're hiring and

whether you want a bunch of job seekers on your doorstep every morning. Describe the requirements of the job. Make it easy for people to respond. Watch out for discriminatory language that mentions sex, age, race, and so forth. Omit salary figures.

- *Get someone off the wall.* In my town there used to be a stone wall next to the unemployment office where day laborers would congregate in the morning, hoping to be picked up by a contractor or other employer. If you hire in this casual fashion, remember that you have no idea who these people are and whether they're right for your needs. Some are OK; many are not. Remember, too, that you have to go through the whole routine of paperwork, deductions, and so forth, whether you hire someone for an hour or a decade. (Anyone who tells you it's OK to pay cash to "casual labor" is misinformed.)
- *Go to an employment or temp agency or a labor contractor.* These companies specialize in screening workers and can theoretically supply you with someone who is qualified to do the work you need. But don't assume the people they send will be any better than what you might find on your own; I once hired a worker through an agency and later found out he was a con artist who faked on-the-job injuries to get workers compensation payments and to sue unwitting employers. I found this out when . . . yes . . . he faked an injury, claiming that mulch had gotten into his eye.
- *Consider chance applicants.* If you advertise a lot and have a high profile business, job seekers will call you constantly. Sometimes these aggressive people are good candidates, so give them a once-over if you're looking for workers.

The Spanish-Speaking Employee

Immigrants, legal and otherwise, from Mexico and Central America are a large portion of the workforce, especially if you live in the Southwest. The language barrier is an important factor in managing foreign employees. Every employer has a story about some minor misunderstanding that led to a big problem. If you hire people who lack English language skills, you and your key people need to be bilingual, at least enough to train and instruct people and to listen to their problems. You also need to keep one English-speaking person on the job at all times, because clients resent not being able to talk to someone during the course of the work. Finally, you need to explain to your Hispanic employees that their chances for advancement will be limited until they learn English. Support good workers that you would like to keep on by letting them know about classes in *English as a Second Language* ("ESL") and by paying for tuition and books if they show interest. This helps them and you. (*Tip*: You learn some Spanish, too. It's only right, and it improves rapport considerably. Besides, suppose you're clearing brush one afternoon and one of your employees hollers, "¡¡Cascabel!!" Wouldn't it be helpful to know that a rattlesnake was about to crawl up your leg? I thought so.)

Legal Requirements of Employers

As soon as you hire someone, you will be subject to many federal, state, and sometimes local laws that are complex and ever-changing. For complete information on federal regulations visit www.dol.gov; for state regulations visit your state employment department website or local office. Here is a summary of the most common federal laws and regulations current as of this writing . . . but please, please check with your local employment development department or follow the links to the various departments that regulate aspects of employment. Important: Be aware that state laws are different and also apply to you, so you must check to be sure you know what the requirements are for your state. I want to be sure you have the latest information, and that's best done online or in person rather than in the pages of a book. Count on official information, not what I provide here. (*Tip:* If you happen to bid work for the federal, state, or municipal government then you will be subject to still more regulations and requirements. Be sure to take this into account if you want to go in this direction, because the extra burden will be considerable.)

Wage and Hour Laws

Employee Recordkeeping: The Department of Labor requires you to keep the following records for every employee:

- Employee's full name and social security number.
- Address, including zip code.
- Birth date, if younger than 19.
- Sex and occupation.
- Time and day of week when employee's workweek begins. Hours worked each day and total hours worked each workweek.
- Basis on which employee's wages are paid.
- Regular hourly pay rate.

- Total daily or weekly straight-time earnings.
- Total overtime earnings for the workweek.
- All additions to or deductions from the employee's wages.
- Total wages paid each pay period.
- Date of payment and the pay period covered by the payment.

Minimum wage: The law establishes a *federal minimum wage*; state laws may set higher standards. You must pay all workers at least the minimum wage.

Full time vs. part time employment: This is not defined in federal law and does not affect compliance with any federal requirements.

Overtime: Employers must pay *time-and-a-half* for any work over forty hours per week. For salaried employees, *compensatory time* (time off in exchange for overtime work past 40 hours, also called "comp time") must be granted at time and a half, and the employee must take compensatory time within the same week as the overtime.

On-the-job time: Workers must be paid for any time that is controlled by and benefits the employer. Exceptions are mealtimes and changing clothes and washing before or after work. *Travel time* must be paid if employees have checked into the office first, but not if you have them show up on the job without going to the office or yard first.

Breaks and mealtimes: Federal law does not require breaks or mealtimes, paid or not. However, short breaks of 5 to 20 minutes are considered compensable (payable) time and have to be taken into account when calculating the 40-hour workweek.

Holidays: You are not required to give time off for holidays or to offer paid holidays.

Calculating hours worked: You may round off to the nearest five-minute period, but you must not pay for any less time than was actually worked.

Flexible Work Schedules: This is not controlled by federal law and is a matter between you and your employees. *Flextime*, and weekend, night, and holiday work are considered the same as regular work in the eyes of the law.

Pay interval: Employees must be paid at least once a month.

Final paycheck: There is no federal requirement, but state laws may regulate how soon you have to give an employee his or her final paycheck after the person quits or is terminated.

Vacations: You are not required to provide paid or unpaid *vacation time*.

Child labor: You can't employ anyone under the age of fourteen, and there are restrictions on the employment of fourteen- and fifteen-year-old laborers, including a prohibition against employment in hazardous occupations.

Free labor: You can't (believe it or not) have anyone work for free, even if they want to do so. You must pay at least minimum wage, even to interns.

Breakages and shortages: If you charge employees for things they break or lose, such charges can't reduce their pay below minimum wage.

Sick Leave: There are no federal requirements for *paid sick leave*, but the Family and Medical Leave Act (www.dol.gov/whd/fmla) does require unpaid sick leave under certain circumstances.

Loans to employees: If you loan money to an employee, you're allowed to withhold a portion from the paycheck, but you can't reduce his or her pay below minimum wage.

Garnishments: The IRS can require you to *garnish* (withhold money from) employee wages to pay back taxes or child support. You can also be required to withhold money for child support payments. You're prohibited from discriminating against or firing these employees on account of the garnishment (subject to certain conditions).

Withholding: You have to *withhold* employee taxes and deposit them in the bank within the time limits set by the government. Failing to do so can result in massive penalties. This is a critical matter for all employers.

Employee Rights

Some of the following laws apply to everyone, whereas others kick in when a company reaches a certain size. Remember that part-time employees have the same rights as full-time ones. (*Warning:* Check with your state labor board for the latest requirements. Don't count on the information included here to cover all the bases. Do your homework.)

Firing (applies to all employers)

The following covers employee dismissals:

Wrongful discharge: The *Employment at Will Doctrine* states that *nonunion workers* have no automatic legal right to their jobs; the employer may fire them at will, for any reason or no reason. Conversely, no employer can force an employee to remain on the job. In recent years, this doctrine has been modified by various court cases that protect employees from *wrongful discharge* under certain circumstances. To protect yourself against a wrongful discharge lawsuit, develop a system of *written warnings* for misconduct. State clearly what will happen if the misconduct continues, and have each employee sign the warning. That way, if you have to fire someone, you can document the fact that the worker was given plenty of opportunity to clean up his or her act.

Blacklisting: Blacklisting is a deal set up with other employers to never hire a person. Illegal. Totally illegal.

Giving notice: Surprisingly, there's no legal requirement for either employers or employees to give *notice of termination*. It's just a tradition.

Severance pay: Any money you choose to pay a departing employee is called *severance pay*. This is not a requirement of federal law, just a custom that is observed by many employers.

Discrimination (applies to all employers in most cases)

Federal laws prohibit you from discriminating against people on the basis of race, color, gender, religious beliefs, national origin, physical handicaps (unless they prevent the person from doing the job), smoking habits, or age. You may also be prevented from discriminating based on HIV+ status, pregnancy, marital status, weight, or sexual orientation. These laws are changing all the time, so check for current requirements. Also, you may be subject to additional state and local laws.

Sexual Harassment (applies to all employers)

Sexual harassment is defined as the creation of an abusive or hostile working environment as a result of unwanted sexually oriented behavior, whether directed at women or men. These actions can include demanding sexual favors, inappropriate touching, or using offensive words or gestures. It can be direct (such as making lewd remarks to someone) or indirect (such as hanging up a Makita Girl calendar in the break room or telling raunchy jokes for all to hear). If someone is offended, it can lead to a big lawsuit. Watch for potentially troublesome behavior in all your employees, encourage employees to report any discomforting incidents directly to you in a timely manner, and then take prompt, decisive action as needed to stop the behavior. Consider holding a training session on this subject for all employees at least once a year.

Other Rights

There are other rights and conditions applicable to the workplace:

Drug testing: Federal law does not require or prohibit drug testing, but state laws are all over the place on this one, so check on applicable regulations before taking on drug testing.

Lie detectors: Except for security-related jobs, the *Employee Polygraph Protection Act of 1988* prohibits the use of polygraphs by employers.

Workplace searches: Except for private storage areas, it's generally OK to search through employees' belongings. It's also OK to monitor phone calls and emails made in the context of the business (via business phones and email addresses). But secret, intrusive monitoring is not OK, nor is any intrusion into the employee's private life. This is a changing issue, especially with respect to electronic privacy, and hard to nail down at the present time.

Credit checks: It's legal to do a *credit check* on a prospective or current employee. These can be done through one of the credit reporting companies.

Dress codes: It's legal to have a reasonable *dress code*, unless you're using it to discriminate against a group for religious, racial, or similar reasons. You're within the law requiring employees to wear clothing that's appropriate for the work being done, that complies with safety requirements, and that is visually appropriate.

Workplace Safety

According to the *Occupational Safety and Health Administration* ("OSHA"), all employers "must report to OSHA any workplace incident resulting in a fatality or the in-patient hospitalization of three or more employees within eight hours." If you have ten or more employees, you have to keep a record of work-related illnesses and injuries. You can't fire or discriminate against an employee for filing a *workplace safety complaint* or for taking part in an investigation. The rules are somewhat complex, and they vary from state to state. You can find the full regulations by searching the index on OSHA's website at www.osha.gov, or give them a call at 1-800-321-OSHA.

La Migra: Dealing with the INS

The federal *Immigration Reform and Control Act* and the *Immigration and Nationality Act* place burdens on the employer that can be devastating to anyone who hires illegal aliens. *La Migra* is what many people call the *U.S. Citizenship and Immigration Services* department (www.uscis.gov). USCIS controls the movement of foreigners into the United States and enforces immigration regulations. However, the *Wage and Hour Division of the U.S. Department of Labor* (www.dol.gov/WHD) governs the complex regulations for hiring foreign workers, and for determining the nationality of all workers. Rules are complex and change frequently, so I urge you to visit their website for the latest details. Briefly, the employer has to have an *I-9 Employment Eligibility Verification Form* on file for all employees within one day of their starting work, along with a *proof of identity* and *proof of eligibility to work in the United States.* (You can obtain I-9 forms and complete information on compliance at www.uscis.gov.) The employee has to produce these documents within three business days of filling out the I-9. The employer is responsible for verifying the authenticity of all documents (this is no small task—the United States is crawling with counterfeit ones) and you will be fined if caught without documents or with falsified ones.

To top it all off, it's illegal to discriminate against anyone on the basis of their country of birth or their status as a naturalized citizen. You can't refuse to hire Latinos, or anyone, because of their nationality. It's also illegal to require that English be used in the workplace. *¿Comprende?*

Pesticide Safety

Pesticides are considered one of the greatest threats to worker safety. Because the landscaping industry uses so many chemicals, many of them highly toxic, we're closely watched and heavily regulated. The *Environmental Protection Agency* ("EPA") oversees pesticide regulations, but state and local laws vary greatly. You have to check (now, not later) with local authorities for a complete set of the regulations that apply to you. Restrictions cover purchasing, storage, handling, disposal, and training. In many states, you need a license to apply pesticides. A permit is required to purchase or apply certain pesticides. Some communities require you to post a list of properties that you spray. And a few places ban conventional pesticides altogether for residential use. (*Tip:* Why not go organic? Your client will love you for it and you won't have to worry about toxics.)

Unions

In many places, unions are no problem for the small business. In others, you have to hire an electrician to plug in your circular saw. No kidding. Unions offer important protections for workers, but for employers unions can sometimes be a pain in the rear. If unions are strong in your area, be sure you understand your obligations and rights, as well as those of your workers.

Shop Categories

If your company is involved with a union, it will fall into one of three categories: An *open shop* is one in which workers aren't required to join the union or pay union dues. (Right-to-work laws in some states require all unionized workplaces to be open shops.) An *agency shop* is one where workers aren't required to join the union but have to pay dues. In a *union shop* all workers must join the union as soon as they are hired. (The legality of this arrangement is in question.) A fourth, illegal, category called the *closed shop* is one where workers must already be union members in order to go to work.

Employee Rights

Employees have the right to discuss union membership on non-work time in non-work areas. They can read and distribute literature and display pro-union sentiments. They can ask the employer to recognize the union.

Employer Limitations

Employers can't grant favors to employees who oppose efforts to unionize. They can't fire, harass, demote, or punish union supporters. They can't close a work site, transfer work, or deny benefits because of organizing efforts.

Union Limitations

Unions can't pressure or coerce employees. They can't encourage the employer to discriminate against employees involved in de-unionization activities. They can't interfere with the employee's freedom to express opinions unfavorable to the union. They can't prevent employees from going to work. They have to bargain in good faith with the employer.

Union Dues

A *check-off clause* may require you to deduct union dues from paychecks and send them to the union.

Prevailing Wage Jobs

Many jobs that are put out to bid by the government require that employees be paid *prevailing wages*, usually union-scale wages, including benefits, even if the employees (or the company) aren't unionized. If you bid one of these jobs, you suddenly have to figure the cost of your labor at many times the normal rate (unless you're already unionized, of course). If you get the job, you have to actually pay people at those rates. This requirement tends to spoil them for everyday backyard-variety work. Before getting into a situation like this, consider the effects, both good and bad, on employee morale.

Hiring

The Job Description

Before you even consider hiring someone, take stock of the kind of employee you are looking for. Write a detailed *job description* that spells out the specific tasks that employee will perform (see "Training Employees" later in this chapter for a sample job description). It can be challenging to think about all the tasks and skills needed for a job, even if it's one you are used to doing yourself every day. Use the job description to accurately convey the nature of the job to prospective employees. A briefer version can be used in any advertising for the job opening, and the full version can be shared with the applicants when they contact you.

The Job Application

There are many limitations to what you can ask prospective employees, and job applications must conform to strict standards. You cannot ask about age, date of birth, criminal record, marital status, health conditions (except as they might affect the performance of the work), pregnancy, anything about family, race, religion, national origin, plans for retirement, or whether the applicant is having his or her wages garnished. It's also not a good idea to inquire about credit rating, home ownership, or whether the applicant knows anyone who works for the company. New legal cases regularly reshape the terrain of the job application. Your best bet will be to go to the office supply store and get a pad of the latest version of a standard job application form. (*Tip:* Be sure to get the applicant's driver's license number and classification so you can check his or her driving record.)

In addition to the standard application, have the applicants fill out a form indicating whether they can operate the equipment you use. Ask them to rate their proficiency on a scale of one to ten. Provide space for them to list any special skills, abilities, or interests.

Remember that job applications are full of information beyond what's actually written down. Naturally, you'll be interested in the applicant's work experience and education, but reading between the lines will tell you more. Look for periods of unemployment or long periods with no advancement. Watch out for job-hoppers with a lot of short-term jobs. Look at handwriting, grammar, punctuation, and spelling. Attention to detail on an application is an indication of attention to detail on the job, and vice versa.

Even if you're desperate for help, don't ever take anything at face value, because a lot of people will lie like crazy to get a job. Before you ever agree to an interview, check references thoroughly. Make sure that a college degree is real, not invented. Call the applicant's previous two or three employers, not just the last one, who may be so anxious to get rid of this person (or get him or her off the unemployment rolls) that he or she will overstate the person's qualities. When you talk to former employers, verify the information on the job application, then ask about the person's duties, promotions or demotions, the quality of the person's work, how well she or he got along with others, whether there were any problems, if she or he was a team player, and whether the employer would rehire this person. Be sure to let them know that all information will remain confidential. Be aware that these days, employers are much less inclined to provide any information about past or current employees, so the sad fact is that you may not get very far with some companies.

Interviewing That Works

Once you've had an opportunity to review written job applications and screen out the ones you're really not interested in (there will be plenty), then contact the remaining candidates to schedule interviews. You might start with brief telephone interviews, which will save time for everyone.

It's illegal to inquire in an interview about any of the things listed as off-limits in the Job Application section above. You want to stay focused on the skills and qualifications necessary to do the job and nothing more. If a candidate brings up one of the forbidden topics, change the subject, bringing the conversation back to safe ground. If you mess this up, you could end up getting sued by a candidate who felt you were discriminating against them, or who is a scam artist setting you up for legal liability. Be careful.

The only thing worse than being interviewed for a job is being the interviewer. I've always felt uncomfortable with this, and you probably will, too. It helps if you understand the purpose of the interview and have specific goals in mind. It also helps if you create a welcoming atmosphere right from the start: Get up to greet the applicant, offer a chair, and sit nearby, not behind your desk. Make a little appropriate small talk to put the person at ease. Remember, it's to your advantage to see applicants at their best. You'll learn a lot about their social skills and self-confidence even at this early stage. Be sure to pay attention to non-verbal information as well as to what the applicant says. Clothing, posture, eye contact, and even a handshake will tell you a lot (for instance, soft hands mean that person hasn't done any physical work for a while).

So, what do you ask them? Here are some key questions:

Previous/Current Job(s): What are/were your specific duties? How many people did you supervise? What equipment did you operate? What did/do you like/dislike most about your job(s)? What did you find most challenging? Why are you thinking about leaving? Why did you leave your previous job(s)?

Past Job Experiences: Can you tell me about a job situation you handled particularly well, or one you're especially proud of? Do you prefer to work as part of a team or alone? What kind of boss do you like to work for?

Education and Training: Why did you decide to go into this line of work? What classes did you enjoy most/do best at in school?

"How Would You . . . " Questions: Pose some real-world problems, technical or managerial as appropriate for the type of job you're offering. For instance, "We've had a problem with sod webworm that we just can't seem to solve. Do you have any ideas?" or "What do you think of those new Toro riding mowers?" or "We have a lot of Monday absenteeism among the laborers. How would you handle it?" A good applicant will really come on strong with this approach.

The Cut to the Chase Question: How about this one: "Why should we hire you?"

(*Tip:* Take time to tell the applicant something about your company—how long you've been in business, the kinds of work you do, the opportunities for advancement, even something personal about yourself. Remember, the interviewing process is a two-way street. The applicant needs to decide whether he or she wants to work for you, so don't be impatient when they ask questions—they have a right to know about you and your operation.)

At the end of the interview, ask applicants if they have any questions. If you're especially impressed, let them know that. Thank them for coming and give them an idea of when you'll choose someone. You may want to do a second round of interviews, going into greater depth with your top 2 or 3 candidates. This isn't as important when hiring a laborer as it is when hiring a foreman or manager. *Important:* Be sure to contact every applicant to let them know you've made a decision. Remember, they took the time to go through this difficult process, and they're anxious to know the results. It's not fair to leave them hanging.

Testing

You might want to test your top applicants. A simple multiple-choice and true/false skills test is a good start. The Sample Skills Test that follows contains a few of the questions I've used. It's not too complex, but it lets you know whether the applicant has basic skills. Add to it as you see fit; twenty or thirty questions should be enough.

Probationary Periods

Always hire people on a *provisional basis*—one to three months' trial period. Make it clear that you can let them go at the end of the period if they're not up to snuff.

For this to be effective and fair, you need to tell employees what's expected of them, and then you need to sit down with them and do an evaluation halfway through the period so that they can correct any problems before the final evaluation. That kind of cooperative approach is a lot better than just waiting three months and canning them.

Hiring Office Help

When you start out as a one-person operation, you'll do all the work, including all the many office tasks. This is good because even if you later become the big shot of the world, you need to learn the basics now. Never delegate anything that you don't already know how to do yourself. Remember, you learn best by doing. And you can delegate best by knowing intimately the work that you're delegating.

Sometime in the near future, you'll get busy and the office won't look so inviting at 7:30 in the evening after you've already put in twelve hours of fieldwork and haven't even had dinner yet. The blinking light on the answering machine and the stack of papers on your desk will remind you that no matter how tired and grubby you are, your work isn't over yet. Sooner or later, you'll realize that it's time to hire someone to help you in the office.

There are usually a lot of people available to do office work. You'll probably start with somebody part time, one or two days a week. You can find candidates by running an ad in the newspaper or on Craigslist, going to an employment agency, or asking around. Asking around is usually the best approach, because ads generate way too many phone calls, and agencies often charge high fees for doing very little work. Start by spreading the word among friends and business associates. You'll be surprised how many good people turn up.

You probably don't need to hire someone full time, at least right away. Remember that office help is overhead, not a profit center like your field employees, so it can be a drain on profits, especially in the first few months. The main financial benefit of hiring office help is that you can do higher-paying work yourself instead of spending time on clerical tasks, and that should more than pay for the office staff. Start out having someone come in two half-days a week. That way, things stay pretty organized without much cost to you. You can increase the workload later if circumstances require it.

Just as you would with a field employee, write out a detailed job description so you can convey the nature of the job to prospective employees. Here are some of the basic tasks you could include:

- Routine bookkeeping (billing your clients, paying bills, posting to the books, etc.)

- Handling payroll activities (paychecks, employee taxes, insurance, etc.)
- Filing (keeping clients' files and other paperwork in order)
- Typing (bids, letters, and such that you have prepared)
- Answering the phone (makes you look very professional)
- Returning phone calls (What a relief!)
- Ordering office supplies

Those are the things that anyone with ordinary office skills can handle, and you can feel comfortable delegating them to a qualified person even if she or he hasn't worked in of the landscaping business before.

There are other tasks that are best done by someone who has worked with contractors or similar service businesses, or with other landscapers. For instance:

- Ordering materials for jobs
- Scheduling jobs and coordinating crews and subcontractors
- Helping to prepare estimates and bids by doing materials takeoffs and calling suppliers for prices
- Measuring properties and preparing plot plan drawings
- Doing landscape design work

These jobs are much more critical and they require skills beyond those needed for ordinary office management. Do these yourself until your business can justify hiring this kind of highly skilled person.

When you interview, go over the job description and make sure the applicant has the necessary experience. Look for someone who is clearheaded, organized, and accurate. I want the same things from an office person that I want from a pilot, a surgeon, or a dentist: calmness, intelligence, seriousness about the job, and a reassuring attitude. As with any prospective employee, check references.

I suggest a simple system for delegating office work. It has two parts:

1. *Recurring tasks:* Set up routine, repetitive tasks in advance; these could include billing clients, paying bills, returning phone calls, for instance. Train the employee yourself and plan on working together over several weeks or months until you're sure things are being done right.
2. *Special and one-time tasks:* Put a file folder somewhere for the office person, and when things come up that he or she can do, stick them in the folder. Special tasks could include reorganizing the filing system, developing forms and systems, or converting a manual list of clients to a computerized database. Discuss special projects in detail with the employee,

and then leave notes and relevant paperwork that they'll need to do the job; check back to be sure that your instructions were clear. Meet as needed during the course of the work, and let the employee know you'll be available for questions or discussion. Finally, go over their work and make any constructive suggestions for final adjustments. Special projects are very enlivening for most people, giving them relief from the tedium of ongoing tasks and offering an opportunity for creativity and accomplishment.

Be sure you convey all your policies and protocols to your office staff, and plan to spend at least a few minutes at the start of every day with your office person, going over what's happening and discussing any hot issues and problems. Try to convey as much detail as you can, because when he or she answers the phone or needs to make a decision, being up to speed will really help.

Warning: Whatever you hire someone to do, discipline yourself to watch over that person to be sure she or he is doing it right. There's a tendency among those of us who prefer gardens over desks to ignore dull things like the profit-and-loss statement, the balance sheet, accounts payable, and so on. That can be fatal to your business because your office person can be cheerfully entering things in the wrong places, letting bills go unpaid, and worse. Even simple things can cause big headaches if they're done wrong. I once fired a secretary (after many other screw-ups) because she put the same zip code on all the pieces of a mass mailing. She explained that she thought it would save time!

Developing an Employee Manual

An *employee manual* is a booklet that details all the policies and procedures your employees need to know in order to do their jobs properly and stay out of trouble. It's also useful in the event of disputes with your employees, perhaps keeping you out of a nasty lawsuit.

It's easy to put off creating an employee manual, but it's an important part of your job as an employer and will result in better relations with your staff and smoother operations. In a personnel management seminar many years ago, one of my competitors described in great detail his employee manual. The seminar leader, impressed, asked him how many employees he had, and he replied, "Oh, well, I don't have any employees yet!" Everyone in the room laughed at him, but he had the last laugh because just a couple of years later he had one of the biggest outfits in the area, with over forty people working for him. Maybe he succeeded because he was prepared for success.

Sample Skills Test

IRRIGATION

1. Above-ground pressure lines may be PVC or galvanized. (TRUE FALSE)
2. Modern drip emitters don't require filtration. (TRUE FALSE)
3. Most digital controllers have a battery backup. (TRUE FALSE)
4. The distance of throw of a Toro 570 spray head is (a) 10–15 feet, (b) 30–40 feet, (c) 18 inches.
5. The flow rate of a drip emitter might be (a) 600 gpm, (b) 1 gph, (c) 21.2 PVC.

PLANTS AND PLANTING

6. Roundup is effective against common weedy grasses. (TRUE FALSE)
7. Malathion is a popular flowering shrub. (TRUE FALSE)
8. Ground covers should be watered (a) one week after planting, (b) after they have died back to the ground, (c) immediately after planting.

HARDSCAPE

9. Nails used in outdoor construction must be galvanized or coated. (TRUE FALSE)
10. A joist is the same thing as a pier block. (TRUE FALSE)
11. Dry-laid brick is usually installed on a sand base. (TRUE FALSE)
12. Which of these is a brick pattern: (a) double runner, (b) basket-weave, (c) salt-finish?
13. A swale is (a) a rock-moving tool, (b) a type of cinder block, (c) a shallow gully for draining water.

EQUIPMENT USE AND CARE

14. A trenching machine may be operated for up to one hour without any operator attention. (TRUE FALSE)
15. Chainsaws run best on straight gasoline. (TRUE FALSE)
16. Rototilling compacted soil should be done at slow speed. (TRUE FALSE)
17. A mattock is similar to (a) a pick, (b) a push broom, (c) a tree stake.
18. Oil levels in gasoline-powered equipment should be checked (a) monthly, (b) weekly, (c) before each use.

SAFETY

19. The mowing height on a lawnmower should be adjusted while it is operating. (TRUE FALSE)
20. Valve solenoids may be tested by applying 110 volts to the coil. (TRUE FALSE)
21. Lifting and carrying railroad ties requires two people. (TRUE FALSE)
22. Injuries should be reported (a) at the end of the week, (b) immediately, (c) only if a doctor's care is required.
23. Heavy lifting should be done by (a) bending at the knees, (b) bending at the back, (c) both.

JOB MANAGEMENT AND COST CONTROL

24. On a crew of three or more, one person is for standby. (TRUE FALSE)
25. A crew leader is responsible for directing the work of his or her subordinates. (TRUE FALSE)
26. Actual hours spent on the job are not important to job cost. (TRUE FALSE)
27. A change order is (a) a refund slip for overpayments, (b) used to add or delete work, (c) just like a purchase order.

In addition to these questions, I strongly suggest a few essay questions. Checking for basic writing skills and the ability to describe a procedure are an important part of the test. By the way, if you find these questions difficult to answer, perhaps you have some homework to do before you go any further with your business.

ESSAY QUESTIONS

Describe the flushing procedure on a new sprinkler system.

List the steps in planting a one-gallon plant.

List some of the major responsibilities of a foreman or crew leader.

ANSWER KEY: 1. (False), 2. (False), 3. (True), 4. (A), 5. (B), 6. (True), 7. (False), 8. (C), 9. (True), 10. (False), 11. (True), 12. (B), 13. (C), 14. (False), 15. (False), 16. (True), 17. (A), 18. (C), 19. (False), 20. (False), 21. (True), 22. (B), 23. (A), 24. (False), 25. (True), 26. (False), 27. (B)

No off-the-shelf employee manual will be right for your company. You need to develop your own policies and procedures, ones that are right for your situation. However, putting them into a standard format makes sense. There are some excellent online resources, books, and even computer software that will help you with this job (see Appendix 1). Find out what your trade association has to offer. Check your library or bookstore for help. (*Tip:* Some of your employees will be only marginally literate. Keep language simple and clear, and keep everything brief.)

Make sure every employee gets a copy of your manual. Have him or her sign a receipt, and keep it in the employee's file. Leave copies of the manual in the toolshed; put a copy on the bulletin board. Update it every year, and distribute new copies to everyone. Provide a Spanish-language version for your Hispanic employees.

Training Employees

One of the most common complaints I've heard from former clients of my competitors is, "He just dropped off some untrained people and left. Nobody seemed to know what they were doing!" You're a pro, but what about your employees? They won't automatically know what to do—you have to teach them! Training is essential to the success of your business, yet many small employers fail to develop and implement adequate training programs.

The Training Program

There are five stages to a good *training program*: (1) decide what training is needed; (2) set goals so you and your trainees can measure their progress; (3) develop methods of training; (4) train the employees; and (5) go back and evaluate the results.

Decide What Training Is Needed

First of all, do you have written *job descriptions* for your employees? No? Better get to work. It's no big deal—just write down the purpose of the job, what tasks you expect the person to do, and what skills she or he will need to do them. Then make a list of specific things the employee needs to learn. For instance:

Job Description: Maintenance Gardener Assistant. Works with lead maintenance gardener in crews of 2 to 3 people on residential and commercial properties to mow and edge lawns, prune shrubs, fertilize, control pests and diseases, water, apply mulch, and clean up walks, patios, and other areas as needed. Also helps with loading and unloading equipment, taking loads of greenwaste to local composting facility, and performing occasional special tasks for clients or company.

Skills Required: Ability to lift and carry up to 65 pounds; ability to use common gardening tools such as rakes, pruning shears, and brooms, and to operate common landscape maintenance equipment such as mowers and string trimmers; general knowledge of basic techniques for applying fertilizers, pesticides, and other garden products; good people skills for talking with customers and working cooperatively with co-workers. Valid driver's license and good driving record desirable.

Training Agenda: Learn the location of tools and equipment in the shop and yard. Learn company procedures for loading and unloading equipment, and for security and safety in the shop and yard, and on job sites. Learn safe and environmentally sound procedures for fueling, routine minor equipment adjusting and maintenance, pesticide and chemical storage and use, and equipment operation. Learn basic emergency procedures for first aid, injuries and accidents, wildfire events, encountering wasp nests, snakes, and other wild animals, and theft. Review operating procedures for all equipment. Review hand tool safety and proper lifting procedures. Learn job route and scheduling, and the names of clients and company personnel.

Well, that's just an example, and more could be added to it. Think of the complexity of even a "simple" job like being a gardener's assistant. There's so much to learn, and it's your job to teach effectively and ensure that the employee has understood everything. It's not so easy for you either, is it?

Plan Your Sessions and Set Goals

No employee can learn everything at once. Break up the training into manageable chunks and set specific goals for learning each chunk. For a brand new employee, start with the most pressing matters they'll need to know: where are the tools, which truck to take, how to get to the job site, etc. Then plan on a training session every week, expanding the employee's knowledge in digestible units until you've covered your curriculum. Of course the employee will also be learning constantly while doing the actual work, and if he or she works with another of your employees (as would be the case for a gardener's assistant) then be sure that the supervising employee also understands the training agenda and methodology.

Develop Training Methods

The best methods are those that teach by example. Remember, your employees usually won't be the academic type, so lots of lecturing and bookwork won't help them. Follow the rule, "Show, don't tell." Here's a good approach:

1. Explain the task—what's to be done, how it's to be done, and what the

results should be. (Explain how to plant a tree.)

2. Show how it's done. (Plant a tree.)
3. Have the employee do it. (Have him or her plant a tree.)
4. Evaluate the employee's performance and make constructive suggestions.
5. Have the employee do it again.
6. Evaluate again.

Be sure to offer plenty of encouragement; don't just tell someone what he or she did wrong. Encourage the trainee to ask questions. Remember that everyone learns at an individual speed. Be an ally, not a punisher.

You may want to develop simple written materials in the form of handouts or little pamphlets on particular subjects, or a big booklet with everything in it, to give to employees so that they can review what you worked on with them. But keep it short and sweet, and let them know that you're always available to go over things with them and that there are no dumb questions. Field employees usually don't like to read, and some may not even be fully literate. Be sure to make written materials bilingual if some of your employees are Hispanic.

Safety training is a special category of training that's recommended by the federal *Occupational Safety and Health Administration* ("OSHA") and its state affiliates, and in some states it is required by law. In California, for instance, employers are required to conduct "tailgate" safety meetings for all employees at least every ten days. These can be brief and informal, but you have to do them. (Regulations in your state may vary, so be sure to check for specifics.) Keep a record of all meetings: who attended, instructor, time and date, subject(s) discussed, new ideas from employees.

Many employers don't have safety meetings because they don't know what to talk about. You'll find a few suggested topics in the list that follows; surely you can think of others, or search online for prepackaged topics and lessons.

Train the Employees

Set aside a time to do employee training. Mornings before heading out to the job are good because everyone is fresh and alert, and the weather is usually cool and comfortable. Consider having a regular training day each week, or as often as needed, keeping in mind that even long-time employees can always benefit from additional training. Special training of new employees can be done when they are hired. Think about whether a new employee will learn better in a one-on-one session or in a group with others (assuming you are hiring more than one person at a time, perhaps for a big job). Think about your time, too; it's easier to train a group one time than to do the same thing over and over for individuals. Training takes time and costs money in temporarily lost productivity and earnings, but it has to be done and really pays off in the long run.

Some training is best done in a classroom setting, but the kind of work you're training most workers to do lends itself better to on-site methods. I recommend that you not do training on actual jobs, because it just isn't very reassuring to clients when they see you training people who you then immediately turn loose on their property, billing for the work they learned to do just moments before. Train at your yard or someplace away from the public, and if you must train people on real jobs, do it quietly and discreetly. Run through the steps outlined above, ask the employee/s for questions, make sure they understood everything, and send them on their way with appreciation and encouragement.

Evaluate the Results

Check up on employees regularly to be sure they're doing things right. Praise them when you can, and correct problems when you need to.

Training Tips: Good training is the basis of quality control. Training never ends; we all have a lot to learn. Encourage a team spirit in your entire staff; be sure everyone is thinking "improvement" at all times. Share your excitement with your people. Provide resources, books, videos, classes, and seminars for all employees. Don't forget about your trade association; most provide an array of training materials, courses, and field training programs. If your association has a certification program, encourage key employees to take the test, and reward them with a raise if they pass (effective training makes them more valuable, and profitable, to you).

Managing Employees

There are a million management books out there. Most of them say the same things. Boiled down, it comes to this: Care about your people. Put yourself in their shoes. Listen. Provide them with a satisfying job with fair pay. Train them well. Recognize their accomplishments. Treat them as you want to be treated. Be honest with them. Be on their side. If you do all this, your employees will be eager to come to work every day because they feel secure and appreciated.

Over 2,500 years ago, the great spiritual leader Lao Tzu had something to say about leadership that still rings true:

A leader is best
When people barely know that he exists,

Not so good when people obey and acclaim him,
Worst when they despise him.
"Fail to honor people,
They fail to honor you."
But of a good leader, who talks little,
When his work is done, his aim fulfilled,
They will all say, "We did this ourselves."

Your role as employer often requires you to help people deal with personal problems that affect their work. How do you do it? After all, you're a landscaper, not a shrink! Well, it's not always easy and there's certainly a point at which you should recognize your limitations and stop trying. But, within those limitations, there's a lot you can do. (*Tip:* Don't assume that an employee with a problem is necessarily a problem employee.)

You can only solve an employee problem by working on it with the employee. Set up a meeting with him or her. Create a nonthreatening atmosphere—no sitting behind the desk. Ask how things are going. Listen. Ask what the employee thinks could be done to make things better; some of it may make a lot of sense. If you can't do some or all of what they want, offer them a detailed explanation of why so they don't feel they're just getting the brush-off. Agree on the course of action, summarizing who'll do what. Send the employee out to give it a try, letting him or her know that your door is open. Now you've both got something to work on, a goal. Check back after an agreed-upon period of time. Readjust and try again.

Topics for Safety Meetings

There are many possibilities for safety meeting topics; these are just a few that will get you started. You'll think up more as you go. Check with your state contractors association or your workers compensation insurance carrier for other topic ideas.

EQUIPMENT

- Safe mower operation
- Using a trenching machine safely
- Chainsaw safety
- Reporting equipment malfunctions

SAFE PRACTICES

- Dig carefully!
- Ways to prevent back injuries

- Using protective clothing
- Refueling equipment safely
- Defensive driving
- Tie down your load!
- Watching out for others
- Stay cool in summer
- Keeping the job site safe for everyone

CHEMICAL SAFETY

- Using a respirator
- Proper mixing of chemicals
- How to handle a chemical spill
- Avoiding spray drift

FIRST AID

- What to do if someone is injured
- Stopping bleeding
- How to call for help

Performance Evaluations

Performance evaluations are a useful procedure for discussing the employee's job performance, setting goals for improvement and advancement, and reviewing the accomplishments, problems, and achievements since the last review. You can quickly find examples of performance evaluation forms with an online search. Periodic performance reviews keep people tuned up, and should be performed at least twice a year. Don't wait to do a performance evaluation until you're so darn mad at the employee that you could pitch him or her out the window. Also, keep in mind that a performance evaluation can be very stressful for the employee, at least the first time around, so make it an opportunity for collaboration rather than a one-sided report back on all the faults you can find. Evaluations aren't meant for beating people up. Reward good behavior and achievements, shine a light on things that could be improved, and listen as well as speak.

Firing People

Giving somebody the ax is just about the hardest thing you'll ever do as an employer. No matter how much the person has driven you, your clients, and your other employees nuts, it still hurts to fire someone. Not only that, it's scary these days: Will the person sue you? Shoot you? Firing is a last resort when all attempts at coaching an employee through their problems have failed.

First, review the section in this chapter on employee rights to be sure you're not firing the person unjustly or exposing yourself to liability. Fire for just causes like dishonesty, theft, repeated absenteeism, substance abuse, insubordination, or inability to do the work. Be sure you've given adequate *written* warning and that the firing is within your company's guidelines (you can find legally reliable employee warning forms online at human resources websites). Give them a termination letter, also available online.

Fire the person privately, quickly, with finality, and without recourse. Which means, don't fire someone without being certain that they are really finished; firing should not be negotiable. Do this in a face-to-face *exit interview*, not by email or through another employee. Some human resources professionals recommend having a witness from the company on hand. Make your explanation brief, since you will have talked about the situation with the employee numerous times in the past and they will be well informed about the problems that are causing the firing. Have the person's paycheck waiting, remembering that severance pay is voluntary and not required by law. Take back keys, uniforms, and other company property. Make it clear that they are to leave the premises at once. Be kind, even if you can't wait to never see this person again. Allow the employee to save face. Say you're sorry things didn't work out, and wish the person luck.

Keeping Good Employees

Sometimes your key employee, the one who learned everything from you, will up and quit on you. It hurts. It certainly will not be the first time it's ever happened, but it doesn't really help to know that. Your first reaction will be, "What good is it to train somebody if they're just going to leave?" How could this situation have been avoided? How can you retain good employees? Here's the bottom line: *People leave because some other situation meets more of their needs than the one you offered them.* Sometimes this is unavoidable, but other times you lost an employee because you were asleep at the wheel.

So what do people want? Money. Do you pay them enough? Recognition. Do you praise them enough? Satisfaction. Do you offer meaningful work? Advancement. Could your people get promoted? Answer these questions often with all employees, then optimize your offerings to them, and you'll have the answer to a stable, faithful workforce. Ignore them and you'll have constant turnover. One of my subcontractors has had the same crew for twenty-five years; they still look happy. But yes, you will lose good people on occasion; it's just part of the game.

Raises

Raises should be given for improved performance and value to the company. A cost-of-living adjustment, given to all employees to compensate for changes in the value of the dollar, isn't a raise. Employees always feel they deserve a raise, and you should give raises whenever you can afford to. When you can't give them one, explain why and suggest (if you can do so honestly) that a raise would be possible if certain *specific* things were improved. Explain what they are, and set a date for a review of the situation. Offer encouragement so the employee doesn't feel totally rejected. People often base their self-worth on their earnings, so it's a touchy subject.

Don't equate a raise with length of service. A person's pay should be based on merit, not just on their ability to stick around. Also, be aware that a long-term employee can eventually reach a pay scale at which it's no longer profitable to have him or her working for you, at which point you really can't increase their pay anymore. If you're at risk of losing a key employee consider offering a profit sharing program or even equity in the business.

Bonuses

Bonuses should also be tied to performance. If the employees do something exceptional and you have an unexpected profit because of it, share it with them. They'll love you for it. Bonuses can be cash payments, tickets to an event such as a ball game, paid time off, a gift of some kind, or just praise or an award that is publicized company-wide. You may also want to give bonuses for special achievements, for ideas that improve service or save the company money, for landing a new client or project, for service beyond the call of duty, or for finding a new employee. You can also provide bonuses for completion of time-sensitive contracts, and in fact some large contracts with public agencies and big general contractors often come with built-in bonuses for early completion that should be shared with your employees (and that type of contract inevitably also comes with penalties for failure to finish the job by the due date, though you had better not try to share those with your workers!). If nothing else, be sure to give employees some kind of holiday gift: a cash payment, paid time off, a box of chocolates, or a holiday turkey are common holiday gifts. (I once had a subcontractor who worked for me nearly every day, and I got to know his employees well. He would completely stiff them every Christmas, and so I started slipping them gifts because I couldn't stand to see them treated so badly.)

Company Events

Speaking of holidays, there's the matter of the company party. Some people love them, others not so much. I would sometimes treat my crew and their families to dinner out at a swanky restaurant, if I could afford it. I suppose some of them may not have been keen on the idea, but everyone always seemed to be happy to get some good grub and a bit of recognition. If your employees like the idea of a party (or a summer picnic or whatever else), and you have the time and money to put into it, then do it. There's nothing like a good time to bring people together. But be aware that these kind of events can lead to problems, having to do with excess alcohol consumption, friction between people, resentment at feeling obligated to take part in activities, and so forth.

Promotions

Promotions are few and far between in a tiny company, but when you can move someone up, based on good performance, then do so. A promotion comes with not only an increase in pay, but also in duties, responsibilities, status, and recognition among peers. A promoted employee, assuming they are up to the demands of their new job, is an employee with a renewed sense of self-esteem and a fresh enthusiasm for the job. Promote from within whenever you can. It's good for morale and easier on you. Be clear about what you expect from people before you promote them—new skills, greater responsibilities, and improved performance. Promotions are an earned outcome based on readiness for advancement and the need to fill an open position, not simply on seniority; be sure people know that.

Benefits

The trend is for employers to offer fewer benefits to employees. Employers are usually not required by law to provide retirement plans, paid time off, life insurance, or sick leave. It's especially difficult for a teeny company to pay for health insurance, pension plans, paid vacations, sick leave, profit sharing, bonuses, tickets to the amusement park, and all the rest. Fact is, you just can't compete with a big corporation when it comes to benefits. Provide what you can, but realize that the real benefits you offer are a personal atmosphere, job satisfaction, and a sense of purpose. Those don't cost you anything, and they'll keep people around just as well as the fancy stuff. (*Tip:* Some employee benefits are required by law; these could include unemployment insurance, workers compensation insurance, time off to vote and serve on jury duty, time off for military service, and family and medical leave. Find out from your state employment development office what benefits you have to provide and make sure your income stream is adequate to provide them.)

Delegating Responsibilities

OK, so now you've got all these employees. What do you do with them? That sounds like a stupid question, but when you wake up that first Monday as an employer, you'll probably be wondering what you got yourself into. After all, maybe you've been used to doing everything by yourself—fixing the mower, returning phone calls, pruning trees, planting plants, buying materials, keeping the books, everything. Now you've got help, but what should you have them help with?

Welcome to the world of delegating. Your first reaction might be, "Look, I didn't mean it. I'll just go on doing everything by myself. Sorry to have bothered you." But you'd be missing an opportunity. Once you get used to the luxury of having somebody clean up the trash, do the bookkeeping, or fix the equipment, you'll be happy you reached this stage in your business.

Here are some tips for successful delegating:

1. List all the work you need to do and then assign some of it to people other than yourself. Keep for yourself the work that only you can do adequately (which shouldn't be all of it!).
2. Have employees do the stuff you don't want to do. You prune the trees, they put the clippings in the trailer. Remember, they start at the bottom. Don't be afraid to hand over the crummy jobs, but give them a balance of work so they don't feel like they're doomed to picking up trash forever.
3. Develop a strategy for who does what and communicate it to your employees by way of a detailed job description for each person and specific daily or weekly assignments. Communicate what you expect and when you expect it. Give them all the information they need to do a good job for you.
4. Learn your employees' skills and strengths so that you can delegate the right jobs to the right people. Then train them to do the work.
5. Where it's possible to do so, assign an entire task to someone. That way, she or he will learn more and find more satisfaction in the work.
6. Be sure to provide resources so that each employee can do his or her job effectively. Make sure employees have the tools they need and that those

tools are in good condition. Give them all the information you can about the job they'll be doing. And let them know they can call on you if they need further support.

7. Evaluate employees' work regularly and be sure to praise as well as criticize. And remember, "Praise in public, criticize in private."

Record Keeping

If you have employees, payroll will be one of your biggest expenses and also one of your biggest sources of paperwork. Federal and state laws require certain record-keeping procedures, and additional records are necessary for reasons of good management. Here's a summary of the records you must keep:

- Time cards for each hourly employee
- Payroll checks
- Detailed earnings records for each employee
- Payroll ledger
- Labor cost information, broken down by types of work (for cost analysis and future bidding)
- Payroll tax tracking forms
- Federal and state payroll forms

Most of your field employees (laborers and foremen) will be paid an hourly wage. If you expand to the point where you need office staff, estimators, and supervisors, you'll probably pay them a salary—the same amount each week regardless of the amount of time they work. At this early stage of your business, you only need to worry about the hourly workers.

Time Cards

Each hourly worker will need to keep a weekly time card that shows how many hours he or she worked each day. Set up your time cards so that they make it easy to break those hours down by job or by category of work, because this will help you bill your clients for time-and-materials jobs and will also give you the information you'll need to analyze your labor costs for future bids.

Many states require that you hold on to time cards as part of your payroll records. Time cards are also needed if you get into a dispute with a former employee over unemployment benefits or the correct payment for overtime.

Employees should be required to fill out time cards themselves. Most employees hate doing this, and often you really have to ride them. Don't count on them to do it right; at the end of each pay period check each time card yourself for accuracy, or have their foreman help. Make it clear that guesswork isn't acceptable. And you know, it is hard to remember what you did all day, so approach this task as a collaborator not a critic. (*Tip:* Require employees to turn in their time cards every day, so you can be sure they don't put off filling them out until the end of the week when it's humanly impossible to reconstruct what happened.)

Time cards like the following sample can be purchased at an office supply store. They're fine for your needs. When you get bigger, you can look into electronic time recording devices that make the process more reliable.

Sample Time Card

DAILY TIME CARD

EMPLOYEE'S NAME Janice Lee DATE 4/2/15

JOB NAME	DESCRIPTION OF WORK	IN	OUT	HOURS
Hawking	Clean up	8:00	11:30	3.5
Travel	Drive to job	11:30	12:00	0.5
Dayton Plaza	Help w/ planting	12:30	2:00	1.5
"	Irrigation	2:00	4:30	2.5
Travel	Back to yard	4:30	4:45	0.25
TOTAL REGULAR HOURS				8.0
TOTAL OVERTIME				0.25

FOREMAN Ted R.

Payroll Checks and Earnings Records

When you do payroll, you add up the number of hours worked, multiply by the hourly wage to get the gross pay, then itemize the various deductions, and subtract them to get the net pay. You then write a check to the employee for the net pay. Later, you deposit the withheld taxes plus employer-paid taxes into a special account at the bank so they can be forwarded to the government. (Yes, that's right. You're not just a landscaper, you're a tax collector, too.) The law requires that you maintain detailed records of withheld amounts. Naturally, you also need to file tax returns of various kinds. Dealing with all this can be confusing and burdensome.

Back in the old days, employers did their own payroll and kept track of when tax deposits were due. Thanks to computers, smart employers now hire a payroll service to handle this job for them. These services do nothing but handle payrolls; most communities have at least one, and online services are available anywhere. All you do is provide initial information on each new employee and then just phone or email in the regular and overtime hours each week. The company handles the rest, including paychecks, tax deposits, tax returns, and a payroll report for you. The cost is amazingly low, especially when you consider that many employers do payroll wrong and end up paying hundreds of dollars in fines. Rather than try to learn all the ins and outs of payroll and subject yourself to constant worry about whether you're doing it right, I recommend that you use this method.

If you hire subcontractors or outside help and pay any one of them over $600 per year, you need to report this to the IRS at the end of each year, using Form 1099-MISC (Miscellaneous Income). Pick these forms up at your local IRS office in January or order them online at www.irs.gov/businesses. Click on "Forms & Pubs" for Employer Forms.

Change-of-Status Form

Use this form to document promotions, demotions, warnings, changes in pay, and dismissals. Nowadays, it seems as though you have to prove everything sooner or later, and if you don't have this stuff in writing, the labor commission or whoever's after you will assume you're guilty. They'll probably do so anyway, but these records might help.

Employee Change-of-Status Form

EMPLOYEE NAME: ______________________________ DATE: ____________________

TYPE OF CHANGE:

____ CHANGE IN JOB DESCRIPTION ____ LEAVE OF ABSENCE

____ INCREASE IN PAY ____ DECREASE IN PAY

____ PROMOTION ____ DEMOTION ____ WARNING ____ TERMINATION

DETAILS OF CHANGE: ____

____

FOR TERMINATIONS ONLY

TYPE OF TERMINATION: ____ QUIT ____ LAID OFF ____ FIRED

REASON FOR TERMINATION:

____ ANOTHER JOB ____ FAMILY REASONS ____ MOVING ____ ILLNESS

____ WORK UNSUITABLE ____ LACK OF WORK ____ MISCONDUCT

____ ATTENDANCE ____ NOT QUALIFIED ____ ALCOHOL/DRUG ABUSE

____ RETIREMENT ____ END OF PROBATION PERIOD

____ OTHER (EXPLAIN): ____

DATE TERMINATION EFFECTIVE ______________

EMPLOYEE PROTEST

If you disagree with the company statement above, explain your reasons below. (Use other side if necessary.)

____

____

____

EMPLOYEE SIGNATURE: ______________________________ DATE: ____________________

SUPERVISOR SIGNATURE: ______________________________ DATE: ____________________

06 Getting Work

Remember Buddy, my partner in the early days of my business? When we were struggling to get started, we made a lot of mistakes. Looking back, I just can't believe some of the things we did. Take marketing, for instance.

One day, while we were out knocking on doors to find some work, a woman asked us for a business card. I hate to even tell you this, but of course Buddy and I looked at each other, excused ourselves, and made a beeline for Buddy's beat up '62 Mercury Comet to have a conference. No, we didn't have any business cards. We had *thought* about getting some, sure, but well, let's just say we hadn't gotten around to it. So we rummaged around on the disgusting floor of this old heap and finally found one of those little raisin boxes from somebody's lunch years ago and a filthy stub of a No. 2 pencil. Tearing off one side of the box, we wrote at the top "landscapers," then our names and a phone number. What excuse we gave to this bewildered woman for our shabby marketing efforts I can't recall anymore, but I remember well how quickly and decisively she shut her front door. Naturally, we didn't get that job.

Well, I've learned a lot since then. You don't have to present a slick corporate image; in fact, it wouldn't be appropriate. But you do have to look professional. Remember, you're asking potential clients to trust you with what is probably their biggest investment and their most cherished possession: their home. You're asking them to spend anywhere from a few hundred dollars to tens of thousands. If they don't believe in you, you're not going to get anywhere, and if you don't make a good first impression they won't believe in you. So how do you present a good image and get lots of work? That's what this chapter is all about.

Serving the Client Well

The most important aspect of marketing has to do with getting your head screwed on right. Let's look at the one basic premise that guides all successful businesses.

Rule Number One: You are in business to serve the needs of your clients. If you do that well and keep them happy, they'll stay with you for years, refer other people to you, and help you to become successful. If you make them unhappy, they'll go elsewhere and (this is the worst part) they'll tell everyone else in town what a jerk you are. Make enough people unhappy and you're finished. There are no other rules worth discussing.

Why is this so hard for people to understand? Most people are well intentioned, but they have a hard time figuring out how to make this principle work on a day-to-day basis. And yes, keeping everybody happy all the time is a big challenge, especially when you're putting in fourteen-hour days and still leaving a lot of stuff unfinished. But if you always think about things from the client's point of view in addition to your own, you'll soon learn a lot about priorities. Let's look at a few common complaints about home-improvement businesses and how to eliminate them.

"I left three messages but no one called me back." This is a great way to end a relationship before it even starts. Why would anyone fail to return a call from a prospective client? Too busy? Sorry, but that just doesn't cut it. The phone call is the heart of your business. Naturally, you can't answer every call immediately, but do take an hour at the end of each day (or sooner if you can) to do so. Start with the oldest ones, leave detailed messages on people's answering machines, and keep trying until you reach someone. Remember: No calls = no appointments = no sales = no work = no money. Too tired? Just do it. I believe that you'll find the process energizing. Think of it: All those nice people want to do business with *you*! Call them back promptly and you'll stand out from the crowd.

With cell phones in everyone's pocket and access to emails and text messages from anywhere, there's simply no excuse for being out of touch. I bet you have no trouble responding quickly to messages from your friends and loved ones; give your business calls at least the same priority. Your phone is your store; keep the doors open.

"We made an appointment, but he was late/never showed up." First of all, always ask the client, "What's a good time for me to come by?" and don't just tell them, "I could come out Tuesday at one." Then be there. I try to be at the door at exactly the time I said I would. It impresses the heck out of people and gets things off to a good start. Remember that everyone has better things to do than wait for you to show up late. Five minutes early is sometimes just as bad as five minutes

late because your premature presence may be intrusive. Five minutes late is never OK, but it is sometimes unavoidable. Use an online map, a GPS, or your knowledge of local driving conditions to accurately estimate the travel time to your appointments. Take traffic conditions into account. Give yourself plenty of time to get there, even if you have to sit in your truck for a couple of minutes. Remember to apologize on the rare occasions when you are late. Pull over and use your cell phone to call and say you're on your way; clients—and potential clients—will be pleased. If you're chronically late for your appointments, start leaving ten minutes earlier.

"He said he'd get back to me within a few days, but I never heard anything from him." People will not call you to find out how you're coming with their bid or design or whatever you promised them. They'll just wait a week, get sore, and give the job to someone else. For crying out loud, if you don't want the job, just *tell* them. This is common courtesy, and failing to observe it leaves a bad impression that will spread around in a hurry. Still, we all drop the ball now and then and, as the days wear on past the due date for a response from us, we find it ever harder to call the person back. My experience is that when I finally do screw up my courage and call them, they're perfectly delighted to hear from me, and we proceed as if nothing had happened. Try it. It'll set you apart from the rest. But more important, develop the "do-it-now" attitude so you don't have a festering backlog of stale bids and forgotten appointments. Mark all due dates on your calendar, set up reminders, and check off work as it gets done. It's better for your clients and for you, too.

Look, I could go on and on about how attitude affects your success, but I think you must have the idea by now. If you find ways to please your clients (and potential clients) and overcome the very human but very bad habit of making excuses for why you've displeased them, you'll do well. Your every action should convey the idea that you care, that you're responsible, and that you can do the job. Don't tell people what you *can't* do, tell them what you *can* do. There are plenty of flaky competitors out there, and with a commitment to professionalism you'll rise above them.

Marketing Basics

Marketing and Advertising Are Not the Same Thing

Marketing is the total of all your efforts and strategies for developing your business. Figuring out what services people in your area need is marketing. Designing a business card is marketing. Wearing attractive clothes to a meeting is marketing. Asking a satisfied client to tell his or her friends about your services is marketing. *Doing a good job is marketing.*

Advertising, on the other hand, is one of the many tools you might use in marketing. Placing an ad on craigslist or in the Yellow Pages, posting flyers on local bulletin boards, developing a company website or blog, or giving out pens with the company name on them are all advertising methods.

Marketing Is the Art of Making Friends

Sometimes people think there's a secret to marketing or that it involves some nefarious techniques of psychological manipulation. True, major corporations use highly sophisticated marketing methods, but they don't have much to do with you and your little business.

Marketing is simple: Meet as many people as you can (either personally or through your ads, handouts, social networking, or other ways of communicating), get their attention, make them like you, tell them what you can do for them, tell them why they should do business with you instead of with somebody else, make them want to hire you, close the sale, then keep them happy so they tell others. (Don't skip any steps or you're not marketing—you're wasting your time and money.)

At bottom, what you're doing is making friends. There's nothing mysterious or nefarious about it.

Advertising May Not Do You Much Good

There's a lot of evidence that conventional advertising methods don't work very well for small businesses. Even the Yellow Pages, trusted (and expensive) friend of businesspeople, isn't very helpful in building a loyal group of quality clients for a service business, and these days people rarely open a phone book anyway, preferring to look online for services. Advertising is often not cost-effective (many kinds of advertising are a total waste of money), the public is suspicious of advertising, and clients that you get through ads are often cheap, difficult, and disloyal. Finally, most small businesses can't afford to advertise professionally enough or consistently enough to make it work. The one exception is your website. It's essential, cheap, and effective.

Word of Mouth Is Your Best Advertising

If you're good, most of your business, and certainly most of your best business, will come from referrals. Referral clients are already sold on you—they've heard great things about you (from more than one person, if you're really lucky), and they've probably seen your work. Unlike someone who responds to your Yellow Pages ad or website, they're probably not shopping the job around to a dozen people or looking for the lowest bid. *They may want you and you alone.* They feel they can trust you;

your performance has spoken for you. There's no better client than a referral client. Nor is there one who will come to you at less cost.

It Costs Less to Keep an Existing Client Than to Get a New One

I lied. There is one better client—the one you already have. You've already gone through all the rigmarole of getting to know each other, explaining the details of how you do business, and making sure you get along with each other. Work harder to hang on to your existing clients than you do to get new ones. Make sure they're thrilled with everything you do for them. Make sure they understand that you're giving them more value for the money than any of the competition could. See to it that their every need is taken care of, 100 percent and on time. I have kept some clients on my active list for 20 years or more. You can too.

There's (Almost) Always More Work Than You Could Possibly Handle

Except for the extremes of economic recession, there's a ton of work out there. Your competition may not realize it. Your clients and potential clients probably won't realize it. But if you realize it, and get creative about targeting opportunities, you'll always be busy. Here are some examples:

1. *Find more work on existing jobs.* Make a habit of constantly looking around your jobs. What else could you do to make them better? Maybe that flowerbed by the front door is getting a bit tacky; why not suggest replanting it? Come up with some ideas and a price and mention it to the client. Chances are they'll appreciate the fact that you care so much and that you're watching out for them. If you make them see how much better a new planting will be, they'll probably agree to have you do it. (Remember that landscaping is always changing and so are the people who own it.)

   Make a habit of stopping by your jobs. If no one's at home, leave a business card and a note in the door: "Mrs. Petersen, I stopped by today and noticed that your mulch is getting a little thin. It would be a good idea to add some more. Give me a call if you need help with this or anything else. Thanks. Jill. P.S. You've got some aphids on your camellias; try washing them off with water." People will be amazed, because no one else ever did this for them. They'll be faithful to you forever.
2. *Talk to the neighbors.* You do a nice front yard. People on the block are watching. Come back in a few months and you may find that neighbors have followed your lead and fixed up their front yards. Kick yourself for not having gone after that business. Next time, knock on a couple of

doors at lunchtime each day, introduce yourself, explain the benefits of the work you're doing, leave a business card and a brochure, offer to provide an estimate. What has this cost you? Virtually nothing. What are the odds of your getting a job from it? A lot better than the odds of your getting a good job out of a newspaper ad.

3. *Find ways to improve the landscaping of total strangers.* Let's say you pull into a shopping center one morning to get a cup of coffee. Naturally, you look around at the landscaping, which is probably not as good as it could be. Find out who owns the place (go to the county hall of records or ask the owner of the coffee shop), then write them a letter suggesting a few things you could do to improve their property. Offer to meet with them at no charge or obligation. Ask them to call you, or tell them you'll call them in a week. Nine letters will probably get ignored. The tenth may land you your best job ever. Your cost? Pennies per letter plus a little of your time. Think of yourself as someone with a cause—improving the landscaping in your community. Then pursue it. You'll leave the competition in the dust.

The moral to the story? Find a need and fill it, as the old saying goes. Find out where the gaps are—gaps in the way properties are being managed and also gaps in the services offered in your community. Maybe there's no one in your community doing sprinkler repair: There's an opportunity for you. Maybe your church has been paying high water bills because its landscaping uses too much water: There's another opportunity. *Solve people's problems.* Business is everywhere; you've just got to develop a nose for it.

Your Competition Isn't Who You Think It Is

You probably think other gardeners and landscapers are your competition. You're wrong. Sure, you may bid against them for work, but they're actually one of your least important forms of competition. Why? First of all, you're better than they are, in a different league altogether. Let them compete with each other if they want to; you go after your own jobs. Second, most of them are so lame that it's easy to outshine them just by showing up on time, being honest with people, and doing a good job. It doesn't take much, just the basics. Third, the other things you're competing with are far more powerful. Here's the real competition:

- *Your client's other interests:* Often a prospective client is trying to decide whether to do the landscaping or get a new car, take a trip, or put some money into the stock market. The dilemma of discretionary spending can take people in many directions. Your job is to convince them that landscaping is their best investment.

- *More powerful marketing forces:* The car manufacturers, the travel industry, and all the other mega-industries have huge advertising budgets and sophisticated marketing people whose only job is to get people to buy their products. The benefits and advantages of spending money on these items are well known. Who helps you explain the benefits and advantages of landscaping?
- *The economy:* When things are slow and money is tight, landscaping is one of the first things to go. When people are feeling anxious about the future, it's pretty hard to convince them to pour their life savings into their yards. For example, when interest rates are low, it can be easy to sell work—people refinance, they move (which gives you two potential jobs: one for the seller and one for the buyer), they have more money to spend. But when interest rates are high or loans are hard to get, there's less discretionary spending.
- *The public image of gardening and landscaping:* In many cultures, people hold the gardener in high regard, but in the United States, the gardener is thought of as an outdoor janitor. The landscaper isn't considered much better. Who's helping you to educate people about your level of professionalism?
- *The reputation of home improvement businesses:* Because there are so many incompetents, fly-by-nights, and crooks constantly preying on people, many of your potential clients have understandably negative reactions to anyone trying to sell them services. You often have to prove yourself to a suspicious public.

You've Got Some Selling Problems

Compared with most businesspeople, you're at a disadvantage. You don't have a store or a showroom, you can't carry your product into someone's living room, no one can test-drive it or taste it or try it on for size, and you can't leave samples. Furthermore, what you offer is complex and hard to explain. You may walk onto a piece of property and instantly have a vision of how you'd landscape it, but how do you convey that vision to the owner?

Marketing Is a Contact Sport

Many people in the trades are passive about marketing. When the phone doesn't ring, they just sit around and wait. That doesn't work. Sometimes you've got to get out and mingle with people, seek out possibilities, tell your story to any qualified listener, and be aggressive.

If You Want to Sell It, You've Got to Tell It

Do your clients know about everything you offer? Do your mowing clients know that you also trim trees? Does the family that you built the deck for know that you also do irrigation systems? How *would* they know unless you told them? Heck, most people aren't really sure what a landscaper does, much less do they have a list of your services in their minds! *You've got to tell them!*

Print out a simple list of the services you offer. Make sure everyone you meet has a copy of it. Go over it with people. Or print your business card on double-size stock, with a short list on the inside; then fold it over so it becomes a little brochure. Develop a good, easy-to-navigate website that lists all your services and shows photos of your work. Tell your story on social media.

Marketing Doesn't Just Happen

Like creating a landscape, marketing requires a plan. You need to decide who your potential clients are, what you have to offer them, why your services are better than those of the competition, what's unique about your services, how you're going to get people's attention, how you're going to tell them about what you're offering, and how you're going to motivate them to do business with you.

Each of those decisions is important, so list them—as questions—right now, each on a separate sheet of paper, and then brainstorm. For example, under "What's Unique about My Services?" you might list, "Offer organic lawn care" or "Only company in town that designs and builds water features." Under "How to Tell Them?" you might list "Print and hand out flyer at malls, canvass in new housing developments, give seminar at home show in May, improve the content of website, run a classified ad for maintenance jobs."

Getting In through the Back Door

One time I needed a place to dump excess soil that we'd removed from jobs. I put a classified ad in the paper. All it said was "fill site wanted" and a phone number. It cost me around $5.00 (this was a long time ago). I got about fifteen calls and learned something astonishing. Seven of those calls turned into landscaping jobs, a couple of them quite nice ones. Why? Well, I hadn't thought of it, but why were these people filling in land? They were going to *landscape* it afterward! I thought I was advertising for a fill site, but I was also advertising for jobs. That's when I began to learn about what I like to call "*Backdoor Marketing*" (not to be confused with various sleazy connotations of the term when used to describe illegal or unscrupulous practices).

Sometimes it's hard to go in through the front door. Sometimes it's just plain locked up tight. For instance, consider the difference between telling a prospective client, "Give me $40,000 and I'll landscape your yard," and "For $100, I'll design a planting for the front flowerbed, then I'll sell you the plants at a discount so you can put them in yourself." Very few people will respond positively to the first offer; it's just too alarming. But a lot of folks who need help with the flowerbed actually need $40,000 worth of landscaping and don't know it. If you can help with their little project, maybe you can get the big one.

That was the strategy behind an idea of mine that worked beautifully for many years, the "Do-It-Yourself Landscaping Kit," subtitled, "We Provide the Design and the Materials, You Provide the Labor." I advertised in the Yellow Pages for years and got a lot of work. Sometimes things would go just the way the ad said, but often (and here's where Backdoor Marketing comes in) the client would get partway into the project and realize that for lack of time, energy, or skills, he or she needed help. I'd step in and finish the project at full price.

One more example: I used to sell sod to homeowners for their own installation. During the course of the sale, we'd discuss sprinklers, weed control, all the aspects of doing the job. Often, they'd want to have part of the work done. Bingo! I had a new client. Then I'd give them my famous excellent service, and they'd never go anywhere else for landscaping.

The back door gets you in, same as the front door. Don't be afraid to use it. Offer a lot of small services, and even products if you wish. Then develop a relationship with the client. Become his or her personal landscaper, the only source to whom that client would turn.

Related to this is the principle that you should never turn down small jobs, especially when you're just starting out. You might do some half-pint little thing for a retired woman, and six months later you get a call from her son and daughter-in-law who did very well in the stock market and need somebody to landscape the new house they're building. Naturally, they'll be happy to talk to the nice young landscaper that Mom liked so much.

What Do People Want from Gardens Today?

As you talk to potential clients, you'll find that they express the same desires over and over again. There are also things that you never hear. In all my years of doing landscaping, nobody has ever asked me for a high-maintenance garden or a high-water-use garden or an ugly garden. Never. They do ask for specific things, though, and you need to know what they are, so let's go into a little more detail.

Here are my top ten picks for "Stuff That's Most Important to Clients." Take care of these and people will just love you.

1. *Low maintenance:* People are busy. Even if they're wild about gardening, they may not have the time to do it. Besides, their idea of "fun" gardening isn't pulling weeds for hours or struggling with overgrown plants weekend after weekend. They want the big things to more or less take care of themselves. People are beginning to realize (and you should, too) that much of the work required to maintain the average garden is the result of bad design: planting things that grow too big for the space they've been given, for example, or using species that are susceptible to pests and diseases when tougher plants could have been used instead. So it follows that if you create a maintenance headache for them, they'll get plenty sore at you, and with good reason. Conversely, learn how to make people's lives easier and you'll prosper. And don't forget to tell potential clients about how simple their new garden will be to take care of. Tell them right up front, because it's music to their ears.
2. *Color:* People really like colorful plantings. If you're designing a garden, talk to your clients about their favorite color schemes and assume that more flowers, rather than fewer, will endear you to them.
3. *Reasonable cost:* No matter how wealthy they are, people are going to ask you about budget. They want to know that they're getting a good deal. Often, people will only look at the design and installation cost of the garden, not realizing that up to 80 percent of the total cost of the average garden is maintenance: labor and materials, water use, and so forth. Let people know that the garden you design for them will require much less maintenance, so that the total cost will be reasonable, even if it's a little more expensive up front. Then deliver on that promise.
4. *Beauty:* Duh. Of course people want beauty; who wouldn't? So tell them (and show them with pictures, sketches, videos, computer imaging, samples of plants, and examples of your work) how gorgeous their new garden will be (or, if you'll be doing maintenance, how you'll make their old garden look better than it ever has). Be a bit of a showman (or woman) here. Let the poet in your soul come out a bit as you describe what you're planning for them. Allow your enthusiasm to be contagious. I often tell people how excited I am about what we're doing. I even say I want a gar-

den like theirs for myself. I never lie or gush; I just let the fun I'm having rub off on them. Beauty. Yeah.

5. *Usefulness:* This means different things to different people. Families want a safe place for the kids to play. Young couples want a place to have a party. People want privacy or storage space or vegetables or improved property value or all of these. So, whatever else the garden does, it must be useful to the owners. Often, people won't express this idea directly, but if you ask them, they'll usually have a pretty clear picture of how they want their property to work for them. Mention the concept of the "outdoor room" to people and you can almost see the lights come on. Get usefulness issues resolved up front and you'll be well on the way to pleasing the client.
6. *Status:* Here's one that no one ever asks for directly, yet everyone wants it. I can't recall a client telling me, "I want to get the attention of those little people across the street," but I know enough to suggest how impressive the new front yard will be. If you had just spent big bucks on something, wouldn't you want to gloat a bit?
7. *Low water use:* This is primarily a consideration out west, but frankly water is getting scarcer, more costly, and poorer in quality nearly everywhere. Cyclical droughts, depleted or polluted aquifers, damaged watersheds, and population pressures all have an effect on availability of good-quality water for landscaping. It's becoming common practice for municipalities to require landscapers to project the water use of new landscaping and to be held responsible for those projections coming true. It's may sound scary, but it's an opportunity-in-disguise for more and better work for the progressive professional. Give people gardens that will be happy on little water and, if you're doing maintenance, find ways to reduce water use: mulches, drip irrigation systems, smaller lawns, drought-tolerant plants, and good water management. You'll have an advantage over your competitors who neglect this important issue. (Keep in mind, too, that many communities and water districts offer rebates for landscaping improvements that lead to water savings. That means that the district will pay your client cash for things like drip systems, lawn removals, and smart controllers, and that money will then be used to hire your company to do the work. Wow.)
8. *Environmental responsibility:* Water use is just part of the much bigger picture of sustainable landscaping. Clients want (or are being forced to think about) a reduction in the amount of greenwaste leaving the gar-

den, the use of fewer chemicals and inorganic fertilizers, and less use of polluting power equipment, just to name a few. As public awareness of the impact of gardens (both positive and negative) grows, you may find people asking you about the source of the materials you'll be using ("Are they made from petroleum? Are they strip-mined? Are they renewable? What's the embodied energy? Are they recycled or recyclable? Were they trucked in from far away?"), their durability ("How long will they last? Will they hold up under hard use? Do they need to be refinished frequently?"), and even about the companies that manufacture them ("Are they socially responsible? How do they treat their workers? Do they do any animal testing? What else do they make?"). They may ask you where you dispose of things, how much refuse is recycled, whether you can use hand tools instead of power tools. They'll want to know what you're going to do to moderate the microclimate around their house, how you'll protect the watershed, what the energy implications of your design are. What answers will you have for them? I think it's good that people are asking these questions. We need to do better, and you should make a commitment to running an environmentally clean operation from top to bottom. After all, give me one decent reason not to do so.

9. *Food:* Growing food is huge. Growers can't produce enough fruit trees or vegetable seeds to keep up with demand. Books on food gardening, permaculture, chickens, and old-fashioned skills like canning are selling like crazy. People in every community are tearing out their lawns to replace them with food gardens. Making the land around people's homes productive as well as just beautiful is about as righteous an act as I can think of. Are you in on this lucrative market? Skill up and then offer home food garden design and maintenance as part of your mix of services.
10. *A good investment:* In the end, clients want to know that the money they put into their landscaping will offer a decent return when they sell their house (and also will save money in the short term by reducing maintenance, saving energy, and providing useful services). Studies show that landscaping is a good investment; you might address this in your proposals and marketing efforts.

To succeed in business, you must master the art of meeting people's needs and desires. Maybe there are other needs that you pick up on when you talk to people. Always ask yourself whether you're truly giving people what they want. It's the key to your prosperity.

Business Opportunities in Sustainable Landscaping and Gardening

What is "*sustainable landscaping*"? In a nutshell, sustainable landscaping is about developing a stable ecosystem, much like a natural ecosystem such as a forest or a prairie. Wild places don't need the kind of "maintenance" we think of when we think of landscaping. There's something fundamentally different about man-made landscapes that makes them more troublesome to live with than natural places. That difference is that people who create landscapes don't give enough thought to how they work. You see, it's not enough to make a pretty place. You also have to set it up right so that the plants don't get too big, or get eaten up by pests, or demand a lot of water or other inputs just to keep them going.

You also have to think about the materials you use to create the landscape, so that you don't generate undesirable environmental impacts at the source of those materials. For instance, concrete is made from rock, sand, and other elements that are strip-mined from the earth and turned into the end product using energy-intensive processes that cause still more harmful impacts.

Finally, a sustainable landscape is maintained without the use of toxic chemicals, polluting power equipment, and other negative impacts.

On an even deeper level, a sustainable landscape offers valuable ecosystem services, such as a reduction in energy use through proper placement of shade trees, sequestration of carbon in plants which can help get the climate back under control, habitat for native animals and insects, and the production of food and other necessities of life.

Our work, at its sustainable best, is healing, restorative, useful, and deeply important. What we do matters so much, and that is the real reason why this is an important business to be in. It's should also be obvious that anyone who is stuck in the old ways, making consumptive, toxic, and useless purely decorative landscapes and maintaining them with obsolete conventional practices, will soon go the way of the dinosaur, leaving the market to you and your sustainable expertise. So don't mess around; make a commitment to working sustainably because it's essential to your future in this business.

There's a lot to know about how to develop and care for a truly sustainable landscape, and this isn't the place to go into detail. For a good introduction to this subject, have a look at my book, *Sustainable Landscaping for Dummies*, and seek out some of the other books and resources on sustainable landscaping to be found in Appendix 1.

How Can You Profit from Doing Things Right?

There are many great opportunities in sustainable landscape design, construction, and maintenance waiting for you. Below are a few of them. Keep in mind that most of these practices are being designed into new projects by forward-thinking landscape architects, yet there are still very few people who know how to actually implement them. That gives you an instant leg up on your competition, as long as you develop the skills to become a sustainable specialist.

Who's in Charge Here?

To some degree, your opportunities will be determined by what your clients want, but they will also be up to you in two important ways. First of all, you are the expert and clients will, for the most part, expect you to propose ideas that make sense to them and to the environment and the community as well. These days, very few people are overtly committed to destroying the planet, poisoning their families, or wasting resources. But on the other hand, most people are unaware of how to do things in a safe and beneficial way, and that's where you and your expertise and your commitment come in. Your job is to advocate for proper practices as well as implement them. Don't be silent when a client asks for something you know is wrong; stand up for the proper ways of doing things and gently educate clients about them. Which brings me to the second point: If a client insists on doing something that isn't in line with your values, you do have the choice of walking away. That can be hard to do when business is slow, and we all have to make compromises now and then. But be aware that you don't have to take on an odious job unless you want to. You are in charge.

Watershed-Friendly Landscaping

One definition of a *watershed* is, "the land draining into a river or other body of water." Everyone lives on a watershed. The watershed begins at the peak of every roof, where water runs off onto the land and finds its way across the yard, into the street, and eventually into your friendly local stream, lake, or ocean. That water picks up a lot of polluting gunk that ends up wrecking water quality. It also causes urban flooding along the way because so much of the urban environment is paved rather than absorbent like a natural, plant-covered area. Landscapers contribute to the problem by installing drainage systems that treat rainwater as waste, efficiently discharging it into the gutter. Rainwater is a good thing, not a waste product. Why throw away fresh, free water and then turn around and buy water to irrigate the garden?

Fortunately, it's landscapers who can come to the rescue, offering solutions that will help land absorb, make use of, and even clean up the pollution so often found in rainwater. Plants are the most watershed-friendly element in the landscape, so in a sense we're already doing this work every time we put in a flowerbed, a meadow, or a ground cover. But there's a lot more to offer, including *pervious pavements* that slurp up rainwater rather than shedding it, *ecoroofs* and *living walls* that transform ugly rooftops and buildings into beautiful absorbent oases, *water harvesting systems* that collect roof runoff and store it in tanks for later use, and *dry streambeds* and *bioswales* that mimic the services provided by nature's brooks and creeks.

Sustainable Landscaping Opportunities

Your clients will benefit from investing in a landscape that is less costly to live with over the long haul. Even if a potential client doesn't give a hoot about protecting the environment, he or she will surely be interested in the savings of money, time, and labor offered by a truly sustainable landscape. The benefit to you is that you can often be the only one in your community offering these features, which, by the way, are an awful lot of fun to create.

Pervious Paving

The typical driveway, sidewalk, or patio sheds water onto adjacent land. That's not always a bad thing, but too much paving causes urban runoff and all the problems we looked at above. In addition, pavement seals up the soil and deprives nearby plants of life-giving rainwater. The idea of *pervious paving* is to create a load-bearing, safe, and usable surface that also allows water to run through it and into the soil below. A simple example of pervious paving is a gravel path, but more sophisticated approaches are becoming common. These include *pervious concrete,* which is made without sand in order to create voids in the material that water can run through, *pervious asphalt,* special *paver blocks* with slots to absorb water, and others. Installing some of these materials takes special training, but it's a wide-open field in most places. Get the training, become the specialist, and you'll have all the work you can handle.

Green Roofs and Living Walls

A *green roof* (also known as an *ecoroof or living roof*) is a roof covered with a protective membrane or shallow boxes, lightweight soil, and a living community of plants. Green roofs absorb, utilize, and bioremediate (that is, purify using natural biological processes) rainwater as it falls on the roof. They keep buildings cooler and help mitigate the *urban heat island effect* that's increasing the air temperature of cities due to the presence of so much dark pavement and roofs. Like all living systems, green roofs produce oxygen and sequester carbon, helping to mitigate global warming. They can provide beauty, habitat for native insects and other living things, and can even be used to grow food for people. Green roofs are becoming more and more common, and are required for new construction in some communities. In some communities there are even tax breaks and other advantages for those who use them on buildings. This means a ready market for your talents, with part of the bill paid by the government.

Living walls are systems designed to cover the vertical surfaces of buildings with living plant communities. This is a less-developed technology than green roofs, but it's up and coming and will no doubt be more common in the near future. Imagine a building completely swathed in luscious greenery, attracting beneficial insects and birds, making fresh air and keeping the building cool. How wonderful is that?

Keep in mind that this work isn't for those with a fear of heights. But if you're intrepid enough to want to scramble around in the stratosphere, you won't find much competition for your services up there.

Dry Streambeds, Rain Gardens, Bioswales, and Constructed Wetlands

A *dry streambed* is simply a ditch filled with attractive, rounded stones and boulders. Its purpose is to attract and hold rainwater, making it available to the roots of nearby plants. Dry streambeds are easily built and can be a wonderful addition to your mix of service. People love having a bit of nature running through their yards, especially when it has so many environmental benefits. A *rain garden* is a dry streambed filled with a mix of plants, often native species, that replicate living waterways, attract wildlife, make use of runoff water, and mitigate urban flooding. A *bioswale* is a special type of dry streambed that has been planted with plant species that biologically treat the water that runs through them. Bioswales are especially useful in cleaning up runoff from streets and other paved surfaces. *Constructed wetlands* are made to hold the water longer than a dry streambed or bioswale; they're used to attract wildlife and restore natural ecosystems. None of these are hard to build, they are becoming more common in both private and public landscapes, and are often required as a condition of development for new projects.

Water Harvesting

As the water available for landscape irrigation grows scarcer, water conservation measures are becoming commonplace in many communities, even in relatively high-rainfall areas. As a result, landscapers are being called on to develop skills that address this growing problem. One of the bright spots in the picture is the practice of *harvesting rainwater* from rooftops. Harvested rainwater can be distributed through the landscape as it falls, using a system of dry streambeds and other distribution methods, or it can be stored in aboveground *tanks* or underground *cisterns* for use during the dry season. This is a fascinating area of work, and I guarantee you'll be hearing more about it as clients become aware of its benefits and as their wells run dry and their water bills steadily climb. You can make good money in this fast-growing field. Check out the excellent books by water harvesting experts Brad Lancaster and Art Ludwig listed in Appendix 1 of this book.

Alternative Materials

You can plan on being asked, by landscape architects and clients alike, for safe, environmentally friendly materials. As the awareness of being "green" spreads throughout our culture, what have been considered "alternative" materials are fast becoming mainstream. For instance, you won't find toxic arsenic-treated wood fence posts at your local lumberyard anymore; they've been replaced by a nontoxic alternative called *ACQ-treated lumber*. Be sure to familiarize yourself with all the greenest materials so that you aren't caught flat-footed when a potential client asks you about using vinegar to kill weeds, making a path with urbanite, or adding mycorrhizal fungus to your plantings. These may sound exotic to you, but they're household terms to plenty of landscape professionals and homeowners. Don't be left behind.

Restoration and Reclamation

Centuries of mistreatment have left much of planet Earth suffering. Ecosystems are in or approaching collapse, native plants and animals are becoming extinct at alarming rates, and the very land itself is washing out to sea after being denuded by deforestation and development. Restoring these areas to their former health is a huge business, and one that most landscapers aren't even aware of.

Restoration work is usually mandated by federal, state, or local governments, often as a condition of development for new construction. Funds for the work come from developers, public monies, and private grants. As with so many of the environmentally beneficial aspects of landscaping, there are few people trained to do this work. It's a far different way of doing business than working for homeowners or private developers, but there's good, steady money to be made and you can feel really great knowing that your work is healing the earth and bringing damaged places back to life. Restoration work is done in collaboration with biologists, and unless you have a degree in a life science you will probably be limited to installation and management work rather than design or consulting. The size and scope of the projects can be massive, nothing like planting a few annuals in a homeowner's flowerbed. You will likely be working in rural or wild areas far from town. Strict conformance with project standards is required, and your work will be monitored by government agencies. This is a rigorous field, and an exciting one where you can do a lot of good. Training programs are available and you should look into them if you want to do this work.

Meadows and Lawn Alternatives

More and more people are coming to see their lawns as a problem. The mowing, the water use, the pollution from fertilizers and pesticides, and other impacts are sending homeowners in search of alternatives. One of the best of these is the natural *meadow*, made up of native grasses, perennials such as yarrow, sedges, and other plants that need less watering, mowing, and fertilizing than conventional turf. Meadows are traffic tolerant, beautiful, and easy to live with, and they also often provide valuable ecosystem services such as nitrogen fixation and habitat for native insects and other wildlife. Solving people's lawn problems in this way can be a huge business opportunity for you. As with all marketing of your services, you can present the meadow as a source of real benefits and advantages to your clients. Meadows require no special skills to install or maintain, may cost somewhat more to install than a typical lawn, but are cheaper over the life of the installation because they need so much less care.

There are other ways to eliminate the impacts of the lawn, by reducing its size, switching to lower-maintenance grass varieties, replacing it with ground covers, or replacing the lawn with a paved area. Each situation presents its own particular opportunities. Become familiar with them so that you can offer clients reasonable, creative choices.

"Food Not Lawns"

One other approach to dealing with lawns is to convert them to food-bearing landscapes of fruit trees, annual vegetables, and other edible and useful plants that also serve as lovely landscape elements. The popularity of food growing is skyrocketing. Fruit tree growers can't keep up with demand. Seed companies can't keep seeds in stock. Considering the many harmful impacts of conventionally farmed food, and the degraded flavor and nutrition of supermarket produce, it only makes sense that people would turn to their yards as a source of something better. Innovative landscapers are retraining themselves to become savvy urban farmers and finding plenty of work making food happen in their communities. Some are even making this their exclusive specialty, developing and maintaining permaculture-based "food forests" for their clients. Help satisfy people's yearning for homegrown, organic, environmentally sound food and you'll stay plenty busy doing wonderful work.

Homesteading in Town

Fruits and veggies aren't the only productive use for home grounds. How many people do you know who are raising chickens or rabbits, growing fiber crops or medicinal herbs, keeping bees, or taking on the other aspects of a fully-integrated home production system? In most communities this is an area of rapidly growing popularity, and it looks like it will be more than just another fad. Is there work for you in all this? Perhaps, if you learn the skills involved and make your company a source of "homestead" design, installation, and maintenance. This goes beyond the conventional bounds of what we think of as landscaping, but there is no reason not to take it on if you are interested in holistic productivity. Look to the Internet and to some great recent books that cover this subject in detail.

Integrated Pest Management

The science of using the *least toxic methods* to control pest and disease problems is called *integrated pest management* (often abbreviated to "IPM" or sometimes "IVPM" to include vegetation management as well). IPM makes use of strategies such as managing the environment so that plants are healthy and therefore resistant to pests and diseases, releasing beneficial insects that eat pest insects, using biological agents such as Bt (a disease that only kills caterpillars), and applying pesticides that are only toxic to the target organism.

There's a learning curve to IPM, but there are plenty of resources and training to help you get started. See Appendix 1 for help with this. In addition to being a great selling point with your clients, going least-toxic with your pest management services keeps you from having to work with poisonous materials that could have a long-term effect on your health.

What's Permaculture?

Permaculture is a system of holistic design that was first developed in Australia in the 1970s and that has become increasingly popular throughout the world. In a nutshell, permaculture is a way of developing and managing land and related improvements to yield the maximum amount of benefit with the minimum of negative impacts. Permaculture uses some key principles, such as *stacking functions* to make any one element in the landscape serve more than one purpose, and choosing living, biological solutions before turning to technological ones. Many people think permaculture is just about growing food or raising chickens, but it deals with much more than that. Many landscapers are becoming certified in permaculture techniques; this can be helpful to you professionally and is a good selling point as well. Visit www.permaculture.org, www.permacultureactivist.net, and www.urbanpermacultureguild.org for more information.

Organic Maintenance

People are increasingly disturbed about the impact of conventional garden pesticides and other chemicals, and are better informed than ever about their negative effects. But they rarely have the expertise to implement an effective organic strategy for their properties. They could use some help, and that's where you come in.

A fully organic maintenance program goes further than IPM alone. Organic maintenance incorporates naturally based fertilizers, bio-activators, use of plants that attract beneficial insects and other organisms, and other practices to assure that there will be no harmful impacts either on the site or at the source of the materials. Whereas IPM considers the possibility of using toxic chemicals on stubborn pest and disease problems, the organic approach does not.

Consider the positive impact of telling potential clients that you will never, ever use toxic herbicides, insecticides, fungicides, or other chemicals, and that everything you bring onto their property will be safe for them, their families and pets, and the environment. It can boost your sales as well as having the obvious effect of keeping you and your operation squeaky clean.

Oh, and yes, organic methods really do work. There's rarely if ever any reason to do things any other way. (*Tip*: in some areas, training in organic methods is readily available, and some organizations offer "organic land manager" certification.)

Watershed-Friendly Maintenance

Now that we've become aware of the impact of landscaping on the watershed (see above), isn't it essential that we gear our maintenance work toward the worthy goal of protecting the watershed? Pesticides, overfertilizing (even with organic fertilizers), overwatering, erosion, and other damaging practices can easily be avoided. In fact, conforming to "best management practices" that protect the watershed are required by U.S. federal law, creating an opportunity for you. So, while you're at it, why not make this a selling point for your clients? How many "watershed-friendly landscape management services" do you see out there? I can almost guarantee you that you'll be the first in your area. People might not immediately understand what you mean, but it will raise interest because it's an unusual claim, and once you explain it to them you'll be points up on the competition for your exquisite care for the environment. (*Tip:* You might consider contacting whatever local government agencies are in charge of managing watershed health to let them know of your availability for this work.)

Fossil-Free Maintenance

Here's another clever way to scoop the competition. Suppose you were to offer a carbon-neutral or even fossil-free gardening service where you use little or no gasoline or diesel fuel to run your operation? Impossible? Well, you'd have a hard time getting to 100 percent on this one, but sometime, check out the website of TerraNova Ecological Landscaping in Santa Cruz, California (www.terranovalandscaping.com). They run most of their operation using bicycles and bike trailers, hand and sometimes electric tools, and of course all organic methods. Their one truck runs on biodiesel. Taking the high road (on a bike!) has been good for Terra Nova and it's worth thinking about for your business as well. And they're by no means the only ones doing this; these practices are spreading in progressive areas. In fact, lawn care using electric mowers charged by solar panels mounted on the roof of the truck is becoming a norm; have a look at http://cleanairlawncare.com for an example of a national franchiser offering these services. Doing well by doing good is entirely possible, especially at this point in history.

Sustainable Landscape Audits

Suppose you were to offer an inexpensive consulting service that assessed the overall sustainability of landscaped properties and provided a point-by-point program for improving the performance of the landscaping and reducing ongoing expenses for the owners? The cost of the service would pay for itself in lower water bills, decreased labor, and other financial benefits, and of course the landscape would work better and look better as well. An experienced professional usually has no trouble finding things wrong with existing landscapes, such as inefficient irrigation systems, poor controller programming resulting in overwatering, shrubs that are too big for the space they're in and cost money to constantly prune to control their size, and so forth. There are also safety hazards and other problems on nearly every property, and alerting property owners can save lives and prevent lawsuits. This is a golden opportunity waiting to be exploited. If you could get it to eliminate belly fat too, you'd be rich.

Quiet Gardening

You may not be aware of it, but a whole lot of people really hate the noise that gardeners make with all their mowers, blowers, and other power equipment. Not only is that stuff polluting; it makes a truly awful racket. There's a gardener in my town who calls herself "The Quiet Gardener." She uses no power tools of any kind. She's a little lady well past her youth. If she can maintain gardens with hand tools, so can you. It's a market niche that might just keep you busy when others are not. And your clients will love you.

Real Estate Services

Realtors usually "stage" properties that are for sale, furnishing empty houses nicely and making other cosmetic changes that improve the appearance and charm of the property. They often overlook the landscape, not realizing that some good maintenance and a little bit of color planting can make a great impression on prospective buyers before they even get out of their cars. Consider offering landscape staging services for realtors. Of course, you should also make yourself available to realtors to freshen up aging landscapes on properties coming onto the market.

Getting Work

As the old saying goes, it's not what you know, it's who you know. The first step in getting work is making contact with the people who need your services, or who know people who need your services. So, ask yourself who in your community can get you work, and how do you contact them? That's the heart of the marketing question. Here's a brief rundown of who can feed you work and how you can attract their attention and their business or referrals. These are the people you need to get to know.

Homeowners

Homeowners take a couple of routes to having landscaping done. The most common is to work directly with a design/build landscape contractor. This means you can approach homeowners directly and expect good results. Naturally, this is also true of maintenance work. There are a number of ways to get the homeowners' attention, including referrals, door-to-door canvassing, flyers, direct mail, a website, social media, telephone solicitation, Yellow Pages ads, newspaper ads, radio spots, home shows, classes and seminars, public demonstrations, sponsorship of events, and advertising specialties like T-shirts and pens. We'll get into the details when we talk about kinds of advertising.

Some homeowners hire a landscape architect or landscape designer to draw plans, and then put them out to licensed landscape contractors for bids. Often, they take the recommendation of the landscape architect about whom to invite to bid, so to get this kind of work it really helps to be on the landscape architect's bidders' list.

Landscape Architects and Designers

Because the *landscape architect* or *landscape designer* (for brevity I'll use the term landscape architect to refer to both) does design work only, he or she is always recommending landscape contractors and gardeners. Every landscape architect has a *bidders list*—licensed professionals with good reputations whom the landscape architect knows and has worked with in the past. Naturally, it takes time to gain the trust of the landscape architect, so it's a good idea to start soon.

There's good reason to ally yourself with one or more landscape architects. First of all, they usually get top-end jobs, ones that are far better than those available to you as a small design/build contractor just starting out. Second, it's good for you to see how others design jobs and to install them according to their specifications. You'll learn a tremendous amount by doing this, even if the style of the project isn't your favorite. (*Tip:* Working with landscape architects can be rewarding or difficult, depending on the person involved. There's an unfortunate tradition of mutual frustration between landscape architects and contractors that's probably never going to go away. It can take some of the fun out of your work. But a good, respectful relationship with a talented landscape architect can be a delightful and rewarding experience.)

How do you get on a bidders list? First, contact the landscape architects—preferably by letter with a follow-up phone call. Ask to meet with them so you can show off your work. Bring in photos of your jobs, letters of recommendation, a job list so they can see your work in person, a list of references, and a list of your services. Put it all into a nice attractive portfolio. Give them a fistful of your business cards. Offer to give them a tour of some of your jobs. Tell them you'd like to bid on some of their smaller projects, and ask if they have anything right now that you could bid for them. If you conduct yourself well, you may walk away with a set of plans. If not, try them again in a few months when you have more finished work to show. Persistence pays.

Building Architects

Architects design buildings but not landscapes, and they usually work with one or more landscape architects and will probably refer you to them. Still, it never hurts to let architects know you're there, because they are involved with virtually every building that gets built. Contact building architects just as you would landscape architects.

General Contractors

General contractors (also known as *generals*, *GCs*, or simply *builders*) build buildings and other structures, either from their own designs or those of a building architect. They usually operate by subcontracting most of the work on a project, hiring electricians, plumbers, roofers, concrete contractors, and so forth. Sometimes, though not always, they will hire landscape contractors as part of their project team. Your chances are better on big multi-unit residential or commercial jobs where the landscaping is part of the prime contract and is not left up to individual owners.

The process of bidding these jobs is complex and risky. Often, the general will call for sub-bids and use them when submitting his or her own bid to the owner or developer. When you bid a job for a general, you need to survive two tests: Your bid has to be the low one for the general to accept you, and the general's bid has to be low for him or her (and therefore you) to get the job. Because it can take a tremendous amount of time to bid a big job, a strategy has been developed in the industry that allows everybody the best possible chance. Each sub finds out which generals are bidding the job and submits the same bid to all of them. Often, generals will call you and ask if you're bidding on the such-and-such job on Tuesday. It's a good idea to contact all the generals you might want to work for and ask to be put on their bidders lists. It'll help if you do the same song and dance as you would for landscape architects.

Another approach is to use the *Dodge Reports* (construction.com/dodge) or something similar to find out what jobs are bidding in your area. Dodge Reports operates an online project listing service that is just for contractors and their listings show jobs by region, describe the kind of work involved, and give other pertinent information. They offer free *lead alerts* for projects that are going to bid.

Other Contractors

Get to know people in the other trades—plumbers, electricians, concrete people, and the like. They're on the job before you are and often get asked about landscapers. They can get you a lot of work.

Believe it or not, other landscape contractors can also get you work, especially when you're starting out. Many larger contractors don't want to deal with small jobs or maintenance. They may not even do residential work, so they need somebody to whom they can refer people. Sometimes contractors just get too busy to handle all the jobs. If they feel they can trust you, they might just send a lot of work your way. So don't be afraid of talking to the competition. Attend association meetings and barbecues; get to know these people and let them know you'd be interested in taking a look at jobs they don't want. Don't forget to return the favor by referring work to them if you can. (*Tip:* Offer to do the ninety-day maintenance on completed projects for large, busy contractors.)

Retail Nurseries

Get to know the managers of the local *retail nurseries* and *garden centers.* They see hundreds of homeowners every day and are often asked to recommend landscapers and gardeners. Sometimes you can even place a display of your brochures or business cards on their counter. Of course, some nurseries also offer landscape design, construction, and maintenance, and probably won't help you in this way.

Realtors

Real estate people know who's buying and selling. They're often asked to recommend tradespeople to buyers, especially those who are new to the area. If you can get their attention, you may get some referrals. Stay in touch with these folks, because they'll quickly forget about you. They tend to hang out at chamber of commerce mixers, Lion's Club meetings, and similar events. (*Tip:* Ask to give a presentation to one of the weekly or monthly gatherings of realtors that are common in most places. Your talk could cover tips on how to "stage" the landscaping for a sale, or on some other aspect of landscaping that would be of interest to them.)

Commercial Property Managers

Large commercial properties, such as shopping centers or industrial parks, usually have a staff person who handles the grounds and buildings. Call and ask for the name of the *facilities manager.* Smaller properties are often managed by a *property management company* that takes care of the properties of many owners for a fee. Landscape maintenance contracts on commercial sites come up for bid every year, and managers are always looking for a better deal. Look in the Yellow Pages or online under "Real Estate Management." (Large estates also have property managers who handle things similarly.)

Public Agencies

Public agencies such as *city public works departments, parks departments*, and other land-based entities have lots of landscaping work. Check the *Dodge Reports* or contact the city manager or another responsible person to find out what's being bid on.

Developers

Developers routinely hire landscape companies for what are often very large projects. Some of them are straight up but many can be very tough to deal with, and may not always be as scrupulous about payment as one might like, so be sure you want to do this and ask others who have dealt with them about the reputation of a particular developer before getting involved. Search online for "Real Estate Developers," "Land Developers," or "Land Companies," for starters. Or ask others in the building trades for possible contacts. Look at public records of proposed developments at your city hall or county *planning and development department*. Remember that these projects are often assigned to contractors early in the process, so don't wait until the buildings are finished to make your pitch.

Landlords

Owners of rental property can often be located by doing a search at the county hall of records or by getting in touch with a local *income property owners' association*.

Garden Clubs

Garden clubs are usually populated by affluent, older garden enthusiasts who can't do all the work themselves anymore. Go to the meetings, get to know them, offer to give a lecture on your favorite topic. It's not always appropriate to give an overt sales pitch to these groups, so check on their policies before you start grandstanding or you will work against your aims.

Social Contacts

Don't forget the value of general schmoozing. Be sure your friends and acquaintances are a part of your sales force. Let them know about interesting projects you're doing, give them a few business cards or brochures, ask them to tell their friends. Make use of social networking resources on the Internet to spread the word about your business, regularly posting news of your services and latest accomplishments, and possibly offering tips and ideas to readers.

Advertising

Since we've already agreed that traditional advertising often doesn't work too well, let's broaden the use of the word to include both traditional and nontraditional forms of making the public aware of you. Here's a rundown of the different approaches and a little about how and when to use them effectively.

(*Tip:* After a few years, possibly sooner, you'll begin to avoid advertising; your reputation alone will bring in more work than you can handle. This is true. In fact, if this doesn't happen to you, ask what's wrong with your service, not with your advertising.)

Important: Whenever clients call you, be sure to ask where they heard about you; that way you can measure the effects of your various advertising programs.

Yellow Pages

With the rise of the Internet as the world's marketplace, old advertising media such as the Yellow Pages are on the decline and it will be interesting to see whether they survive the next few years. It's much cheaper to develop a website and do social networking than to buy a Yellow Pages ad. Think about how you do your own shopping, and ask yourself how many times you have used the Yellow Pages in the past 5 years. OK, I'm just going to say this: If I were a startup company I wouldn't pay a penny for Yellow Pages advertising. Sure, I did it back in the Dark Ages, but times have changed. And even back then, most of the prospective clients I got through my Yellow Pages ads were, shall we say, not of the highest caliber. You'll pay hundreds, or even thousands, of dollars every month, on an inflexible long-term contract, for decent-sized ads (you'll be tempted to show up in ALL the many directories that litter everyone's driveway once a year) and you may get no response at all. In fact, many of the calls you get will be cheapskates and cranks, not good clients. You will probably not get a good return on this investment, and the cost may suck you dry just when you need to run lean. I'd like to see you work your social media hard and effectively, spending practically nothing for placing yourself in where people shop these days. Unless you know that the Yellow Pages is heavily used in your community, stick with your small, free listing and move on to greener pastures. After you have a good base of clients and some money to put at risk, you could try a display ad in a directory if you are so inclined.

Newspapers

Newspapers are another moribund medium that seems to have no future and may not be a good place for your advertising dollars. But some people still profit from print media advertising. There are two kinds of newspaper advertising: *classified* ("want ads") and *display*. Perhaps your paper has a special "Services Offered" classified section where trades people advertise; the cost can be reasonable and results can be pretty good. Display ads are outrageously expensive and generally not cost-effective for a tiny startup company. (Remember, though, that it doesn't matter what an ad costs; it only matters how much profit it brings you.)

Try a classified ad for starters; they're especially good if you're looking for maintenance work. Make your heading bold or use all capital letters, and include enough text to tell what you do. If you decide to use display advertising, have the graphics professionally done; don't rely on the hacks at the paper.

Don't run an ad for a week or two and decide that it doesn't work. Successful media advertising depends on consistency. Make a commitment to a strategy and stick with it for at least six months; if it's still not working, change your strategy. You can vary your ad during this time, especially the text, to see what works best. Use coupons or special offers to help measure the effectiveness of your ads. At the end of your campaign, evaluate your return on investment, in net profits from new clients who you got through your ads. If you haven't made any money, even if response was good, drop the ads or change them.

Many papers have a garden section one day a week; it can be a good spot for your ad. Saturdays and Sundays are good, too, and don't overlook seasonal special sections. Get to know the paper's garden writer. They're always looking for stories and may feature your work, which is great *free* advertising!

Radio and Television

Forget television; it's just too expensive and the results aren't good. Radio can be helpful and is surprisingly cheap—a thirty-second spot can cost as little as a few dollars if you run it consistently. (*Tip:* The rates that radio stations quote you are fictitious; dicker with them for a better deal.) One problem with radio is that it's hard to tell if your ads are doing you any good. You can test effectiveness by offering listeners a special discount available only to them or a free consultation or small gift if they mention the ad. (But as with other conventional media, give yourself time to develop your operation before you jump into this, because your startup won't have the cash to risk on speculative ad campaigns, and if you do end up getting a lot of response you won't be ready for it. First things first: Get your operation running right, then take over the world.)

Choose a station that's listened to by affluent homeowners. Your favorite rock station is probably not the one; try a station with a classical or easy listening format. News stations and talk radio are especially good because people are really paying attention.

Internet

The Internet is the current marketing powerhouse. It's where we all shop now. Use it to your advantage by developing a *website* and maybe even a blog, and by using social networking tools to make connections and stay in touch with people. Most established landscapers have their own websites these days. You should too. A company website can act as an electronic showroom, with pictures of your jobs, letters of reference from happy customers, a list of your services, photos of your crews and equipment, and whatever else you want to include. You can even have video tours of gardens you've done. How about an online newsletter or blog? Or answers to frequently asked questions (FAQs)? Or seasonal gardening tips? Let your imagination be your guide.

You can create your own website using ready-made templates or simple design applications, or pay a company to do it for you. It can be hosted for little or no money on your regular Internet account, or for a tiny bit of cash you can register your own domain name, which looks more professional and is easier to remember. For ease of recall, use a domain name that's as close as possible to your name or that of your company. (Tip: The more often you post useful information on your website, the higher your rankings with the search engines and the closer you get to the top of the list when people search on keywords relevant to your business, making it more likely that they will find your site. This is called *search engine optimization*, or "SEO," and it's a complex science. You can pay companies to improve your rankings, or study how to do it by . . . searching online for "SEO.") Some small companies have good results with *online ads* such as Google's AdWords. You pay per click or per call, and your costs are controllable. I haven't done this myself, so I can't speak as an expert, but you might check with owners of different kinds of small local businesses to see what their experience has been.

Sign up for accounts on the leading *social networking sites*, such as Facebook, Linked-In, Twitter, and others. Develop robust profiles and keep them up-to-date. Post announcements of new services, advice about seasonal garden tasks, and other information. You can advertise on Facebook, but the reading I've done seems to indicate that it's not all that productive. I'm sure that some people love it, though, so don't rule it out. Tweet people with gardening news and other items of interest.

Don't use these resources for blatant marketing; make sure you offer something of value to those who are following you so they don't tune you out. Try running ads on Craigslist. They're free and will reach a lot of people. You need to update them regularly, but it's easy to do. The brave new world of *online marketing* is complex beyond the scope of this book. A bit of research will open your eyes to the many possibilities and give you an idea of how you can profit from your online presence.

Finally, consider *email campaigns* using one of the inexpensive services that offer page setup, mailing list management, and more. Search the Web for "email marketing" to find out more. (Oh, and never, ever spam people. Avoid sending out unsolicited emails to your mailing list, and don't send mass email blasts to people you don't know because it could get you kicked out by your host. It'll make people angry and your service provider may drop you. Legitimate email marketing services have opt-out and other features, some required by law, that will keep you on good terms with recipients.)

Direct Mail

Direct mail is anything you send through the mail to potential clients—postcards, brochures, newsletters, special offers. Direct mail is a great way to build your business; it's also a way to stay in touch with your regular clients. Though response to direct mail is usually only 2 to 3 percent, the profit per dollar invested is often excellent. You can vary your mailings with the season to highlight services that may be appropriate at certain times of the year. By generating your own mailing list or using the services of a *list broker*, you can target a select group, such as new homeowners, high-income families, or people in a certain neighborhood. Response to a direct-mail campaign is quick and easy to measure. There are companies online that will print a mailer of your design or from their templates and mail it directly to your list for a very reasonable price, at much less trouble on your end. (*Tip:* If you buy a list from a broker, be sure it doesn't include names of renters.)

The first job of a direct mail piece is to get the recipient's attention; it's not easy when everyone's mailbox is full of junk mail every day. Use a *teaser*—a line of copy on the outside that creates interest. Classic teasers are "FREE!" or "Increase the Value of Your Property!" Inside, you need to make an *offer*, such as a week's free mowing with a three-month contract, a free half-hour consultation, or a free plant with every estimate. Describe all your services. Use personal, direct language, as if you were talking to the person face-to-face. Then, tell them what *action* to take: "Call today," or "Return the postcard for more information," or whatever. Repeating the offer never hurts. Be sure to appeal to the readers' needs and desires. They want to hear about greener lawns, less yard work, and more beauty; they don't want to hear about you. They do want to hear why you're the one to do the job. Finally, give them reasons to respond. (*Tip:* Unless you're really good at graphic design, have a professional lay out the ad for you or use a ready-made template; a hokey mailer is worse than none at all.)

Door-to-Door Canvassing

Going door-to-door is a lot of work, but it can really bring in the business. It's especially good when you're just starting out. Dress up in your good clothes and hit the streets. (*Tip:* You may need to get a permit from your city or county before you can legally go door-to-door.) Choose affluent neighborhoods, either new ones where everybody needs landscaping or older ones where a lot of houses could use a face-lift. You could send out a mailer first to build name recognition, or just show up unannounced. (*Tip:* Consider giving out a free gift, perhaps a small plant or a packet of seeds, to each person you contact. If no one's at home, leave it on the doorstep along with a flyer and a business card, and then come back the next day.)

There are four steps to canvassing:

1. *Making contact with the person and making a good first impression:* This is where clothing, grooming, and demeanor count. You've got about five seconds to do this well. Be friendly, positive, outgoing. Be yourself, but be on your best behavior, as if you were meeting your fiancée's parents for the first time.
2. *Qualifying the person:* Find out if it's likely these people are in the market for your services. Some of this you do simply by avoiding unpromising homes: those that show no pride of ownership, that have no landscaping, that have dead cars on the front lawn, or that are probably occupied by renters, for example. After you've talked with a homeowner for a while, you'll be able to tell whether he or she is interested in your services and able to pay for them. Don't waste your time on people who aren't likely to do business with you.
3. *The presentation:* Once you see that there is some interest, make your pitch. This is your opportunity to describe your services, to tell why you're better than the competition, and, specifically, to paint a picture of what you can do for the person to whom you're talking. This is where you have it all over other door-to-door salespeople, because you've checked out the owner's front yard on the way up the walk and developed a mental list of things you could do to make the place better. When people demonstrate any interest, take them out and show them.

   The presentation could take a while, especially if the owner is really interested. If someone is truly engaged, don't be in a hurry to go. If the person walks you around the yard, you know you've got a serious potential client. However, don't waste your time with someone who just wants to chat; remember, you're there to get work, not to pass the time of day.

   It helps to ask questions: "Who does your yard work now?" "Is there anything you've been wanting to do to improve your landscaping?"

Listening is important; it helps you get to know people a bit so you can customize your presentation for them. If you've done any work in the neighborhood, mention it. Be professional and be proud of what you're offering. (*Tip:* You have to give away some of your knowledge to prove that you know what you're doing, but don't tell them so much that you come back later and find they've ripped off your ideas. See "Designing the Project" at the beginning of chapter 8 for more information on this touchy subject.)

4. *The close:* This describes the way you complete the sale. If you don't close the sale right then, you'll probably never hear from the person again. (See "Closing the Sale" at the end of chapter 7.)

Flyers

Print an 8 ½-by-11-inch, one-page (or even a half-page) *flyer* and hand it out to a specific audience or put it under windshields at the mall. This is a simple, inexpensive way to get attention. It's especially good for seasonal or introductory offers. You can also post flyers at retail nurseries or on your local supermarket bulletin boards. A flyer can double as a direct-mail piece. Don't put flyers into people's mailboxes; it's against the law to do so unless you have adequate postage on the material. (*Tip:* You can track response to your flyers by offering a discount or gift for responding to them, or you can simply ask people how they heard about you.)

Job-Site Signs

Have some signs professionally made that you can put in the front yard on jobs you're doing, and leave them there for a couple of weeks after you've finished (assuming that local regulations permit you to do so). They attract a lot of attention and are a way to show off your work. Custom-made plastic, metal or masonite signs, mounted on a steel stake, will cost $50 to $100 apiece, and they're well worth it. If you're feeling cheap, go on line where you can find adequate signs for as little as $25. Make them easy to read, with large letters. Use color tastefully to attract the eye. However, be sure to ask your clients if it's okay before you place a sign in their front yard. Some people may object and it's important to respect their feelings.

Truck Signs

People look at your trucks and they will pay close attention to any signs you place on them. Use *magnetic door signs*, or mount signs on the sideboards. Put a sign on the back of your truck, too; it'll get read more often than the traditional ones on the side. Make your signs easy to read, with big, clear lettering and a simple design. They may not generate any jobs, but they will reinforce other advertising and help build your name recognition. Be sure to keep your trucks clean and in good condition.

Home Shows and County Fairs

Renting a booth at one of these events can cost you several hundred dollars, and decorating it can run much more than that. Getting ready for the show and taking things down afterward can consume a lot of time. Still, landing a couple of good jobs can make it all worthwhile. Just be sure to avoid sleazy shows that will make you look bad. Choose a show with a long track record, ask for local references, and consider contacting the Better Business Bureau to see if there are any complaints against the organizers.

Alternative Forms of Marketing

Some of the best advertising doesn't cost anything. You may find the following ideas helpful.

Teaching and Lecturing

Teaching a class or giving a lecture establishes you as an expert and puts you in touch with people who are doing landscaping. Organizations that may be able to sponsor and advertise a class or lecture for you include adult education programs, botanical gardens, garden clubs, service clubs (like the Rotary or the Lions Club), and private learning centers. You might also be able to speak at a special event such as an Arbor Day tree planting. Get on the radio or TV if you can. Take advantage of occasions such as Water Awareness Month or special community gatherings. Become the local expert on something—water conserving landscaping, organic pest control, whatever. Just be sure you know your stuff; b.s. won't do. (*Tip:* If you're not a confident public speaker, think about joining a group like Toastmasters to improve your speaking skills.)

Public Service

You should do some public service just because it's good to give something back to the community that supports you. But there's no denying that public service has its marketing advantages, too. It's a great source of leads. Possibilities include environmental workdays for groups like the Nature Conservancy or the Sierra Club, community tree plantings, and urban creek cleanups. You may eventually be asked to chair a committee or become a member of a public board or commission; consider that an honor and say yes if it's something you're passionate about and if you have the time to take the job on. Your expertise will be welcome, and you'll make friends with a lot of good people who will recommend you to others. You can even think up your own cause. Is there a problem in your community that you could solve? If so, ponder the possibility of starting a grass-roots group to address the issue.

You can help these causes by donating materials, equipment, labor, and, most of all, your expertise as a professional.

Political Activity

Also consider political activity, especially environmental issues, but be aware that taking a visible stand on a controversial issue (such as abortion or gun control) can alienate a lot of potential clients. Being obvious about your membership in or support of a particular political party or candidate could likewise alienate potential clients who are lifelong loyalists of the other party. Whether it's issues or candidates, political bumper stickers on your trucks are probably not a good idea; save them for your car. That having been said, I personally have always been very open about my political leanings and I believe it has been good for my business. I know that some folks on the other side won't work with me, but I probably don't want to work with them either, and the folks who think like I do make the best clients. So I consider having a strong political profile a net benefit. But that's just me, and I've been fortunate to live in communities where most folks are on my side of the issues.

Donations

Donate something to local charities, such as the boys' or girls' club, preschools, churches, and service organizations such as the Jaycees. These are just a few suggestions; look around your community for other possibilities. You can give of your time and expertise on a project, donate a consultation or other services to a fundraiser, or just write a check. Be sure they mention your company when thanking donors.

Press Releases

Many businesses large and small promote themselves very successfully by using *press releases*. Whenever you win an award, hire a new key employee, donate your services to a worthy cause, or give a talk, send a press release to the local media. Although there's no guarantee that it will be published, it's always worth a try and doesn't cost you anything. You stand a better chance with this strategy in small towns than in big cities. Be sure to use the standard format for the release, which can be found online by searching for "How to write a press release." Write in the style of the publication you'll be submitting it to so that they can use it with a minimum of editing. Remember the five "Ws" of journalism: who, what, when, where, and why. And don't get your feelings hurt if they do edit it or don't use it at all. Now, don't wear out your welcome by sending releases too often; 3 or 4 times a year is about all you should do. (*Tip:* Send your release to local bloggers as well, and of course post everything on your Facebook page.)

Keeping Track of Potential Clients: Contact Report

The *contact report* form holds the basic information about a potential client. There are two parts to a good contact report: The first part contains basic data about the client (name, address, etc.). If you plan on running a credit check on the client, find out what your local credit bureau requires and include that. Include a place to indicate how the client found you—your website, the Yellow Pages, a referral, a newspaper ad, or whatever. This bit of information will be important in evaluating the effectiveness of your marketing and advertising.

The second part includes information about the project (address, type of project, work to be done, schedule, etc.). If you're bidding plans drawn by a landscape architect, include the name, address, and phone number of the firm; the person in charge; drawing numbers; dates and revisions; specification section numbers; and dates. If you will be subcontracting out part of the work, have a space to list the various trades and the names of potential subs. If you'll be working as a subcontractor, provide a place for the name, address, and phone number of the general contractor. Also have a place for the job phone number and the name of the superintendent or contact person.

Sample Contact Report

DATE ____________ BY ______ 4/10/15 JW

PROJECT

Name Seaboard Shopping Plaza
Address 2121 W. Thompson Ave.
City/State/Zip Allenton, CT 00760
Phone (123) 555–7497
Contact Joe Marston
Fax (123) 555–2242
Type: Residential ______ Commercial X Other ______

Name Seaboard Group, Inc.
Address 10476 S. Elm.
City/State/Zip Allenton, CT 00761
Home Phone ——————
Work Phone (123) 555–1797

Name Marshall Design Group
Address 172 E. 4th St.
City/State/Zip Stone Valley, RI 00814
Phone (123) 555–7121
Contact Peter Marshall
Fax (123) 555–0070

Name Hanson Contracting
Address 907 Placid Lake Dr., #201
City/State/Zip Allenton, CT 00760
Phone (123) 555–1994
Contact Jim Petrie
Fax (123) 555–2747

Drawing Nos./Dates/Revisions Sheets L-1 through L-4, #L-417-00, 2-2-03, rev. 2 (2-19-00)
12, 2-4-03

Specification Section No./Date ______

Submit proposal to: Owner ______ L.A. ______ G.C. X Other ______

Bid date/time 4/24/15
Date work to start 5/29/15

Budget $40,000
Getting other bids? Y ______ N ______

Landscape plantings and irrigation, 2 retaining walls, mulch — in front and
s. side of 2 new buildings

— excavation and grading
— concrete

Referred by Landscape architect

07 Bidding

Seldom will anyone offer you a job without wanting to know what it will cost. It's your responsibility to provide clients with a price before you actually do the work, and that's what the science of bidding is all about. Your price has to be both attractive to the client and profitable to you. Accurate bidding is one of the keys to your success. Bid too high and you won't get any work; bid too low and you'll go broke.

The Main Elements of a Bid

Boiled all the way down to the basics, a bid consists of *costs* and *profit*. First you figure what the job is going to cost you, then you add on a fair profit, and you've got yourself a bid. The Elements of a Bid outline, which follows, shows the way it looks in detail.

Note: Contingency is an allowance for things you can't foresee (delays caused by others, price increases, weather conditions, etc.). Some people call it the "fudge factor." Contingency can also be used to include what I call *courtesy padding*—a little extra money in the bid so you won't have to nickel-and-dime the client every time some little change comes up on the job.

Important: Remember that you have to recover all your costs before you can make a profit. Most important, *the business never pays for anything; it's always the client who pays.* The client pays for your labor and materials, your overhead, your truck and tools, and (if you make that profit) your house and groceries as well.

How a Bid Differs from an Estimate

A *bid* is a commitment. When you submit a bid, you are agreeing to do the job for the bid price and the client is counting on you to meet this obligation; if you back out, you can be sued for non-performance. An *estimate* is a way to let the client know approximately how much a job will cost without making an actual commitment to do the work at that price, or to do it at all. Be clear with clients about whether the figures you submit are an estimate or a bid; write one of those two words in big letters on whatever written material you submit to them, and add clarifying language on estimates stating that they are not bids.

About Rough Estimates

At some point in the early stages of a discussion with a new client, they will inevitably want to know what the project will cost. It's an awkward moment because there's nothing concrete to go on—no design, no specifications, nothing but a barren or overgrown mess that everyone is looking forward to turning into a paradise. This puts you in the difficult position of giving prices out of thin air. Yes, you may have a sense of the overall cost, and after years of doing this work you will probably be right. But you have no control over how the project will flesh out in the design stage, and you haven't had an opportunity to measure, to fully understand the scope of work, or to work up some numbers in a methodical way. So there you are, wanting to answer this most difficult of all questions, and if you're like most of us, you will say something like, "Well, it's pretty early to say, but, now don't quote me on this, but, um, I think it should run between, um, X and X dollars." You take the bait and you set yourself and your client up for disappointment. That part about not quoting you? The client will never hear that, and later they will get sore because the job cost more than what they remember you said and yes, they will quote the heck out of you and let you know that they think you are not competent or honest or a nice person. Also, they will only hear that first "X," the low one. It's human nature. The solution? Tell them you want some time to work up a rough estimate, and then put it in writing with plenty of caveats about it being rough, approximate, preliminary, and probably totally cuckoo in places. Give a wide range of costs, and an explanation that there are a million ways to do the job and time will tell what you end up with and what it will cost. Assure them that you can work within any reasonable budget, adjusting the design so that it fits what the client wants to spend. Meet with them again to present this, to discuss it, and hopefully to win them over as a new client.

Time-and-Materials Jobs

Sometimes a firm bid isn't appropriate. Some things, such as cleanups or demolition, are difficult to bid fairly. Others, such as small repair jobs, are so trivial that a bid isn't necessary. That's when you'll work on a *time-and-materials* basis, also

Elements of a Bid

Costs (money you have to put out to do the job)

Direct: (things that go into the actual job)
- Labor
- Materials
- Subcontractor costs
- Equipment costs (both owned and rented)
- Fees (dump fees, permits, etc.)
- Contingency

Indirect: (things that keep your company running)
- General conditions (job costs not part of the actual job)
- Overhead (what it costs to run your business)

Profit (money you earn for doing the job)

known as "T&M." You do the job, then bill for the actual hours spent on labor (at a profitable rate) and for the materials used (marked up from wholesale to retail or at least to a profitable price). A common variation is called "*T&M not to exceed*," in which you place an upper limit on what you'll charge for the job; this approach is used when the client doesn't want to write you a blank check.

There are good and bad things about doing business this way. It's great to know that you'll get paid for everything you do (unlike a bid, which may turn out not have been high enough to cover costs and profit). When you've built up a relationship of mutual trust, both you and your client know that everyone will be treated fairly. Still, some clients will look over your shoulder all day, and when you present your bill, they'll complain because someone showed up at 8:33 instead of 8:30 a.m.

To be successful with the T&M approach, you have to make your billing policies clear. Let the clients know that you'll charge for time spent off the site (going to the dump, picking up materials, etc.), and tell them what prices you'll be charging for labor and materials. Give them an estimate of the total costs, and let them know about anything that might increase those costs. If during the course of the work you find yourself spending more time or needing more materials than you originally estimated, then let the client know that right away. That way there won't be any nasty surprises for either of you at the end of the job.

Bidding and Contracts Questions and Answers

Q: When should I submit an estimate instead of a bid?

A: You should submit an estimate under the following conditions:

1. The scope of the work is not clear or you don't know what problems might arise. You might want to provide a range of costs for parts of the work, such as $700–$1,000 for the cleanup phase.
2. There are several alternative possibilities that are being considered.
3. The client isn't sure what she or he wants and is "just getting some prices." It's reasonable to educate people about the cost of your services, but it's not reasonable to spend hours on a very detailed bid for someone who may not be serious about hiring you (or anyone).

Q: How much detail should I include in a bid?

A: Spell out as much as possible about what you will and won't do. An incomplete bid creates several problems. First, it doesn't make clients feel very comfortable. They don't know exactly what you'll be doing or what each element costs. They may also feel that you don't understand what's involved or that you've padded the price. Second, you're not protected. Clients could (and often will) claim that you said you'd do something that you never intended to do. This can lead to arguments, delays, damage to your reputation, refusal of the client to pay you, and possibly a lawsuit or revocation of your contractor's license.

Q: When do I need a written contract?

A: Legal requirements vary from state to state. Often a written contract is required if the total price of any one project exceeds $500, or some variation on that. If you are a licensed contractor, learn what is required by law to be included in your contracts; this can be very specific and complex and you must do things precisely or you'll get stung. Get something in writing before you begin any job, no matter how small it is, even if you only get the client's signature on a job work order.

Q: Should I have written contracts for my maintenance jobs?

A: It's not a bad idea. Just as with a landscaping job, you need to include detailed information on what you will and won't be doing.

Unit-Price Bidding

Suppose you install a lot of sod lawns. There's no point in going through the whole complicated routine each time you bid a job. Instead, you do it once to set a fair *unit price*, say $1.50 per square foot, and then you use that price every time you bid a lawn. If conditions are unusual (a long carry into the backyard, extra weed control, difficult soil), you adjust accordingly. If you're smart, you'll still *cost out* every job (see the section on "Job Costing" later in this chapter) to be sure you did OK. If you're consistently making less than you should at a given unit price, adjust it. You should check your unit prices every few months to be sure you're still making money.

(*Tips:* A badly figured unit price will lose you money every time you use it, so do your homework. Don't just imitate somebody else's prices; their costs may be different than yours and they may even be losing money. Base your unit prices on your own situation. Don't use unit prices for everything, just for simple things like plants, lawns, and other routine tasks. Never unit-price bid a large or complex job; go through the regular full bidding process.)

Bidding Maintenance Jobs

Maintenance is mostly labor, so bidding can be somewhat simpler. Otherwise there's no difference. But remember that you have to live with your bid not just once but every month for at least a year or until you can justify a price increase.

When to Charge for Bids

In most circumstances, charging for estimates or bids is not appropriate. *Insurance estimates* are an exception. Many times, when landscaping is damaged, the owner will use your free estimate to get money out of the insurance company and then spend it on something else. You'll probably never get the work, so you can justify charging a modest fee up front for the estimate; you might make it refundable if you get the job.

The same goes for design work. A common con, often tried on inexperienced landscapers, is for the owners to pick your brains for *exactly* what you'd do to the backyard, and then use your ideas to do the work themselves. That hurts enough that you'll soon start charging for design work, as you should. Estimates and general ideas are free; specifics should not be. (You could offer to refund part or all of the design fees if you get the work.)

The Bidding Process, Step-by-Step

Bidding can be intimidating to newcomers because there are so many little but important details and because there's so much at stake. There's nothing worse than getting a job because you were the low bidder and then realizing you will be losing money because of some dumb mistake or oversight (remember that in a formal bidding situation, if you were awarded the job, you are obligated to do it for the price you bid, except in certain special circumstances). But if you take a methodical approach, you'll find that bidding is not all that complicated. Try following these steps to make the process less overwhelming.

Step One: Do You Really Want This Job?

Some jobs are best left to your competitors. To be successful you need to be selective; don't try for every job that comes along. Here are some of the questions you'll learn to ask.

Will this job make me a profit? Did you hear about the landscaper who won $1 million in the lottery? When they asked him what he was going to do, he said he'd probably just keep on doing landscaping until the money was all gone. Well, there's no point in going to work unless you can make money, so you have to be sure you're not going up against all the low-ballers in town or that owner who wants a Mercedes for the price of a Ford.

Is this the kind of work I'm good at doing? If the project is beyond your abilities, let it go. To do otherwise is to ask for trouble. It's OK to stretch yourself with new aspects of a familiar kind of work, but to charge people for work you really have no idea how to do is just wrong.

Is it the right size? Big jobs aren't for beginners. You won't be able to bid it right, do it right, or finance it right. Evaluate your available personnel, equipment, subcontractors, and financial capabilities before you get involved.

Is it in the right location? Don't take work that's located 200 miles away. You'll go crazy commuting and your travel costs will be outrageous. When the job's done and the client wants you to come out every three days to see if the plants are doing OK, you'll realize you should have stuck closer to home.

Do I have time for it? Overextending is a major cause of failure. Learn how much work you can handle at one time, and take on only what you have the time to do properly. Although you want to provide service as promptly as possible, clients will wait for you if you have a good reputation. In fact, knowing that you're busy seems to make people feel better. (I used to have a message on my answering machine that included a comment about my three-to-four-week backlog; I discovered that it made people more eager to get in line to have me do their landscaping. Strange but true.)

Is the client a turkey? Sometimes you look at a job and something just doesn't feel right, something about the way the guy looks at you or whatever. Maybe you can't put your finger on it, but after a few bad experiences, you learn that the little voice inside that was telling you to flee was right. Sometimes you'll take on a job with a potential turkey because things are slow (we've all done this); then, sure enough, a week into it you'll wish you'd never seen the place. (Apologies to actual turkeys, who are more intelligent and certainly more decent than some clients.)

Evaluate potential clients for sincerity (weed out tire-kickers), integrity (don't fall for that stuff about "give me a good deal on this job, and I can get you lots of work"), ability to pay (the bank does credit checks; why not you?), agreeability (when some people complain about every other contractor or gardener they've ever had, you can bet they'll be talking about you the same way soon enough), and sanity (some people are just too loony to do business with). Apply the same tests to the project landscape architect, general contractor, or anyone else who may have power over you.

Is the project a turkey? Is this a hideous job that you'll be ashamed to be associated with later? Are there unreasonable risks involved (erosion, soil problems, safety hazards)? If a landscape architect designed it, is it a dreadful design? Are there unreasonable conditions (too little time to bid it or to complete it, outrageous guarantees, etc.)?

How do I get rid of a funky job? If you don't want it, just say so. True, some people will go ahead and bid sky-high—but that can give you a reputation you don't want. Others just don't call such clients back, but that looks bad, too. Just tell them it's not your kind of project or (if you feel you must lie) that you're too busy to take it. Thank them for their interest, and move along.

Step Two: The Plans and Specifications

Study the *plan drawings* and *specifications* with utmost care because they describe the job and set the standards to which you'll work. Be sure you have the latest version of the plans plus all addenda and revisions. Ask the landscape architect specifically if this is the case. If you're doing design/build, you'll be setting your own standards, which makes things a lot easier.

Many people have gone broke because they missed some little note or detail that cost them everything. For instance, what if you misread the scale of the plans and bid on 4,000 square feet of lawn instead of 16,000? What if you missed the part that said, "Contractor shall obtain and pay for all building permits"? Plans often include lists of plants and other materials; check the quantities shown on the drawings against the materials lists for discrepancies. (Often the specifications state whether the drawings or the lists take precedence in the event of an error.) Read the specifications several times; do the same with detail drawings and any other attachments. Call the landscape architect with any and all questions; the landscape architect is obligated to help you understand his or her intentions.

Step Three: The Site Inspection

Anyone who bids on a job without doing a *thorough* inspection of the site is plain crazy. Site conditions can make a big difference in the cost of the job. Some of the things to look for are soil conditions (Is digging easy or difficult? Are there rocks?), terrain, and existing features (structures, trees and shrubs, weed growth, underground utilities that affect digging, overhead wires that affect equipment operation, accessibility for equipment and materials delivery). Compare the actual dimensions of the site with what's shown on the plans, because plans are often horribly inaccurate. Look at the finish grade: Is it high or low, indicating potentially expensive earthmoving work? Think about where you'll park trucks, where the staging area will be, where people will go to the bathroom. Think the job completely through from beginning to end. The *Site Inspection Report (Landscaping)* will help you with this process. For maintenance work, use the *Site Inspection and Bid Worksheet (Maintenance)*. Both forms appear later in this chapter.

Step Four: The Takeoffs

A *takeoff* is a list of all the direct costs (materials, labor, equipment, and subcontractors) required to do the job. The takeoff will follow you through the job, serving first as a basis for your bid, later as a shopping list, and finally as a way to do your job costing once the work is completed. Have a look at the *Bid Takeoff Worksheet (Landscaping)* later in this chapter to see how to organize the information in a usable form. (This process will get easier as you gain more experience. For starters, stick to small, simple jobs.)

Materials

List your materials first. As you go along, mark the plans with a highlighter to make sure you counted everything. Be methodical and careful to get everything. Remember that the plans may show certain items, like plants, but not others, like staking materials or soil amendments. You need to allow for shrinkage, too; for example, when you compact soil, it can shrink up to 30 percent. There's wastage in almost all materials, so include more of everything. Don't forget supportive materials like concrete forms that might not be reused. Finally, be sure to include sales tax on a separate line. (*Important Tip:* The key to successful bidding is building the job in your mind. You've got to visualize every act from start to finish: killing the weeds, digging the holes, hauling the mulch up the hill. That way, you'll get a good idea of the materials, labor, and equipment required, not just a wild guess.) Remember, when you get to doing the actual job, you'll need what you need, and it'll cost what it costs. Now's the time to face it.

Labor

The materials takeoff was the easy part: it's just counting. Now you've got to figure your labor. Labor is usually what makes or breaks you. It's also a lot harder to estimate than materials because you're dealing with people.

There's nothing on the plans that you can count to get your labor costs, so how do you do it? One way is to get a book of *time-and-motion studies*, often available through trade associations. You'll find information on how many one-gallon plants a laborer can plant per hour in different soils, how much area a mower can mow per hour, and so forth. Of course, these figures don't have much to do with *your* people on *this* particular job, do they? So use them only as a guide, adjusting for the particular circumstances you face. A better way is to base your labor on what you and your people have done in the past. As you do more jobs, you'll be able to develop your own time studies as well as adjustment factors for different soil conditions and other contingencies. Include plenty of *fudge factor* in your labor takeoffs, because you'll need it. (When I started hiring other people to do work that I had been doing myself, I was shocked to find that they took twice as long to do things as I did. They were doing their best, but they didn't understand how to work efficiently, so I was faced with training people not only in the technical aspects of the work but also in the art of eliminating wasted motion. For instance, because my mother used to tell me to never go anywhere empty-handed I was accustomed to carrying things with me wherever I went, taking a few plants into the back yard on my way to hauling some refuse from the back yard out to the truck. I watched with growing dismay as my employees would turn that sort of thing into two trips. I would have to show them that they could make things easier for themselves as well as more profitable for me by using their noggins.)

What about your own salary? Well, if you'll be working on the job, pay yourself an hourly wage. But even if you never leave the office, you need to apportion an appropriate amount of your salary to the job, based on the amount of time you'll spend on it. Don't assume you'll just take your living expenses out of the profit; profit is another matter entirely.

Equipment

Next, list the equipment you'll need. If you're going to rent a tractor, figuring the cost is easy: calculate how many days or hours you'll need the equipment and what the rates are per day or hour, plus delivery charges, taxes, etc. But you will also need to recover costs on your own equipment. One way to do that is to charge what the rental yards would charge you if you had to rent the item. Their business is making money on equipment, so if they don't know costs, who would? Just remember to deduct your best guessstimate of the profit they include, because you don't want to add profit on twice (well, you do of course, but it doesn't help you to be competitive). The other way is to figure actual costs of ownership: Purchase price plus maintenance, less salvage value, divided by the estimated hours of useful life will determine a rate per hour. Naturally, you do this only on trucks and mechanized equipment, not rakes and shovels.

Subcontractors

Include the cost of any *subcontracted work* you may be hiring out. To do this, you need to get bids from your subs. Allow plenty of time for this; don't wait until the last minute and expect them to come up with a price. After all, they've got to go through the same routine you do. Get them involved right at the start. It's up to you whether to get more than one sub-bid for each trade. Do it if you need to be low bidder; otherwise, stick with your regular subs and don't pit them against others. (*Tip:* Some states don't allow you to hire subcontractors. In that case, you can get bids from subs but you'll have to set the deal up so that the client pays the subs directly. Or you can simply have the client handle that portion of the bidding and you will just bid on work that you and your employees will be doing.)

General Conditions

Finally, you've got to deal with a category called *general conditions*. These are costs that don't become a part of the finished job but have to be paid for anyway. Examples include time spent every day to clean up the site, loading and unloading, travel time, portable toilets, roll-off rubbish bins, moving equipment on and off the job (called *mobilization*), record drawings, and photos. And what about time spent looking for plants, replacement of plants that die and other warranty work, and dump fees? There are lots of general conditions, and they vary from job to job.

Total Direct Cost

Now add all these factors up to get your *total direct cost*. That's what you can expect to pay to get the job done. Oh, and be sure to add one more item: a *contingency* amount to account for still more unexpected things that will (will) come up. Depending on the project and the bidding situation, two to five percent is prudent. This is guesswork, of course, but like everything else you'll get better at guessing as you do more and more jobs.

Step Five: Figuring Overhead Recovery

Remember *overhead*? It's the cost of running your business (telephone, insurance, gasoline for the trucks, etc.), and it gets paid only if you charge it to the jobs you do. Where else would it come from—the overhead fairy?

You know from your business plan what your overhead should be in the first few years. You also know that your overhead will be low as long as you work out of your home and do things yourself. When you've planned in advance for overhead recovery, you'll know that overhead won't have to come out of profits because you failed to account for it in your bids. (*Tip:* You need to recover most of your overhead from your labor, because labor causes more of it in the first place. After all, if you were just selling materials, you wouldn't need trucks and equipment and tools, you wouldn't have to pay worker's compensation insurance, and so forth. So a job that's labor intensive needs to have more overhead charged to it than one that's materials intensive.)

Now, divide your projected annual overhead into daily chunks. When you bid a job, figure out how many days it will take and add the overhead amount to the bid price.

Another approach is to pre-calculate your overhead as a percentage of direct costs. This works better after you've been in business a year or two; it will then be more accurate than the previous method. Let's say your overhead is 15 percent of your direct costs; you mark up the direct costs of the job you're bidding by 15 percent. (*Crucial Warning:* Adding on 15 percent doesn't *recover* 15 percent! If you have a "markup/markdown" key on your calculator, use it to get the true markup. If you don't, or if you're setting up a bid form on a computer spreadsheet, *divide* your direct costs by the *reciprocal* of your overhead—85 percent—to arrive at the 15 percent. Or add on 17.67 percent to arrive at the same figure. Play around with this on your calculator until you get the idea. This same principle is true of any markups or markdowns. See the markup chart to better understand how it works.)

Step Six: Adding On Your Profit

Now you know what this job is going to cost you, but you haven't yet figured out what you're going to make on it. (If you're feeling guilty about the prospect of making a profit, go back to chapter 3 and reread the section on net profit/loss.) Remember that profit is your reward for investing in your business and for taking the risks involved in the jobs you do. In fact, the riskier the job, the more profit you should add on.

So, the least profit you should accept is equal to the interest rate the bank would pay you on your savings, plus maybe 2 percent to cover your risk (interest rates are low these days, at least at the time of this writing, so this is usually not enough to compensate you for your efforts). The highest acceptable profit is what will still get you the job and not make you feel like a gouger. When you've got twenty years of high-quality work behind you and people are beating down your door, you can probably ask whatever you want for your services. But that doesn't mean you need to be a lowballer now, just because you're the new guy. Setting prices too low gives people the idea that you must do crummy work.

Markup Chart

To achieve a gross profit of	Add this amount to your cost	
5%	5 1/4%	(5.25%)
10%	11 1/9%	(11.12%)
15%	17 2/3%	(17.67%)
20%	25%	
25%	33 1/3%	(33.34%)
30%	42 6/7%	(42.86%)
35%	53 4/5%	(53.80%)
40%	66 2/3%	(66.67%)
50%	100%	

EXAMPLES

COST PRICE	+ MARKUP	= GROSS PROFIT
$100.00	$33.34 (33.34%)	$133.34 (25%)
$100.00	$25.00 (25%)	$125.00 (20%)
$100.00	$11.12 (11.12%)	$111.12 (10%)

PROFIT POINTERS: Remember that you can't expect the same profit on a commercial or competitively bid job as you can on a residential job. Smaller jobs should earn more profit than big ones. You may have to lower your profit margin when times are lean and money is tight. Going against lowballers may make it impossible to do the job at any profit. (Here are a few reasons lowballers can bid jobs so low: They may not be licensed and may not pay worker's comp or other insurance.

They might do all the work themselves, dig smaller holes and shallower trenches, use cheaper materials or use less than what's called for, and do sloppy work. They could be using money from the next job to pay for the last job, or they may not pay their suppliers or their taxes. Some have a rich spouse or parents who support their little hobby of landscaping. Most likely of all, many lowballers are in the process of slowly going broke.)

No one can help you any more than that; your profit margin is your decision. Just remember that good work isn't cheap and cheap work isn't good.

Bidding Secrets

Here are some things it takes the average person years to learn:

Front loading (for jobs where you receive progress payments): Get your profits out of the job early on by putting a higher markup on the things you'll be doing first: demolition, earthwork, and so forth. To do this, you need to do a separate bid sheet for each segment of the job and submit a price for each segment. Prices for early stages of the work will include more of the overhead and profit than later stages. You also need to base your progress payments on completion of specific segments.

Loading "sure thing" items: Sometimes the client will get your bid and start eliminating frills like lighting or water features. By putting most of your profit into the basic portions of the work, you're sure to make your money. Since they can't cut out weed control or grading, put more of your profit there.

Rounding off: I once had a sub who would always turn in bids that look like this: $43,167.16. That's absurd. Round everything up to cover some of your contingency. Turn in round-number bids.

(*Tip:* If you're doing bids by hand rather than on a computer, use a printing calculator to run a tape so you can double-check your addition; save the tape with the bid sheets for later reference.)

Step Seven: Checking Your Bid

Double-check everything—your takeoffs, your assumptions, your arithmetic. If you have a partner or someone else who can go over it too, then so much the better. Remember, your livelihood is riding on every bid. Who needs to go to Las Vegas when you risk everything every day?

Look at the *Bid Summary Sheet (Landscaping, Lump-Sum Bid)* later in this chapter to see how to organize your final bid information.

Alternates

Many times the client will ask for other, possibly cheaper, ways of doing the job. They're called *alternates*, and you need to provide a separate bid for each alternate. Many people hate having to bid alternates, but they're really one of your best selling tools. By getting the client involved in whether to use brick or gravel for the walks, you make it easier for him or her to say yes to the job. Use alternates even when people don't ask for them—everybody appreciates a choice rather than a take-it-or-leave-it approach. It shows that you're thinking. Besides, you can make the same profit on the alternate simply by marking it up higher.

Conditions, Limitations, and Exclusions

Most bids include a section where the contractor clarifies the work beyond what's on the plans and specifications. This part of the bid document is commonly called *Conditions, Limitations, and Exclusions*. Often it's used to tell what you won't do. For instance: "Painting not included," or "110-volt supply to irrigation controller to be installed by others," or "Not responsible for survival of transplanted trees." Often there's a *rock clause*, limiting your liability for unobservable soil conditions and establishing a billing procedure for extra labor required to deal with the problems that might arise from boulders and other junk buried underground.

The Bid Package

On a private residential job, you'll usually submit your bid directly to the homeowner, or in some cases to the landscape architect. Be sure it's neatly printed on your letterhead and that all details, exclusions, and other necessary information are included. The bid package is your showroom, so make it professional and attractive. Include the contract (where applicable), a list of jobs you've done that the client can drive by and look at, a list of references, your brochure or other sales literature, a credit application if you wish, and a cover letter. Put it all in a nice folder with your business card stuck to the outside where people can see it.

There are a lot of approaches to the format of the bid presentation. The example in the *Sample Bidding Forms* section that follows shows some of the information you should include; this is a format that works well for me. Remember: Presentation will vary depending on the circumstances.

Submitting the Bid

On a residential job, it's traditional to meet with the client and go over the bid. Always have a personal meeting with the client; sending a bid through the mail or by email won't give you the opportunity to explain your pricing and answer any questions the client may have. Generally when you send a bid you never hear from the people again. On a big, competitively bid job, there's often a formal bid opening that all bidders attend. Whatever the circumstances, this is your moment of truth. Below are a couple of things that can happen at this stage.

So You're the Low Bidder?

One of the scariest outcomes is to be the low bidder on a competitively bid job, especially if you're a *lot* lower than the other bidders. What did you forget? How much is it going to cost you? Is this the end of your career?

Generally speaking, once your bid has been accepted, you're obligated to do the work. Still, there are certain circumstances under which you can back out or adjust your bid. For example, courts have found that if an error is so obvious that even the client can see that something's wrong, the bidder can withdraw or re-bid. If this ever happens to you, see an attorney at once. (*Tip:* Always get the bid results of every competitively bid job you bid on so you can see how the other contractors are bidding.)

What If You're over Budget?

Usually clients have a number in the back of their minds, the price for which they think you ought to do the job. In some cases, the landscape architect has provided them with a cost estimate. Naturally, they won't tell you what that number is until you've submitted your bid. If your number is a lot bigger, you've got problems. The client may be shocked. The landscape architect may be embarrassed. They may want to throw you bodily into the street. What do you do?

Let's say they really want you to do the work, but the price is just too high. You have an opportunity to salvage the situation by telling them what you can do for *their* price. What can you change or delete? Naturally, they won't get as much work as the original project (*Never* lower your bid price to get a job. *Never.*), but surely you can change something. Start stripping the bid of nonessentials (those low-profit frills like lighting and ponds). Show them on paper how the price drops every time you take something out. *Downsizing* plants—fifteen gallon to five gallon, fives down to ones—can cut costs in a hurry without changing the nature of the project much. If this doesn't get you to their price range, suggest doing the work in stages, half now and half in the fall, for example. Go as far as you can without cutting quality or profit (I hope I don't need to explain why you should never cut either of those things!). Usually this works as long as people's expectations aren't wildly off the mark.

Sample Bidding Forms

When you look at the sample forms in this chapter, remember that there's no one right way to do bidding; you'll surely develop your own approach over time. The examples that follow will help you understand the basics. *Note:* These forms are provided for illustration only. All the figures are fictitious and should not be used in your own bids. (*Tip:* You may want to provide a line or box on the bottom of each page of any legal documents for clients to put their initials. That's a standard way to protect yourself against later claims that they "never saw that page.")

The Contract

The *contract* is one of the key documents in your business. Required by law, the contents of the contract will vary, depending on the regulations in your state. You must not get creative with these requirements or you risk losing money or even your contractor's license. Check with your attorney or the *contractors license board* to find out what you need. You can make up your own contract (with the help of your attorney) or if you prefer, preprinted forms are sold at contractors' bookstores and office supply places. Another good source is your state *landscape contractors association*. *Warning:* Sometimes the standard forms are incomplete or out of date, because laws change so often. Compare the form to the law before you use it.

If you're submitting a bid to a general contractor, developer, or landscape architect, they may give *you* a contract rather than the other way around. Many times these contracts are heavily weighted against you. Read them carefully and negotiate changes in any clauses that are unfair to you. Run the contract by your attorney if you're not absolutely sure you understand it.

Some people turn in the contract along with the bid, which makes it easy for the client to say yes just by signing on the dotted line. Other times, you turn in the bid and wait for the client to say yes before you send or bring a contract. It's best to meet with the client to sign the contract. For one thing, she or he may have questions. More important, people often get cold feet at the last moment, so you want to be there to help them make the final decision in your favor.

Job Costing

Logically, this topic belongs at the end of chapter 8 on project management because it's done at the end of the job, but *job costing* is so closely allied to bidding that we need to discuss it right now.

Job costing is the flip side of bidding. It's adding up your actual costs at the end of the job to see whether you made any money. To do it, simply use the bid form to enter actual costs (taken from invoices for materials and equipment, payroll

Site Inspection Report (Landscaping)

Job Name Seaboard Shopping Plaza

Job Location 2121 W. Thompson Ave., Allenton

Client's Name and Address Hanson Contracting

907 Placid Lake Dr., #201, Allenton, CT 00760

Client's Phone (123) 705–1994

Landscape Architect Marshall Design Group

General Contractor Hanson Contracting

Date Bid Due 4/24/15

Start Date 5/29/15 Completion Date 6/20/15

Access Open

Distance/Driving Time 18 mi., ± 30 min.

Vehicle Parking Ample

Suppliers Nearby Irrigation 3 mi., Nursery 12 mi.

Water/Power/Temporary Improvements Water in by 6/5±

Bathroom Facilities Portable toilets by G.C.

Staging Area Adjacent to G.C. Staging—NEED FENCE

Soil Conditions Clay loam—stays wet 2–3 days after rain

Digging Conditions Med. difficult, no rock

Existing Grade Flat

Weed Growth To be scraped by G.C. prior to start

Vertebrate/Other Pests None observed

Existing Plants 3 mature beech

Existing Structures New construction—2 retail bldgs.

Other Considerations Other trades will be present during construction

Site Inspection and Bid Worksheet (Maintenance)

Job Name ______________________ Job Location ______________________

Client's Name and Address ______________________________________

Client's Phone ______________________

Work Area ______________________________________

Duration of Work ______________________ Visits per Month ______________________

Lawn: Mow (sq. ft.) ______________ Edge (lin. ft.) ______ Times per Week ___________

Area (sq. ft.): Front ______________ Rear ___________ Total ______________

Type: Equipment: Rotary ______________ Reel ___________ Other ______________

Mowing Height ______________________ Remove Clippings? ______________________

Edging: Mechanical ______________________ Chemical ______________________

Fertilization: Frequency ______________________ Type ______________________

Weed Control ______________________ Pest Control ______________________

Disease Control ______________________

Watering ______________ Times per Week ______________________

Overseeding ______________ Aerification ______________ Dethatching ______________

Reseeding ______________ Resodding ______________ Topdressing ______________

Special ______________________________________

Weed Control Beds ______________ Slopes ______________ Other ______________

Pest Control Trees/Shrubs ______________ Beds ______________ Other ______________

Fertilization Trees/Shrubs ______________ Beds ______________ Other ______________

Pruning Trees/Shrubs ______________ Beds ______________ Other ______________

Watering Trees/Shrubs ______________ Beds ______________ Other ______________

Irrigation System SPRINKLERS DRIP VALVES BACKFLOW REPROGRAM CLOCK

Special Water Features ______________ Drains/Gutters ______________________

Snow Removal ______________ Composting ______________ Other ______________

Other______________________________________

Labor Hrs.	Per Visit: ________	Per Month: ________	Rate: ________	Total: ________
Materials	Per Visit: ________	Per Month: ________	Rate: ________	Total: ________
Dump Fees	Per Visit: ________	Per Month: ________	Rate: ________	Total: ________
Driving Hrs.	Per Visit: ________	Per Month: ________	Rate: ________	Total: ________

Total Bid

Comments Date: By:

Bid Takeoff Worksheet (Landscaping)

QTY./ UNIT	BID ITEM	UNIT COST	MATERIALS	LABOR	EQUIPMENT & OTHER	TOTAL
3,000 S.F	**Grow & Kill**					
1 pt.	Herbicide	22.00	22.00			
1 hr.	Labor	11.00		11.00		
	SUBTOTAL		22.00	11.00		33.00
	Demolition					
30 hrs.	Weeds on slope	11.00		330.00		
6 hrs.	Remove shrubs	11.00		66.00		
	SUBTOTAL			396.00		396.00
	Lawn					
3,000 S.F.	Fescue sod	0.27	810.00			
1 L.S.	Sod delivery		40.00			
10 C.Y.	Compost	30.00	300.00			
50 lb.	16-6-8	1.50	75.00			
30 hrs.	Till & F.G.	11.00		330.00		
20 hrs.	Lay sod	11.00		220.00		
1 day	Tiller rental				100.00	
	SUBTOTAL		1,225.00	550.00	100.00	1,875.00
	Planting					
2 15 g.	*Ulmus parvifolia*	40.00	80.00			
14 5 g.	*Ligustrum texanum*	9.00	126.00			
73 1 g.	Assorted (see list)	3.50	255.50			
4 C.Y.	Compost	30.00	120.00			
50 lb.	16-6-8	1.50	75.00			
450 ea.	Fertilizer tabs	0.09	40.50			
26 hrs.	Planting	11.00		286.00		
	SUBTOTAL		697.00	286.00		983.00
	Mulching					
18 C.Y.	Walk-on bark	40.00	720.00			
20 hrs.	Apply mulch	11.00		220.00		
	SUBTOTAL		720.00	220.00		940.00
	General Conditions					
4 hrs.	Mobilization	11.00		44.00		
3 hrs.	Cleanup	11.00		33.00		
2 hrs.	Hauling	11.00		22.00		
1 L.S.	Dump fees				22.00	
1 day	Truck use				200.00	
	SUBTOTAL			99.00	222.00	321.00
	Subcontractor					
1 L.S.	Electrician				125.00	
	SUBTOTAL				125.00	125.00
	Maintenance (90 days)					
52 hrs.	4 Hrs./wk. x 13 wks.	9.00		468.00		
1 L.S.	Fertilizer		10.00			
1 L.S.	Herbicide		5.00			
1 L.S.	Pesticide		5.00			
	SUBTOTAL		20.00	468.00		488.00

Bid Summary Sheet (Landscaping, Lump-Sum Bid)

QTY./ UNIT	BID ITEM	MATERIALS	LABOR	EQUIPMENT & OTHER	SUBCONTRACTORS
3,000 S.F.	Grow & Kill	22.00	11.00		
1 L.S.	Demolition		396.00		
3,000 S.F.	Lawn	1,225.00	550.00	100.00	
1 L.S.	Planting	697.00	286.00		
18 C.Y.	Mulching	720.00	220.00		
	SUBTOTALS	2,664.00	1,463.00	100.00	
	General Conditions		99.00	222.00	
	Subcontractors				125.00
	Maintenance	20.00	468.00		
	ADJUSTED SUBTOTALS	2,684.00	2,030.00	322.00	125.00
	Labor Burden (30%)		870.00		
	Sales Tax (7.5%)	201.00			
	TOTAL DIRECT COST	2,885.00	2,900.00	322.00	125.00
	Contingency (10%)	289.00	290.00	32.00	13.00
	Overhead	(15%) 509.00	(30%) 1,243.00	(10%) 36.00	(10%) 14.00
	TOTALS	3,683.00	4,433.00	390.00	152.00
	SUMMARY:				
	Total materials 3,683.00				
	Total labor 4,433.00				
	Total equipment 390.00				
	Total subcontractors 152.00				
	Total direct cost 8,658.00				
	Profit (17%) 1,774.00				
	Grand total 10,432.00				
	BID PRICE $10,500.00				

Bid Presentation (Landscaping)

GREEN WITH ENVY
Landscaping Co.

221 S. Marchant Rd., Turfburg, PA 07468 (555) 771–2239 andy@gwe.com

PROJECT: Harrison Residence, 701 E. 4th St., Turfburg
INFORMATION: Bid on Proposed Landscaping Work
DATE: July 12, 2015

LOCATION OF WORK: Front yard only, at the above address.

GENERAL DESCRIPTION OF WORK:
Kill existing weeds in turf area. Remove weeds and shrubs. Trim and prune shrubs and perennials in beds around lawn. Install new automatic sprinkler system to irrigate lawn and surrounding beds and bed along driveway. Install hybrid fescue lawn to replace existing one. Install plants per list below. Mulch all beds.

DETAILS OF WORK:
1. GROW and KILL: Spray weeds with herbicide (two sprayings max). Owner to water area three days prior to each spraying.
2. DEMOLITION: Remove weeds (including roots, as practical) on west slope above lawn. Remove shrubs along driveway from sidewalk to mailbox. Trim hedge behind east flowerbed. Prune foundation plantings.
3. IRRIGATION: Install 1 Hardie RD600-EXT controller, wiring, and 5 WeatherMatic 11024F electric valves in valve boxes. Install 32 Toro 570P heads in lawn and adjacent borders, including pipe and fittings.
4. LAWN: Prepare soil per sod grower's specifications and install 3,000 sq. ft. of "ToughGreen" hybrid fescue sod.
5. PLANTING: Plant 2 15-gal. Ulmus parvifolia, 14 5-gal. Ligustrum texanum, 73 1-gal. assorted plants per sketch approved by owner.
6. MULCHING: Apply 3-inch-thick mulch of walk-on bark to all planted beds in front yard.

CONDITIONS, LIMITATIONS, and EXCLUSIONS:
1. Owner must locate and flag buried water main and sewer.
2. Extra work due to large rocks or other buried obstructions to digging will be billed at regular rates.
3. Small flowerbed under dining room window is not included in irrigation work.
4. Work includes ninety days maintenance on all newly installed landscaping, including mowing and edging, weed and pest control, cleanup.

GUARANTEES:
All work is guaranteed against defects in materials and workmanship for ninety days from date of installation, except irrigation system, which is guaranteed for one year.

PRICE OF WORK: $11,930.00

PAYMENT SCHEDULE:
Ten percent deposit on acceptance, balance due on completion of work.

SCHEDULE:
We can begin work the second week in August, except for grow and kill, which will be done immediately on acceptance of the proposal and after watering by owner.

CONTRACT:
A written contract will be prepared for all work.

LICENSES:
State Contractor's License No. 77462; City of Turfburg Business License No. 1773.

REFERENCES:
References and a job list are enclosed.

CONTACT:
For more information, please contact Andy Tomlinson, owner (555) 771–2239 (office) or (555) 771–9903 (cell), andy@gwe.com.

Thank you for allowing us to provide you with a proposal. Please get in touch if you have any questions. We're looking forward to working with you!

Respectfully submitted,

Andy Tomlinson, owner

records, and subcontractor billings) where before you entered projected costs. It's a simple and absolutely necessary procedure. Force yourself if you need to, but do job costing on all your jobs. Then adjust future bids to account for what you've learned.

Sales 101

To get the job, you have to do more than provide a good price. In fact, price is often of less concern to potential clients than other things. As my old marketing guru used to say, you never sell your product or service; you sell the benefits and advantages for the buyer. To get the job, you have to convince the prospective clients that they will get what they want, whatever that is. Some want the beauty of a new garden; others want the convenience of low-maintenance plantings or an automatic sprinkler system. Some are looking for improved resale value or status or better relations with their spouses. And everyone is interested in hiring a capable, friendly, honest company. To get potential clients to do business with you, you have to figure out what they want, and then prove you can give it to them. Do that and you've got the job; fail and you're down the road, no matter how low your price is.

The idea of "selling" is disagreeable to many people, but we actually sell ourselves every day in many ways to many kinds of people for many reasons. Selling your services is nothing more than the following perfectly honorable set of actions:

1. Find out what the client wants.
2. Figure out how to provide it.
3. Tell (and show) the client what you propose, stressing benefits and advantages.
4. Answer any questions the client has.
5. Overcome any objections the client has.
6. Share your enthusiasm for the project.
7. Close the sale.

Tips on Making the Selling Process Pleasant and Effective

Never mail, fax, or email a bid. Nine times out of ten, when you send people a bid rather than meeting with them, you never hear from them again. Always set up a meeting so you can go through the seven steps of selling (above).

Relax. Your life doesn't depend on this job. Take it easy, be yourself, and let the process happen naturally.

Talk people's language. If the client is an artist, talk about how beautiful the garden will be when you're done with it. If the client is an accountant, talk about the cost-effectiveness of your proposal. Be more formal with formal people and more casual with casual people, but never lose your professionalism. Don't swear just because the client does, for example.

Dress well. Set your appointments for the morning, before you've had a chance to get dirty, or at the end of the day when you can go home and clean up first. Nobody expects you to arrive in a three-piece suit, but they'd just as soon you didn't track mud from your last job all over their carpet.

Don't bad-mouth the competition. It's tempting to tell stories about how lousy your competitors are. Don't do it. It makes you look bad, and besides, you might get sued for slander. If you know that the client is looking for other bids, give the names of a couple of the best (and hopefully most expensive) competitors. That way you'll be bidding against qualified people, not hacks. You might even tell these competitors you've given out their names and ask them to do the same for you in the future. It sure is nice to be able to choose whom you're bidding against.

Listen. You can learn so much by paying attention to what the client says. Don't just walk in and do your song and dance. By being attentive, you make the client confident that you care about him or her.

Show. Bring photos of your other jobs (a photo portfolio on a tablet is great for this). Walk clients through their yard and paint a word picture of what it will look like when you're done. Make them see the hammock under the trees, next to the new native meadow, and themselves lying there with a cold drink and nothing to do all afternoon.

Never say no. No is the worst word in the English language when you're trying to sell someone something. When they ask, "Does this plant flower all year?" say, "It flowers from March through October," not "Well, no, actually it doesn't." Who wants to hear "no"?

Be flexible. Remember, you're there to meet the needs of the clients. If they want something, figure out how you can get it to them.

Watch for closing signals. People act differently as soon as they've made up their minds. Here are examples of signs that you should stop talking, answer any specific questions, and then try to close the sale:

KINDS OF QUESTIONS THEY'LL ASK

1. How long would the job take?
2. When could you start?
3. Would you be supervising the work yourself?
4. Does the flagstone come in any other colors?

BODY LANGUAGE

1. Relaxing, settling back, unfolding arms
2. Studying plans or proposal in detail
3. Any sudden change in attitude

Selling isn't about bullying people into buying something; it's about educating them and presenting yourself and your company well. Remember, every good business deal is a win-win situation. The client gets a landscape (or care of a landscape); you get a job.

Closing the Sale

Lots of books are written on how to close a sale. There are dozens of manipulative closing techniques, most of which you won't need if you've done a good job so far. To me, the only dignified close is to simply say something like, "So, shall we go to work, then?" Just give them the opportunity to say yes to your proposal. You don't have to act like a stereotypical used-car salesman.

After they say yes, try something like this: "Great! Well, I'll order the plants in the morning so they'll be here on time. Listen, I'm really excited about this job. It's going to be beautiful! Thanks for letting me go to work for you. Here's my cell phone number in case you can't get me in the office; call me any time you need anything. I'll call you Friday to let you know what day next week we'll start. Now if you'll just sign here, we'll be all set." (*Tip:* In some cases, you have to offer clients a *Three-Day Right of Rescission*, giving them three days after they've signed the contract to back out of the deal. In most cases it will be wise to not start work or order materials until that waiting period has passed.)

What if they say they want to think about it? There are numerous variations on this: "I'll have to talk it over with my wife." "I've got to ask my business partner." "We're still waiting to hear from one other bidder." Books on the art of selling will tell you that you're losing the sale at this point, and it's time to dig in your heels, ask what you could do to sign them up right now, offer them extras, do any desperate and ungracious thing to close the sale on the spot. I've never been able to make myself do this. I suggest you remind them of a few of the benefits that you've mentioned and, if you're so inclined, throw in a couple of new ones for good measure. Don't give them a long spiel, just make one more try, then thank them, ask them when they'll be making a decision (so you can call them for an answer), and leave.

Call back in a few days to see whether they've made up their minds. If you thought up something else that you could offer to help close the sale, offer it. And accept the fact that you're not going to get all the jobs you bid. In my experience, a *capture ratio* of 50 percent is decent, though you can do better under some circumstances.

Good luck!

08 Finally You Get to Do Some Real Work

Designing the Project

Doing installations based on your own designs is called *design/build*. In most regions it's legal for a licensed landscape contractor to design private residential projects, as long as she or he also intends to build them (you have to be a licensed landscape architect to do just design). Regulations vary from state to state, so check with your contractor's license board.

Before you get into design/build, be sure you're qualified. Many landscape contractors are good installers but they do a really bad job of designing. Just because you can build things doesn't mean you can also design them. Design is complex and this is not the place to cover it in detail. There are lots of great books on landscape design and plenty of other opportunities for you to educate yourself. As with any aspect of landscaping, start with small, simple projects.

Homeowners are the best source of design/build projects. The best ones will come as referrals, people who have seen or heard about your work from their friends or neighbors. You can also solicit design/build projects through advertising or by going door-to-door.

The design process usually goes as follows:

1. *The Initial Meeting.* The purpose of your first meeting with the client is to evaluate the project, learn the client's needs, and define the basic elements of the design. Usually the client will have a list of problems and questions for you. The first step is to have the client show you around, while you listen and take mental notes. Then it's your turn. Walk around again, this time asking questions and proposing solutions. By the end of this one-hour to two-hour meeting, you should have established a general approach to the design and an overall budget (be prepared to provide per-unit prices for the installation and

give a rough idea of what the entire project will cost). At the end of this meeting, you should measure the property so you can prepare drawings. (*Tip:* Ask the client if she or he has a set of house plans that you can make a tracing from; this might save you much of the measuring.) You won't need to draw a set of plans for a very simple project such as adding a few plants to a bed, but the ability to prepare an attractive quick sketch makes a good impression and helps the client visualize your proposal.

2. *The Conceptual Design.* Design is the process of going from the general to the specific. The conceptual design is a scale drawing that shows the general outlines of proposed improvements (where the patio is going to be, the location of shade trees, the shape of the lawn) but not every last detail (an exposed aggregate patio, six 24-inch boxed *Ulmus parvifolia*, such-and-such variety of hybrid tall fescue). At this stage you also prepare a preliminary list of plants, with several options for each area (two or three varieties of shade trees, several kinds of hedge plants, etc.) and some alternatives for the hardscape features (tile versus textured concrete for the walks). Preparing the conceptual plan and plant list could take four to ten hours. (*Tip:* It's helpful if you can color in your sketch with marking pens or colored pencils; it makes the plans more readable, and clients really like the way it looks.)
3. *The Second Meeting.* When you present your conceptual design, bring along photos of the plants on your list (bring some picture books or have images in a file on your tablet or laptop) and also photos of some of your projects that might be similar to this one. And bring a more detailed cost estimate that reflects the current level of detail of the design. At this meeting you'll make decisions on the specifics of the design, tentatively choosing materials, plant varieties, and so forth, and confirming the wisdom of whatever overall scheme you have laid out. Spend time out on the site going over details with exquisite care—this is a critical moment and decisions made now will likely be incorporated into the final product, so it's important to get it right at this stage. The second meeting should last one to two hours. In some cases you won't need to do much more designing than this. If the client understands and likes your approach, you can provide a written confirmation of the decisions you've made, a final list of plant varieties, and a final bid and contract, and then get on with the installation. But don't let a fidgety or budget-conscious client talk you into doing less design than is needed to be sure the project will turn out well. You need to be in the driver's seat on this and insist on a properly detailed

project; if you proceed with a half-baked plan you will be responsible for an unsatisfactory and possibly catastrophic outcome. As legendary architectural and industrial designer Charles Eames once said, "The details are not the details. They make the design." Be a stickler for details now and everyone will benefit.

4. *The Final Design*. Where the complexity of the project warrants it (simple jobs often don't), you'll prepare a final drawing that shows specific locations, varieties and quantities of plants, and exact dimensions and construction details for all hardscape features. If the irrigation system is intricate, you may want to do an irrigation plan on a separate sheet. The final plans should take six to twenty hours to prepare. (*Tip:* Take a class in landscape drafting. The drafting skills of most contractors need major improvement. It helps if you're artistically inclined, but anyone can learn to produce a professional-looking set of plans.) Naturally, you'll have another meeting to go over the final plans and the final bid.

Specifications

Whatever the complexity of your design, you should provide the client with a set of written *specifications* for the work. Specifications detail exactly what you'll be doing and how you'll be doing it. As with design, this is a complicated matter and is too much to go into here, but suffice it to say that every aspect of a project—planting, hardscape construction, irrigation, lighting, water features, all of it—must be explained in meticulous detail in the specifications. Specifications are always evolving and are the subject of much study and discussion within the profession. Remember that whatever you propose to do on the project must be covered in the specifications, and whatever you say in the specifications must be included in the finished product. Here's an example of a specification for soil preparation:

"Soil shall be rototilled to a depth of 5 inches. Any rubbish and loose stones larger than 2 inches shall be removed and disposed of off site. Soil shall be amended with nitrolized fir bark compost at the rate of 4 cubic yards per 1,000 square feet; compost shall be spread evenly over the surface and fully blended with the tilled soil by tilling a second time. Area shall then be finish graded to plus-or-minus 1 inch."

(*Tip:* Trade and professional associations publish books of specifications that you can use as they are or modify to suit your particular needs. If you use them as-is, just be sure you're prepared to do the work as it is described.)

Specifications protect the client, but they can also protect you by defining the limits of your responsibilities. Here's an example:

"Owner will be responsible for all care and maintenance of plantings after completion of the work, following instructions of contractor."

There are other protective clauses that you should always include in any set of specifications. A *rock clause* limits your liability for buried obstructions that were not reasonably foreseeable. A *site conditions* clause defines what you expect the condition of the site to be when you show up—cleanliness, finish grading, access, and so forth. A detailed *guarantee* explains what is and is not covered and for how long. You should state that guarantees are valid only if the client has complied with payments and other terms of the contract.

There are many other protective clauses. Check with your trade association and possibly your attorney for specific information. Also, if you do jobs designed by landscape architects, you'll get to see the specs they use.

How to Charge for Design Services

Some contractors do designs for free, in the hopes of getting the installation. This is foolish because it makes you look desperate and unprofessional, and cuts you out of a legitimate source of income for an important service you are providing. It also exposes you to the danger of getting your design ripped off when an unscrupulous client (trust me, there are plenty of them) uses your design to do the work on his own or to hire someone cheaper to do it. If you feel you must offer an incentive, refund part of the design fees on completion of the installation work. Once you've built a good reputation, you should charge full price for designing.

You can work by the hour or do the design for a set price. Charging less than $40 to $80 per hour for designing makes you look like a beginner, because licensed landscape architects usually charge from $100 to $200 per hour or more for the same work. Charge what you think you're worth, but never undervalue yourself. As you get better, gradually raise your prices.

Many people find it difficult to do installation work all day, manage the business, and then have energy left to do design work at night and on weekends. At first, avoid complex projects that require a lot of designing; doing so will make it easier for you to get things done right and on time. As your business matures and you hire people to do the labor, you will be able to spend more time on design and other critical aspects of your business.

Project Management

As you become more successful and get bigger, more complex projects, you'll need to keep track of more and more details. Jobs don't manage themselves. Developing project management skills will be a key to your success. The following techniques

Should You Do a Free Visit?

Many people are uncomfortable with paying you for your first visit. That's understandable. After all, in most cases they haven't even met you yet. So there's a lot to be said for popping by at no charge or obligation in order to meet and greet, to have a look at the site, and to find out more about what they want. On the other hand, some people would love to get a full hour or more of helpful free design advice so that they can do the work themselves, leaving you with nothing. If you do free initial sales calls, be sure to make it clear that you will come out for a limited time (half an hour is reasonable) and that you will not be offering concrete advice during that meeting, just a quick look, a conversation about what they want and what you can do for them, and maybe a very rough estimate if you're comfortable doing that. At the first contact with a prospective client (via email, on the phone, or in person) I offer them a choice of whether to start with a half-hour sales call or roll right into a paid consultation. People who already know your work and reputation, and who are eager to get going, will usually opt for the consultation; the rest go for the freebie.

and methods will help you. So will the "Job Checklist" located in Appendix 2, which itemizes all the conceivable tasks to be accomplished on a typical job. It's a pretty long list, one you certainly won't be able to keep in your head when you're first starting out. Use the checklist on every job to help you stay organized and stay out of trouble.

Scheduling

The day will come when you find yourself overbooked—you have too many projects and not enough time, personnel, and equipment to do them all on schedule. Even if you're working by yourself or with one or two helpers, scheduling projects is a challenge. As the complexity of your services grows and you add more people, scheduling becomes an important part of your job. One of the most common complaints about service businesses is the broken promise: You said you'd be there Tuesday, and you still haven't shown up a week later. Whether you'll be doing maintenance, landscaping, or both, your approach to scheduling is the same. Set up a master job calendar on your computer or on a paper desk calendar. Every time you get a job, put the job name on the calendar on the days you promised you'd do the work. Scheduling software is readily available if you want to go hi-tech.

Here are the main factors that will govern your scheduling of work:

1. Size of jobs (number of worker hours required)
2. Number of jobs awaiting completion
3. Available personnel
4. Available equipment
5. Urgency of each job
6. Availability of materials
7. Weather conditions
8. Season of the year
9. Needs of the clients

Getting a big job means tying up your crew, making it necessary to delay other work. Getting a lot of small jobs means you'll spend a lot of time running around setting up and closing out jobs. Consider the efficiency of your routing when you schedule jobs, so you don't have people driving from one end of town to the other unnecessarily. Scheduling is especially important for maintenance routes. Use a map to route jobs by area and by day.

If you have a lot of jobs stacked up, it means clients are waiting; this is a possible source of dissatisfaction. But if you're honest about your backlog, most clients will understand and wait for you. On the other hand, if you constantly make promises you can't keep, you'll make people unhappy.

If you get more work, you have to decide whether to add more employees or create a longer backlog. If you don't have the equipment you need, should you rent it or buy it? Will you need purchased equipment after the big job is finished?

How urgent is each job? Will you have to interrupt the job because some of the plants are on back order? This can cause inconvenience because you have to move your equipment to another job and then back again when the plants come in, and it can also make the client unhappy. Bad weather can throw your schedule off; you need to let clients know if there's a possibility of delay due to weather. Remember that it often takes a few days for the soil to dry out after a rain. You can go back to work in sandy soils sooner than you can in clay soils, which may affect which jobs you get back to first after a rain. (*Tip:* Communication is important to keeping clients happy; contact them verbally and in writing whenever there are delays or changes in your schedule.)

Some work such as tree pruning, fertilizing, planting, and lawn installation is done in specific seasons. Other jobs like cleanups, hardscape construction, and irrigation aren't as dependent on the season. Finally, and most importantly, what are your clients expecting from you? If they feel they're not getting it, your scheduling has failed. (*Note:* Sometimes a starting date and completion date aren't negotiable, especially on commercial projects. You do the job on the client's schedule, or you don't get to do it at all.)

Getting to Work

When you've gotten all of the nitpicking little details out of the way, you're ready to begin to do the actual job. But wait, there's one more thing you need to do before this little miracle can take place. You need to define the exact details of the work to be done. This is especially important if you'll be sending someone else out to the job without you. If things aren't written down, how will they know what to do?

Fortunately, there's a form that can help you. It's called a *Job Work Order* (see the two-page example that follows). This form is often used as the starting point for small jobs. It can serve as instructions for your crew (where to go and what to do), a final invoice for the client, and on the back, a record of materials and labor used and a quick job-costing form, all in one. It's one of the cleverest forms around and can be purchased at any office supply store.

The Pre-Job Walk-Through

Before you start any job, spend some time inspecting the site. If you have employees, bring them along, especially if someone other than you will be in charge of the work. A walk-through shouldn't take much longer than an hour, even on a fairly large job. It's time well spent, because it can make the work go more smoothly and prevent problems. The client should accompany you on the walk-through so you can agree one more time on the details of the work and answer any questions he or she might have. You might want to reserve some time for meeting with just your crew so you can discuss the sequencing of the work, the equipment that will be needed, and who will take responsibility for which parts of the job.

Keep your eyes open for potential problems that you hadn't noticed before. Also make a written inventory (preferably with the client present) of any existing damage such as cracked or displaced pavement or broken light fixtures, so you don't get blamed for it later. You might even want to get the client to sign it. Be sure the client gets a copy. And take lots of photos or make a video of your walk-through. They can help you later if there's a problem, and the images can also be used in "before-and-after" shots in your portfolio.

Locating Buried Utilities

Before doing any digging, be sure to locate buried utilities. First, contact the *underground locating service* in your area by calling 811 (from anywhere in the United

(FRONT)

Wilson Landscape & Design
6602 12th Street
Greenville, OK 00020
(405) 222–8888

JOB WORK ORDER

	DATE 7/14/15		
JOB NAME Bundy Residence	SEND BILL TO (Same)		
JOB LOCATION 93 Oak St.	ADDRESS		
CITY Lawndale, OK	CITY		
PHONE 222–1121	STATE	ZIP CODE	
DESCRIPTION OF WORK 1. Remove weeds in parkway		STARTING DATE 7/17/15	
2. Prep soil in parkway		DAY OF WEEK Monday 8:00	☒ A.M.
3. Plant 2 flats ivy in parkway			☐ P.M.
4. Trim shrubs in front of house		FOREMAN LR	
5. Check sprinklers. May be a leak in back lawn		LABORER (S) TS, ML	
near veg. garden. Repair as necessary.			

☐ Total amount due for above work, or
☒ Billing to be mailed after completion of work

I hereby acknowledge the satisfactory completion of the above-described work:

____
CUSTOMER'S SIGNATURE

WORK ORDERED BY	ORDER TAKEN BY
Mrs. B.	TW

(BACK)

MATERIAL AND LABOR RECORD			
QUANTITY	**MATERIAL USED**	**PRICE**	**AMOUNT**
1 L.S.	Organic fertilizer		9.00
1 C.Y.	Soil Amendment		28.00
2 Flat	Ivy	12.00	24.00
1 ea.	1/2 ST ELL, PVC		.29
Job Completed?	**TOTAL**		61.29
☒ Yes ☐ No	Less Returned Materials		
Date Billed 7/19/15	Net Cost of Materials		61.29

DATE	**EMPLOYEE**	**WORK DONE**	**HRS.**	**RATE**	**AMOUNT**
7/15	L. Rodrigues	Parkway	3	11.00	33.00
7/15	T. Sanders	Parkway	3	11.00	33.00
7/15	M. Lewis	Shrubs/Sprinklers	3	16.00	48.00
				TOTAL LABOR COST	114.00

TOTAL MATERIAL COST	61.29	TOTAL SELLING PRICE	255.00
TOTAL LABOR COST	114.00	LESS TOTAL COST	184.29
SUBCONTRACTOR COST		GROSS PROFIT (28 %)	70.71
OTHER DIRECT COSTS*	9.00	LESS OVERHEAD (14 %)	35.70
TOTAL COST	184.29	NET PROFIT (15 %)	35.01

*Dump Fees

States); they will then contact all the utility companies that serve the property (gas, electric, telephone, cable, water, sewer, etc.) and send them out to mark the location of their pipes and wires where they enter the property. The call and the service are free. Using them is not optional; it's required by law. If you damage something and you haven't called, you can be liable for *very* expensive repairs and possibly legal action against you.

Next, you have to ask the client about any water mains or other utilities within the property lines. You can also hire a locating service to find the utilities before you dig. Mark everything with flags or marking paint before you do any digging. It's also a good idea to make a drawing of the property that shows all the buried utilities, drains, etc. For a listing of locating services in the United States, check out www.digsafely.com/contacts.htm.

Building Permits and Related Requirements

In most communities, most of the work you do won't require a *building permit*. Some things, like backflow prevention devices, decks, fences, and retaining walls, may require permits. Before you do your first job, visit the city and/or county zoning and building departments or look at the regulations section of their website to find out all of the many requirements you'll have to follow. Tree removal may be prohibited or controlled. Structures will have to be built in conformance with the setbacks on the property. And so on. Do your homework and play by the rules or you'll end up in a lot of trouble.

Getting through the permit process can be lengthy and trying, so allow something extra in your bids to cover the permit fees, at least one visit to city hall, and numerous inspections. Though most are reasonable, some building officials can be arbitrary and obnoxious. Force yourself to be nice to them even if they're difficult, because they have total power over you and can make your life miserable. It's an unpleasant reality that'll never change. Don't get a reputation as a troublemaker with the folks downtown. (*Tip:* Put a clause in your contract that exempts you from any consequences of unanticipated and unforeseeable decisions made by building officials or agencies. That way if an inspector makes a sudden, on-site arbitrary decision that will require more labor or materials than you had anticipated, you're not going to have to pay for them. This doesn't exempt you from doing the job as it was permitted, but it will cover you for later changes.)

On-the-Job Management Techniques

Loading the Truck

It's 7:30 in the morning; you're wide awake and going full steam ahead, bursting with enthusiasm for this bright new day and the start of yet another fun, profitable job. Then again, maybe you're just a bit groggy from a long weekend and not thinking too clearly yet. Your helpers are waiting for leadership, and you're waiting for the caffeine to kick in. You know there's a lot to think about, but you can't seem to remember what it is.

Fortunately, you took the time yesterday to plan ahead a bit. You filled out your *Job Work Order* and made lists of the materials and equipment you'd need. Now, you can pull this all out and look like the true captain of industry that you are. In no time, you and your team will be on the road.

It helps if you have a preprinted form or two to help you. *Loading lists* for equipment and materials can be very handy. (Examples follow later in this chapter.)

Keeping Track of Daily Activities

Once you're out on the job, you still need to keep track of many things. You'll be buying materials and taking deliveries at the job site, subs will be coming and going, the landscape architect might stop by for an inspection, and the owner may request changes in the work. You may pick up, use, and return rental equipment.

You'll also need to keep a record of the work you've completed today and any problems that came up. Finally, you'll have to plan for tomorrow—what equipment, materials, and labor will be needed and the goals for the workday. If you don't keep after it, you'll lose control of the job in no time. Believe me, it's worth the trouble. Besides, if there's a dispute or (heaven forbid) a lawsuit, you'll need lots of documentation to protect your interests.

Guess what? There's yet another handy form that prompts you for this information. It's called a *Daily Job Report*. Fill one out every day, or have your lead person do it. (See example later in this chapter.)

Keeping Track of Materials and Labor

One of the worst and most common experiences is to get to the end of the job and realize that you haven't kept good records of materials and labor. If it's a time-and-materials job, you can't get paid without providing this information on your invoice. If it's a bid job, you'll have no way of knowing how you did unless you keep track of what has gone into the job. Sometimes the information can be laboriously reconstructed from crumpled invoices you discovered under the seat of the truck and from people's week-old best guesses about who worked when, but sometimes it's just not possible to go back and sort it all out.

Like everything else about business, developing good habits early on will help you eliminate this problem. Keep a *daily record* of the materials and equipment that you use and of everyone's labor. You may even want to keep track of the hours of use on each piece of major equipment.

The best way to do this is to start a record at the beginning of each job and add to it every day. Then at the end of the job, you're ready for billing and/or job costing. The standard approach is to use a *Material and Labor Report.* An example of one that works pretty well follows later in this chapter. You may want to customize it for the peculiarities of your own operation.

Site Management

Train yourself and your employees to keep the job site clean and safe. Let everyone know that they have to clean up at the end of every day. Make site safety everyone's responsibility—everyone has to watch for, report, and immediately eliminate hazards, including unmarked open trenches, tools left in walkways, unsecured chemicals, vehicles or tractors with the keys left in them, and so forth. Safety also has to do with behavior: Never assume that the client or the client's children are smart enough to watch out for you. Put up caution tape or barriers to keep the public away from all activities, especially things like power equipment, tree trimming operations, and laborers swinging picks. Remember that regular safety training for all your employees is not only a good idea, it's also often required by law.

Job site security is another concern. Thefts of equipment and materials are common, and you need to keep all valuables guarded by day and locked up at night. Leaving that chainsaw on the sidewalk while you're around back looking at the flowerbeds is asking for trouble. Things will disappear from the backs of trucks, side yards, and garages, and unfortunately even from securely locked tool chests and storage yards. Getting insurance to cover theft from vehicles and job sites can be next to impossible, and even when available, it will cost you plenty.

Finally, you've got to think about courtesy to the clients. To you it's just a job site, but to them it's home. Prohibit radios, dogs, drugs, and alcohol. (A radio tuned to a loud rock station and left playing all day long is a sure way to lose a client.) Train people to behave themselves—no shouting, swearing (in any language), peering in windows, or behaving in a rowdy manner. Provide uniforms for employees or enforce dress codes banning really shabby clothing, T-shirts with vulgar sayings printed on them, or anything else that might be offensive to your most straight-laced clients. Get rid of anybody who won't comply. One of the most awkward issues is where employees go to the bathroom. Unless the client is providing on-site bathroom facilities for your workers, rent a portable toilet for each job and be sure you recover the costs in the price of the work. The easiest way to do this is to make "toilet facilities" a line item on your bid and then remember to charge for it when you do your progress billings.

Purchasing

Where You Buy Things

If you're a gardener, you may have to buy your supplies from retailers, which cuts you out of a lot of profit. If you're a licensed contractor, you can buy directly from growers and wholesalers, at about half the retail price in many cases.

The *retail nursery* is a source of small quantities of plants and supplies. Retailers usually offer a modest discount (10 to 20 percent) to professionals and are happy to cultivate your business. They will usually be willing to order in plants for you, which wholesalers often are not.

The *wholesale nursery* grows plants and sells them to retail nurseries and to licensed landscaping professionals. Many wholesalers offer a *cash-and-carry discount* for immediate payment and no delivery, usually an additional 10 to 20 percent off the regular wholesale prices. Wholesalers prefer to deal with large orders, but they will usually sell any quantity to regular customers. Some wholesalers also carry soil amendments and other planting supplies. Many specialize in certain kinds of plants. Some wholesalers also act as *brokers*, ordering plants from other growers and possibly supplies of other kinds, and assembling a complete shipment for your larger jobs. There are also *independent plant brokers* who do the same thing.

You'll need things other than plants: irrigation materials, fertilizers, lumber, rock and gravel, other building materials, lighting and electrical supplies. It's usually better to do business with companies that supply professional contractors because the quality and service will be better than at the big box stores. Visit suppliers and get to know them. They're an important part of your team.

Discounts aren't as generous on most building materials as they are on plants. For example, the typical discount to contractors at a lumberyard is 10 to 20 percent. Take that into consideration when pricing your jobs. Irrigation materials, on the other hand, are usually heavily discounted to contractors. (*Tip:* You have to ask for these *contractor's discounts*; no one's going to give them to you automatically.)

EQUIPMENT LOADING LIST

In addition to the regular tools and equipment, take/rent the following special items for this job:

Power Equipment

1	Rototiller
	Lawn renovator
	Aerator
	Reel mower
1	Sod cutter
	Hedge trimmer
	String trimmer
	Spray rig
	Vibratory plate compactor
	Jackhammer, electric
	Jackhammer, pneumatic
	Tamper
	Power auger
	Chainsaw
	Circular saw
1	Tractor w/box scraper
	Tractor w/backhoe
	Tractor w/bucket
	Skid steer loader
	Flatbed truck
	Dump truck

Layout Equipment

30	Flags (10 yellow, 20 blue)
	Flagging tape
	Mason's twine
	2 x 12 stakes
	2 x 2 stakes
1	100 ft. tape

General Equipment

2	Tarps
2	Planks
6	Tie-downs

Nonpower Equipment

	Fertilizer spreader
	Lawn roller
	Wheelbarrow
	Hand truck
	Tree dolly
	Backpack sprayer
	Hoses

Hand Tools

	Tripod ladder
	Extension ladder
	Climbing gear
	Posthole digger
	Hand tamper
	Stake driver
	Sighting level
	Measuring wheel
	Chalk box
	Sledgehammer
	Hand pruning saws
	Loppers
	Pole pruners
	Brush hooks
	Ax
	Grading rakes
	Come-along
	Rebar cutters
	Bolt cutters
	Plumber's torch
	Carpentry tools

Other

	Water meter key

MATERIALS LOADING LIST

Job Name Francis Residence

Job Address 1117 Marsh Rd.

Date 7/9/15 Prepared by: Joe

LOADED	QTY.	MATERIAL	SIZE	PRICE	TOTAL	YARD	VENDOR	SUPPLIER
		IRRIGATION:						
	200’	CLS 200 PVC Pipe	¾"			X		
	600’	CLS 315 PVC Pipe	½"				X	Irrig. Supply
	42	Toro 570 P Heads					X	"
	1	Blue Glue	Pt				X	"
		Fittings Boxes				X		
		SOD LAWN:						
	6	ORGO-Mulch	C.Y.	30	180		X	Turf Supply
	50	16-5-5	Lbs.	11	11		X	"
	1100	Bluegrass Sod	Sq.Ft.	.25	275		X	Green-sod
		PLANTS:						
	17	Raph. ‘Ballerina’	1 gal.				X	Tim’s Nursery
	7	Ilex cornuta	5 gal.				X	"
	2	Strawberry	Flats				X	Cal. Growers
	1	Planter Mix	Scoop			X		

DAILY JOB REPORT

Job Name: Eastside Shopping Center
Job No.: 10-112
Job Address: 414 E. 37th St.
Job Phone: 717–2207
Supervisor: John Peters

Date: 7/7/15
Temperature: 94 High
78 Low

Weather: (Clear) Snow Windy Rain Overcast

INVOICE #	VENDOR NAME	MATERIALS	INVOICE #	VENDOR NAME	MATERIALS
70724	Irrigation Central	Pipe & Ftgs.	9171	Henry's Equip Rentals	Tractor
A4717	Landscape Depot	Mulch			
2376-22	Statewide Nursery	Trees			

SUBCONT	NAME	WORK PERFORMED	START/STOP/HRS.
	Electricians 'R' Us	Install J-Box for controller	10:30–3:00/4½
	We Are Boring Co.	Bore concrete curb for drain	8–10/2

CHGS	NO.	CHANGE ORDERS/ADD'L WORK	AMOUNT ±	VISITORS TO SITE/REMARKS
	07	Add 1-24" Elm tree	$375.	Cheryl Peterson—Landsc. Architect
	08	Add weeding on slope	125.	(Spot trees in parking lot)
	09	Deduct 3 flats ivy	<–140.>	Earl Yamamoto—Bldg. Dept.
				(Inspect backflow device)

EMPLOYEE NAME	JOB FUNCTIONS/HRS.								TOTALS
	PLANT	FINISH GRD.	MULCH	IRRIG.	CLEANUP				
Janice Cartwright	8								8
Ernesto Muñoz		2		6					8
Robert Dowd	4	2	1						7
Lupe Rodriguez	8								8
Sonny Kline					8				8
TOTALS	20	4	1	6	8				39
EQUIPMENT									
Dump truck					4				4
Kubota		3			5				8
TOTALS		3			9				12

(Front)

WORK COMPLETED TODAY

WORK	LOCATION
1. Planted 24 in. trees	Entry
2. Finish graded	Front of main bldg.
3. Mulched	Entry
4. Sprinklers	Entry
5. Cleanup	Behind bldg. 2

WORK SCHEDULED FOR TOMORROW

WORK	LOCATION
1. Finish planting 24 in. trees	Entry
2. Finish mulching	Entry
3. Test and adjust sprinklers	Entry
4. Start planting	Main bldg.
5. Hook up controller #2	

NEED FOR TOMORROW

TOOLS & EQUIPMENT:	Kubota
	Small Trencher
SUBCONTRACTORS:	Electrician (box for controller #2)
MATERIALS:	12 24 in. Elms
	3 C.Y. Planter mix
	14 C.Y. Mulch

Follow-up Needed

1. Find out why no power to controller
2. Restake 1 tree at entry

PREPARED BY: John Peters **DATE:** 3/14/15 **TIME:** 4:40 p.m.

(Back)

MATERIAL AND LABOR REPORT

Job Name Francis Residence

Date 7/9/15

Job Address 1117 Marsh Rd.

Explanation of Work Sprinklers & Lawn

Phone 707–1103

Job Number 15-1104

DESCRIPTION	QTY	COST	TOTAL	DESCRIPTION	QTY	COST	TOTAL
½ CLS 315 PVC Pipe	200'	.12	24.00				
¾ CLS 200 PVC Pipe	100'	.20	20.00				
½ SS ELL PVC12"	12"	.25	3.00				
¾ SS ELL PVC6"	6"	.32	1.92				
½ SSS TEE PVC	3	.32	.96	EQUIPMENT			
¾ X ½ X ½ SSS TEE PVC	2	.47	.94	Small trencher, hours	4	20.00	80.00
½ ST ELL PVC	12	.29	3.48	Total Equipment			80.00
½ Poly cutoff risers	12	.38	4.56				
TORO 570P Heads	12	4.55	54.60				
Champion ¾ ASV	1	9.40	9.40				
¾ x 18 Galv. nipple	1	4.90	4.90				
¾ x TEE, Galv.	1	1.27	1.27	VEHICLES			
PVC Cement, qt.	1	9.40	9.40	Flatbed truck, hours	6	15.00	90.00
Teflon tape roll	1	1.40	1.40	Total Vehicle			90.00
Subtotal Irrigation			134.91				
Sod, bluegrass, S.F.	1100	.25	275.00				
Amendment, C.Y.	6	30.00	180.00	MISC. EXPENSES			
Fertilizer, sacks	1	17.00	17.00	Delivery—sod			50.00
Subtotal, Lawn			472.00	Total Misc. expenses			50.00
TOTAL MATERIALS			606.91				

TIME AND LABOR

EMPLOYEE	IN	OUT	HOURS	RATE	TOTAL AMT.
J. Martin	7:30	3:00	7	11	77.00
T. Orlando	7:30	3:00	7	11	77.00
W. Hadley	8:00	4:00	7.5	15	112.50
M. Fisk	8:00	4:30	8	18	144.00
TOTAL					410.50

MISC. TOTAL	50.00
EQUIP. TOTAL	80.00
VEHICLE TOTAL	90.00
MATERIAL TOTAL	606.91
SALES TAX	42.83
LABOR TOTAL	410.50
TOTAL	1,280.24

SIGNATURE Anna Johnson

Picking Things Up versus Having Them Delivered

You can spend all day running around from supplier to supplier, picking up materials and delivering them to the job. Sometimes it makes sense to pick things up, especially small orders, but delivery is often a better option, even if there's a delivery charge. After all, your time's worth something, not to mention the wear and tear on your truck and the problems that sometimes can occur when you're not on the job.

Vendor Credit

Many vendors will be happy to establish a *line of credit* for you, even though you're just starting up, as long as your personal credit rating is good. Try this with businesses you already have relationships with, then after a few months of paying your bills on time, use them as a credit reference to open accounts with other vendors. (A friendly lumberyard clerk by the name of Sig gave me a $500 line of credit when I was just starting out, and I remember well how good it felt to have earned his trust, and how important it was to my later success.) Then, whether you need a few sacks of fertilizer for spring feeding or $1,000 worth of materials for a patio installation, you can charge it and pay the bill in thirty days, hopefully long after the client has paid you.

Neat, huh? That's the standard way of doing business—letting your suppliers carry your materials purchases so you can get through the job on their cash instead of yours.

Just remember to pay them off on time every month or you'll lose this most important of privileges.

Until you establish credit everywhere, you may have an alternative: All but the very smallest vendors will accept Visa or MasterCard. Because you'll be charging thousands of dollars per year on your credit card, get one that offers frequent flyer miles or other benefits with every purchase. Be sure to pay credit card bills on time, because the interest rate can exceed your profit margin on the job.

The Purchase Order

When you have open accounts at vendors, you're vulnerable to a stranger (or a competitor) walking in and charging materials to your account just by telling the clerk he's a new employee of yours. Send all vendors a certified letter telling them not to charge anything without a signed *purchase order* from you. Then use the purchase order to document and clear your purchases with the vendor. The purchase order also helps you keep track of your purchases, making job costing easier. Match the purchase orders to the invoices when you receive them to verify purchases and prices. Look at the sample Purchase Order that follows later in this section; it's filled out so you can see how it works.

Changes on the Job

The morning you finally start a job, you're certain that everything's perfectly organized. Everyone knows what to do; you've talked it over a million times. The only thing left is to do it. There can't possibly be any changes after all this planning.

Umm . . . wrong. Every job has changes, often lots of them. There are various reasons for changes on a job. There's the "While-You're-Here-Syndrome": The client wants something pulled out or put in or trimmed and, well, you're there after all so why not do it? There's the "Oops Syndrome": You can't get one-gallon junipers, only fives; or the family dog ate all the hollyhocks in the middle of the night. Soon your perfect little game plan is a mess of additions, deletions, and alterations, and your head is swimming with details. It's easy at this point to lose control of the project, especially where costs are concerned, the result being that you will have no idea how to bill out the job, taking into account all the changes. You have to keep things strictly under control, starting on Day One.

The solution to this problem is a form called a *Change Order*. (See the example that follows later in this chapter.) If you don't document changes, the client may not realize there are additional charges and might refuse to pay you, and if you try to force their hand in court the judge will almost certainly disallow your additional charges. You could even lose your contractors license if someone wants to press the point with the state license board. Most contractors are terrible about using change orders. They're afraid to tell the client the price of that birdbath that he or she asked for at the last minute, or they're too busy to figure out how much the additional planting will be. Ignore change orders at your peril.

Change orders should also indicate any additional time required to do the extra work, extending the completion date by the amount of time required to do the additional work (or, of course, reducing it where elements of the project have been eliminated). Use a change order even if there's no price change; it's important to document any and all alterations to the scope of the work. If you do something extra at no charge, put it on a change order so the client knows what a generous, peachy person you are.

Getting Along with Others

Business is about people: liking them, making them feel good, bringing out the best in them. Every interested party on a job has his or her own agenda, and it helps if you understand what it is and how to deal with it. The client wants the job completed beautifully, for the promised price, and with a minimum of mess and inconvenience. Your employees and subs want good working conditions and fair pay. Your vendors want to get paid on time. Communication is vital to your success; keep everyone supplied with all the information they need to stay aware of what's going on. Keep in mind that in the absence of information we all tend to fill in with the worst possible outcome, even though we're just totally making it up. Have you ever thought to yourself, "So-and-so didn't return my phone call; she must be ignoring me," only to find out later that she was down with the flu or didn't get your message? We all do that, and that's why you need to keep people informed so they don't do it to you.

Then there's the matter of getting your information through to people. Studies show that people hear only a third of what you say. That means you've got to say things three times to be understood! That's why writing things down is such a good idea. Whenever something occurs on a project that might affect your interests, send an email to the parties involved to advise them of where you stand. Keep all written documents, including all emails, permanently in your job file; doing so could prevent big problems later on.

Keep people (especially the client) *delighted*, not just satisfied. Remember that a problem that you consider small can be a big annoyance to your client, and it can spoil the whole experience for him or her, no matter how good everything else was. (Think about the last time you went to a restaurant where the food was great, the atmosphere was wonderful, and the service was OK except that you never got your coffee. What did you walk away grumbling about? Did you go back?)

Make common courtesy part of your every interaction with people. Use these old-fashioned phrases regularly: "Please," "Thank you," "Excuse me," and "I'm sorry." And when you're wrong, admit it. What's the big deal?

Working with Your Employees

This is simple: Develop a team spirit in all your employees. Help them work together. Explain the job to them before they start doing it. Share your enthusiasm. Encourage people to come up with good ideas and reward them when they do. Work hard and have fun.

At the same time, watch how your employees relate to the client and others on the job. They may not be as sensitive and personable as you are. Because they don't know all the details of the work, they may also make statements that are well intentioned but end up being detrimental to your interests. Train everyone to treat others with respect and courtesy and to defer to you or the supervisor when a client asks a question that he or she can't answer. Also, make sure your

Sample Purchase Order

Wilson Landscaping & Design

6602 12TH STREET
GREENVILLE, OK 00020
(405) 222–8888

Purchase Order

NO. 2329

Show this Purchase Order number on all correspondence, invoices, shipping papers, and packages.

TO

Green Gulch Sod Farm
1717 Benson Road
Greenville

DATE OF ORDER	JOB NO.
7-25-15	15-712
JOB NAME Dennison	
JOB ADDRESS 201 25th St.	
	JOB PHONE 700–1121

WHEN SHIP	F.O.B. POINT	SHIP VIA	TERMS
7-27	Job site	Vendor	Charge

QTY. ORDERED	QTY. RECEIVED	ITEM/DESCRIPTION	UNIT PRICE	TOTAL
1500 sq. ft.		"Tall Green" Hybrid Fescue Sod	.22	330.00
		Delivery		50.00
		Sales Tax		19.00
		Total		399.00

Kim Wilson
AUTHORIZED BY

ORIGINAL

Sample Change Order

Wilson Landscaping & Design
6602 12TH STREET
GREENVILLE, OK 00020
(405) 222–8888

Change Order

TO Mr. and Mrs. T. W. Francis	CHANGE ORDER NO. 01
ADDRESS 1117 Marsh Rd.	DATE 7/9/15
Ashton, OK	PHONE 707–1103
JOB NAME AND LOCATION Same	JOB NUMBER 15–1104
	DATE OF EXISTING CONTRACT 6/25/15

1. ADD: Prune shrubs by front door	75.00
2. ADD: Plant 2 flats annuals (including soil prep)	67.00
WE AGREE hereby to make changes as specified above, at this price ☛	142.00

DATE 7/9/15	PREVIOUS CONTRACT AMOUNT	$ 2,714.00
Kim Wilson AUTHORIZED SIGNATURE	REVISED CONTRACT TOTAL	$ 2,856.00

ACCEPTED: The above prices and specifications of this Change Order are satisfactory and are hereby accepted. All work to be performed under same terms and conditions as specified in original contract unless otherwise stipulated. This revision becomes part of the existing contract.

DATE 7/9/15 SIGNATURE Tom Francis

employees don't do work that's not part of the contract, but only do work they're assigned to do.

Working with Landscape Architects and Designers

If you work from plans prepared by a landscape architect or designer, your activities will be partially under their control. They may inspect the project at various stages, often following a schedule they provided you along with the plans and specifications. For example, you may need to call for an inspection after the main irrigation lines are installed and pressurized but before the trenches have been backfilled. Many times the landscape architect will place the plants in their exact planting locations before you install them. Often, you will have to submit copies of your invoices for materials (to prove you purchased the right kind and quantity) and you may be required to provide extra plants that can be inspected for root growth and condition. It's your responsibility to give the landscape architect advance notice of inspections and to be prepared for them.

Working with a landscape architect can be a delicate balancing act. You're in the middle, trying to satisfy both the client and the landscape architect. Sometimes you'll find a problem with the plans—a shade plant that's being planted in the sun, for instance—and then you have to decide how to proceed. If you keep your mouth shut, then when the plant fails, they can hold you responsible: You were the *proximate cause* because you knew there was a problem and didn't say anything. On the other hand, if you tell the client (who pays you) what a stupid design she got, then you're finking on the landscape architect, and you may never get another job from that person. But if you tell the landscape architect, she or he may get haughty about a mere contractor telling him or her what to do (landscape architects can be that way). The best approach is to tell the landscape architect first, privately, using your most diplomatic walk-on-eggs behavior. If the landscape architect refuses to do anything about it, and you're sure you're right, give a written notice to all parties that you aren't going to take responsibility for that portion of the work.

Include some extra fudge factor in your bids when there's a landscape architect involved. You'll have to spend time dealing with him or her and may get sucked into doing extra work because of some capricious decision that's been made halfway through the job. Some landscape architects can be a pleasure to work with; others can be an absolute pain.

Working with General Contractors

If you're working as a subcontractor under a general contractor, you'll have little or no contact with the client, especially on commercial jobs. You'll have to be a team player and do things the way the general wants. You'll also have to get along with the other subs on the job, often under difficult conditions. Fortunately, the landscaper is the last person on the job, after many of the other subs are out from underfoot.

Some generals are great and others can be pretty hard-boiled. Many of them eat landscapers for their midmorning snack, so be prepared to deal with someone who's way ahead of you in the construction game and isn't afraid to make you dance. It's a great learning experience but not one for the fainthearted.

Working with Your Subcontractors

Subs know more than you do about their specialties. Once you know they're capable, stand back and let them do their thing. To meet your obligations to the client, you need to coordinate the work of subcontractors and keep things moving. You also need to monitor the quality of the work and make sure it complies with the plans and specifications and with standard good practice. To meet your obligations to the sub, you need to provide firm dates for the work and be sure you're ready for the sub when he or she shows up. You also need to pay your subs in accordance with the terms of their agreement with you.

Sometimes a subcontractor will create a problem for you. Let's say the concrete guy leaves a big mess that you have to clean up. Because you owe him money, you can deduct the cost of the cleanup from his bill. This is called *backcharging*. You might even backcharge one sub to pay for work done by another. Backcharges are an effective way to make subs really angry at you and should only be used after discussing the matter and trying to reach an agreement on what's to be done. First, give the sub a chance to correct his mistakes, and use backcharges only as a last resort.

Other Outside Services

There are other resources that you may want to tap at times. Your county or state may employ *pathologists* who diagnose pest and disease problems. Check with the County Agricultural Commissioner or similar agency. The *cooperative extension specialist* (also known as a *farm and home advisor*, or simply *farm advisor*) can also help you with horticultural problems at no cost, and their department often has publications available on a wide range of subjects.

Overlooked by many beginners, *consulting engineers* and *laboratories* can keep you out of trouble. Say you have an area that just won't grow anything, and you can't figure out why. Send a sample of the soil to a *soils laboratory*, and have them run a series of tests to determine the nutrient levels, salinity, pH, and other factors, and make recommendations for correcting whatever problems they find. Or maybe a client has asked you to plant a slope that you think may be geologically unstable. Call in a *consulting geologist*. Can't figure out how to build a retaining wall? Call a *civil engineer*.

In certain situations, the city or county may require that you hire a consultant to make certain that a complex project is done right. Some things will always be beyond your abilities. Don't try to do it all. Whenever somebody knows more about something than you do, hire him or her. Be sure the cost of the consultant's services is reimbursable under the terms of your contract, or have the consultant bill the owner directly (the latter is the best way to go because it protects you against any liability for the work done by the consultant).

Getting Paid

Maintenance work is billed at the end of the month. Small landscaping jobs are billed when you're finished. For larger landscaping jobs (those lasting more than a week), you should arrange for progress payments (see below).

Progress Payments

You specify in your contract when *progress payments* are due. In many cases you can ask for a deposit on acceptance of the contract. The law often limits the amount of this deposit. You can require that the balance be paid in weekly payments or on demand. You'll base the amount of the payment either on completion of specific work items (such as demolition, sprinkler system, lawn, etc.) or on the percentage of all work that has been completed at the end of the week. To receive a progress payment, present the client with an itemized list of completed work, showing the contract amount and any change orders, all payments made to date, the amount of the current payment you're requesting, and the balance due on the contract. (*Tip:* It's a good idea to state in your contract that failure to make a progress payment within three days of the due date is a material breach of contract. That gives you the right to stop work until you get paid.)

Final Payments

On a landscaping job, you collect the *final payment* when all the work is completed to the client's satisfaction. The first step in getting a final payment is to do an *end-of-the-job walk-through* with the client to see if there's anything that's been left undone. During this walk-through you make a list that's called (for some reason I never understood) a *punch list*. On it you write things like, "Nozzle missing on sprinkler head in east lawn," and "Need to stake peach tree." You give the client a copy and agree on when the work will be corrected. (*Tip:* An even better idea is to do this walk-through on the last day of the job and have one or two of your workers follow you around actually taking care of the punch list items as you identify them. Now that's service! Plus, it saves you the trouble of going back to see if the punch list work was done right.)

When you go to get your final payment, be sure you present a complete itemization of all billings, change orders, and payments to date and a final invoice.

If you're working for a general contractor, through a landscape architect, or on a public or commercial job, you may have to wait thirty days or longer to get the final payment because of a requirement called *retention*. Retention is a way to protect the client by holding on to some of your money until the lien period runs out (see "Stage Three: The Lien Laws," later in this chapter) and until you complete the work satisfactorily. It's also a way to be sure you honor your guarantees and, incidentally, a way for the client to earn a bit of extra interest on your money.

Invoices

Invoices can vary a lot in style. A *time-and-materials job* is billed differently from a *lump-sum job*; maintenance might be billed differently from a landscaping job. If you're using handwritten invoices, it's easy to use any format that works for the occasion. With a computer, I've found it necessary to set up several kinds of invoice templates, because computers can lock you into rigid formats for everything.

Always present a neat, complete invoice so the client understands what the bill covers. Make your terms of payment as short as possible—no longer than ten days. After all, you're not in the loan business. (*Reminder:* If you're charging for materials, you need to show sales tax as a separate line item.)

As with all forms, consistency is important, but it seems to be more elusive with invoices because of the varied nature of the work. Whatever system you use, try to do the same thing every time, if possible, because this will make it easier for the client (and you) to understand. (Sample invoices are shown later in this chapter.)

Credit Card Billing

If you accept Visa or MasterCard charges (which you should, even though you do have to pay a 2 to 3 percent service charge), you'll have to use the bank's system for recording a sale. You still have to fill out one of your own regular invoices, though, or you'll end up with no way to track those jobs through the bookkeeping system. Keep the fees in mind when you bid on a job that you know will be paid by a credit card. *Credit card merchant accounts* are a lot easier to get these days, thanks to technology that allows you to swipe cards on your smartphone or tablet wherever you are. These *point of sale systems* are easy to operate and very economical as well. Every businessperson should have one.

A contractor friend of mine used to let people charge entire landscaping jobs to their credit cards until he realized that the bank was taking 2 or 3 percent of $10,000 or $20,000. That was eating into his 10 percent profit margin in a big way. Credit cards are best for small purchases, but paying the bank charges is better than losing the job. Just be aware of what it's costing you.

Handling Credits and Refunds

Sometimes you have to give money back for some reason. It doesn't happen often, but if you don't document it correctly, a credit or a refund can throw your book-keeping off.

The standard approach is to use a *credit memo*. A credit memo looks pretty much like an invoice but is used to document refunds or credits to clients. One simple approach is to use a regular invoice, clearly marked credit memo at the top and credit at the total line. This indicates to the client and you that this time the money went to the client or was credited to his or her account. Computerized systems have special credit memo forms built in.

Sending Out Statements

If you have credit sales (you shouldn't, but it does come up now and then), or someone wants to pay you off in installments, or if you've sent out a slew of invoices to one client and haven't gotten paid for all of them, you need to send out a *statement*. It's a listing of what's been paid and not paid in chronological order. Notice how the arithmetic works on the Sample Statement that follows later in this chapter; it's a standard presentation.

Slow Pays

Sadly, not everyone will pay you on time. The best ways to avoid this are to choose clients carefully, do good work, and make sure your clients are so happy that they can't wait to reward you for your great service with a nice fat check. You should also come calling with your invoice at the end of the job, making sure your body language says (in a nice way), "Yes, as a matter of fact, I *do* want to get paid right now, thank you."

Sample Maintenance Invoice

INVOICE

INVOICE NO.
6751

JOE'S GARDENING SERVICE
601 CARTER BLVD.
WEST PLAINS, NJ 03947
(201) 717–2271

CLIENT NAME			JOB NAME		
Pete & Brenda Thomas			Thomas Residence		
STREET & NO. 1045 N. Locklin St.			STREET & NO. Same		
CITY West Plains	STATE NJ	ZIP 03947	CITY	STATE	ZIP

WORK PERFORMED/DATE	TERMS	DATE
Maintenance / June	Payable on receipt	7-10-15

1 BAG	16-6-8 Organic fertilizer	$17.50
1 PT.	Kelp soil treatment	19.00
	Subtotal	36.50
	Sales tax	2.19
	Total materials	38.69
1 LOAD	Dump fees	12.00
	Monthly maintenance	120.00
	Total	$170.69

Sample Time-and-Materials Invoice

INVOICE NO.
6752

INVOICE

HARRIET'S SPRINKLER REPAIR
101 TEANECK BLVD.
SAWTOOTH, VT 00310
224–2424

CLIENT NAME			JOB NAME		
Ted Meyers			Meyers Residence		
STREET & NO. 22 Barton Lane			STREET & NO. Same		
CITY Sawtooth	STATE VT	ZIP 00310	CITY	STATE	ZIP

WORK PERFORMED/DATE	TERMS	DATE
Sprinkler Repair, Back lawn – 7/13/15	Payable on receipt	7/17/15

1 PC.	½ Slip-Fix		$2.79
3 PC.	Rain Bird nozzles	.54	1.62
2 PC.	Cutoff risers	.35	.70
	Subtotal		5.11
	Sales tax		.31
	Total materials		5.42
2 HRS.	Service call	45.00	90.00
	Total		$95.42

Sample Lump-Sum Invoice

INVOICE NO.
6753

INVOICE

GARDENSMITH LANDSCAPES

29357 45TH ST.
PEACH GROVE, GA 17462
947–2212

CLIENT NAME			JOB NAME		
Mrs. C.W. Rubenstein			Rubenstein Residence		
STREET & NO.			**STREET & NO.**		
93 Tipton Terrace			Same		
CITY	**STATE**	**ZIP**	**CITY**	**STATE**	**ZIP**
Peach Grove	GA	17462			

WORK DONE/DATE	TERMS	DATE
Backyard Landscaping (per contract of 5/22/15)	Payable on receipt	7/9/15

1 L.S.	Landscaping - Per Contract	$7,490.00
	Add: Change Order #1 - Additional irrigation work	315.00
	Add: Change Order #2 - Extra trees/mulch	270.00
	Deduct: Change Order #3 - Downsize privets	<-105.00>
	Adjusted Total	7,970.00
	Less: deposit Rec'd 5-22-15	<-749.00>
	Less: progress payment Rec'd 6-14-15	<-2,200.00>
	Balance due	$5,021.00

Sample Statement

STATEMENT

Wilson Landscaping & Design

6602 12TH ST.

GREENVILLE, OK 00020

(405) 222–8888

Peter Howard & Brenda Ryan
217 Elm Rd.
Greenville, OK 00021

AMOUNT PAID ____________

PLEASE DETACH HERE AND RETURN UPPER PORTION WITH YOUR REMITTANCE.

6-30-15	Balance Forward		70.50
7-3-15	Maintenance - June	221.00	291.50
7-11-15	Payment-Thank You	<–70.50>	221.00
7-17-15	Sprinkler repairs	107.20	328.20
7-26-15	Potted plants	157.00	485.20

WILSON LANDSCAPING & DESIGN

Getting Your Money When They Won't Give It to You

Stage One: The Polite Phone Call

You know how it is. Sometimes we all forget to pay a bill or lose it or just need a little more time. Clients are no different. If you've waited a little too long to get your money from someone, start by giving him or her a friendly phone call. Diplomacy is important, because you don't want to sound like you're dunning the person, even though you are. Sometimes the conversation will actually go like this:

> YOU (nervously): Hi, Mr. Jensen, this is Mary of Mary's Lawn Care.
> CLIENT (even more nervously): Oh, hi Mary. Say, I've been meaning to call you. I'm going to send you that payment tomorrow morning.

But you typically won't be that lucky. There are right and wrong ways to approach this delicate matter. Take this example:

> JENNIFER: Mr. Dennison, this is Jennifer of Green Side Up Landscaping. We haven't gotten paid yet for the new lawn we put in for you, and I need to get a check from you right away or we're going to wind up in court.
> DENNISON: What are you talking about? Why should I pay you when you were four hours late the first morning, and you forgot to hose down the sidewalk, and I still don't know whether this lawn is going to take or not?! I'll send you a check when I'm sure the lawn isn't going to have any problems. Take me to court if you want to. I don't care.

Oops! That was the wrong way to approach a slow-paying client. If you want to get your money, you need to be diplomatic and consider the other person's feelings. People usually know when they haven't paid a bill, and they feel guilty about it. This makes them defensive and ready to attack back, even though they're wrong. You have to deal with this, because if you make them angry, they'll never pay you, and yes you will end up in court. You also have to deal with the possibility that the check got lost in the mail, or that they thought they had paid you, or that they actually did pay you and you have a bookkeeping error. Let's send Jennifer to sensitivity training and have her try again.

> JENNIFER: Hi, Mr. Dennison. This is Jennifer from Green Side Up Landscaping. How are you?
> DENNISON: Oh, hi, Jennifer. I'm fine. How are you?

JENNIFER: Fine. Do you have a minute to talk?

DENNISON: Sure. What's up?

JENNIFER: Well, I was looking at my books and I see we don't have a record of any final payment for the lawn we put in for you. This might be a bookkeeping error of ours, but I wanted to check with you and see if you had sent it in, or if not, whether there was a problem that we could resolve for you.

DENNISON: Well, Jennifer, as a matter of fact, I haven't sent the check. I've been busy and I just haven't gotten to it yet. I'm sorry if I caused you any trouble. Actually, there is one thing that concerns me. The lawn looks kind of thin in places and I'm wondering if you should have a look at it in case we need to do something.

JENNIFER: Sure, no problem. Sometimes we need to add a little more seed. Sometimes it just takes a while to thicken up. I'd be happy to take care of it for you. When would it be convenient for me to come take care of it?

DENNISON: How about Thursday around five o'clock?

JENNIFER: That'd be fine. And I'll pick up the check then.

DENNISON: No problem. See you Thursday.

JENNIFER: Great. Thanks so much.

Notice that the outcome was much more successful this time because Jennifer treated the client with respect. By suggesting that she might be in error, Jennifer made it easy for Dennison to tell the truth, which was that he'd been ignoring the bill. It also created an opening for him to voice a legitimate concern, one that may have contributed to his hesitation in paying her. Finally, Jennifer proved her willingness to stand behind her work, and this made it easier for Dennison to keep his end of the deal.

Stage Two: Collection Notices

When payment is more than sixty days past due and you've called several times to no avail, you may have to goad people into action with a written notice. Some office supply stores sell a set of forms that you can use; there are usually three or four, each one more strongly worded than the last. Start with the mildest one, wait thirty days, then graduate to the next, and so on. It's best to avoid written *collection notices* until things look really hopeless. They offend a lot of people, and you could lose a good client with this approach.

You could also take the bill to a *collection agency* at this point. Getting a call from a collection agency can be more motivating than getting a call from little ol'

Tom the gardener, and you might get your money sooner, though not all of it. If the agency folks collect anything, they'll keep anywhere from 10 to 50 percent for their troubles and give you the rest.

Here is some sample language that you can use or modify if you get to the point of sending out collection notices. There are a few things to keep in mind about collection notices. First, always be sure to include the client's name and address, the date, a description of the work done, and the amount owed. Don't allow a lot of time to go by between letters; keep the pressure on. Remember, if someone owes you money, he or she probably owes a lot of other people money, too, and will pay the most insistent creditors first. Send collection notices by *certified mail* with a *return receipt* and always enclose a self-addressed reply envelope. Be polite and businesslike; no personal attacks. Try to appeal to the client's sense of fairness first; later remind him or her of the need to protect one's reputation and credit rating. If all else fails, then threaten legal action.

- **First Notice**

  This is a friendly reminder that we haven't received payment for the work we did for you. If there's a problem with the work or a question about the bill, please call us at once so that we can take care of it. Otherwise, would you send a check today? Thank you for your cooperation. P.S. If you've already sent in your payment, please disregard this notice.

- **Second Notice**

  Recently, we sent you a reminder that your account was overdue. Unfortunately, we still haven't received a check from you. We believe that you want to treat us fairly. If you aren't able to pay this bill right now, please contact us at once to make arrangements for payment. Otherwise, please send a check immediately to avoid further collection efforts. Thank you.

- **Third Notice**

  Your account is long past due. Avoid legal action and damage to your credit rating by paying this bill in full today.

- **Final Notice**

  Because you have not responded to our previous attempts to collect the past due amount owed to us, we will begin legal proceedings against you on ____________ (date). You can be sued in Small Claims Court and your payment history can be reported to credit reporting agencies. We can also file a mechanic's lien and foreclose on your property. Send a check now.

Note: Check with an attorney about the legal status of collection methods in your area and modify the language of these notices as required by state or local laws. If a maintenance client is past due, you can always suspend service until the bill is paid in full. This action almost always results in prompt payment. On the other hand, the client could drop you, but what's to lose, really? Why work if you don't get paid?

Stage Three: The Lien Laws

Anyone who performs work or supplies materials on private property is entitled to be paid. The *mechanic's lien* is a special statutory protection that permits you to make a claim against the client's property if the client doesn't pay you. By attaching the property, it could be sold and the proceeds used to pay you. Naturally, this hardly ever actually happens, but it certainly is motivating, and the person usually finds some money to pay you real fast. The lien laws are particularly helpful if you're working as a sub, having little contact with the owner of the project. In order to preserve your lien rights, you need to follow certain specific procedures during and after the job. Requirements vary from state to state.

Discussion of the lien laws is much too complicated to get into here, but you must learn about them and how they work. If you've gotten your contractor's license, you've already been exposed to this information. If you haven't, call the contractor's license board, your trade association, or your attorney for help with this. It's important, so do it. (*Something to NEVER EVER do:* Once you've completed the work, you have no right to repossess it by taking plants out of the ground, ripping up the new patio, or jacking the controller off the wall, even if the client owes you a ton of money. You will THINK quite passionately about doing these things, and that's legal, but if you actually do them you could wind up in jail. Seriously.)

How the Lien Laws Work

Each state has its own take on the *mechanic's lien laws*, but they are universally used throughout the United States. The first and most important thing to know about the lien laws is that in order to take advantage of them, and to stay out of trouble, you need to comply precisely with strict requirements. You have a right to lien (which means to assert a claim against) the real property (that is, the house or other property) on which you worked as a contractor, materials supplier, or other vendor, if you are not paid for your work that was incorporated into the property (for instance a patio or plantings or an irrigation system). To protect your lien rights, you have to provide very specific documents to the owner within specified time periods during the course of the work. The commonest of these documents is called a *Notice to Owner*, which formally alerts the owner to your lien rights. This notice contains very specific language and must be presented within a limited time period. But there are other notices as well, and the subject is intricate. If you find yourself in the unhappy situation of needing to file a lien against a property, you will need to do so within a certain time after completion of your work. Filing is also complex and exacting and is probably best left to an attorney because any little mistake could invalidate your claim. Another consideration is that your suppliers, who also have lien rights to the properties they supply materials to, may send *Preliminary Notices* to the owner as well. This can cause upset when owners receive legal documents that might mislead them into thinking they are being sued. The contractors laws in many states require you to provide yet another written notice as part of your contract when you take on the job, explaining all this to the owner in specific language. But nobody ever reads them, so you should consider walking them through it during the signing of the contract. It all sounds gruesome, but these laws are there to protect you. Get the details down pat, relying on information specific to your state that can be found in the state contractors law, and then develop a systematic approach to providing the required documents for each project you work on.

Stage Four: Legal Action

Litigation is costly, time consuming, and often unproductive. The only time I got into a major lawsuit, I won, but my attorney's fees (which I had to pay) exceeded the amount of the judgment. Sometimes it's better to just drop the matter. Other than doing that, you have three alternatives: small claims court, municipal court, and arbitration.

Small claims court deals only with small monetary judgments, usually limited to a maximum of $2,500 to $25,000 (see chart at www.nolo.com/legal-encyclopedia/small-claims-suits-how-much-30031.html). This approach is fast, inexpensive, and often effective.

Neither party can be represented by an attorney. The atmosphere is informal, and all proceedings are conducted in plain English. The defendant can appeal, but the plaintiff (that's you) can't. Unfortunately, the court doesn't collect the money for you or even guarantee that you'll get it. But once you win a judgment, you have other methods of getting the money; the court will explain those to you.

Municipal court is for larger claims and is more cumbersome and expensive. You will probably need to hire an attorney to handle the case. Think three times before you get into a lawsuit in municipal court.

Arbitration is an informal alternative to going to court. Cases are often heard in a conference setting by attorneys and experts in your business. You can use an attorney or represent yourself. The results of an arbitration hearing are often not appealable. Some contracts include a provision for mandatory arbitration; decide if this is agreeable to you before you sign it.

Following Up on Your Jobs

Site Visits

One day you'll drive by a job you did a couple of years before, and it'll be a horrifying mess—dead plants, weeds, bad pruning, trash everywhere. It beats me why anybody would pay thousands of dollars for landscaping and then let it run down like that, but some people do. Naturally, it's bad advertising for you. Besides, maybe they didn't know how to take care of it (*you* were supposed to have *told* them) and they just gave up.

It's your job to make sure this doesn't happen. Schedule regular visits over the first year. I suggest you come back two weeks after the job is finished, then a month after that, then every two to three months. Normally, you don't charge extra for this. You can either arrange these visits with the client or do them as a surprise (as we discussed in chapter 6, but of course don't let yourself into a client's property without his or her permission). Regular follow-up of this kind helps the client learn to deal with the new landscaping and keep things in good condition. It gives you an opportunity to prevent dissatisfaction and to sell the client more work, including, perhaps, maintenance.

Another approach is to include ninety days of *establishment maintenance* in all landscaping proposals. The cost to the client is minimal, the landscaping will perform much better than if the client struggles with care during this critical period, and you may get hired permanently at the end of the ninety days. It's such a good idea that many landscape architects specify a ninety-day maintenance period on all their jobs.

It's also a good idea to provide written information on the care of the landscaping, especially for the plants. This could be a printed brochure, specific information for the plants you used on that job, or both.

The other document you should provide the client with is a *record drawing* of the irrigation system, showing the location and size of pipes, valves, wires, and anything else that might be hard to find without a diagram. It'll help you, too, if you get called back five years later and need to find something. You might want to do the same for lighting, drainage, and other underground systems.

Quality Audit

It pays to find out if clients are satisfied with your performance. A *quality audit* gives you an opportunity to correct any problems, and it also alerts you to changes you need to make in your operation. It's a great goodwill builder.

Include a questionnaire with your final bill (or annually for maintenance clients) that gives the client an opportunity to comment on the quality of the work, the service, the employees, and other reactions to your company. Allow people to answer anonymously if they wish and supply a postage-paid envelope for them to use to return the questionnaire. You can also use an online survey website; surveys are easy to set up and use. If they do include a name, respond personally to any complaint (or compliment!) as soon as you receive the questionnaire back from them.

Thank-You Card

How many people take the time to do this? Imagine failing to thank someone who just paid you thousands of dollars! Also send thank-you cards to people who refer you to others. It's best to do this the old-fashioned way, with a nicely printed card sent by snail mail, but even a friendly email at the end of the job is a nice gesture.

Business Nightmares: Keeping Your Nose Clean

Used to be, businesspeople were free to do just about whatever they wanted. Unfortunately, over the centuries ne'er-do-wells took advantage of this freedom one way or another, and laws and regulations were gradually put into effect to protect the public. Most of these laws are well intentioned, and some of them even work the way they're supposed to work. Today, there are hundreds of them, and if you run afoul of even one, you can be in a world of trouble, especially since the courts usually assume that because you're in business you must be the one who's wrong. Never mind that most businesspeople are decent and struggle day and night to keep their customers happy; never mind the extremely high failure rate of business start-ups in this country (between 50 and 90 percent, depending on whose statistics you believe and how you interpret them); never mind that the average self-employed person earns slightly less than he or she would in a "real" job, doing the same tasks for someone else. Everyone just assumes that you're rich, corrupt, and not to be trusted. The businessperson is often presumed guilty even after being found innocent.

Worse than this is the proliferation of lawsuits that has affected nearly everyone in business. Even if you haven't been sued, every action has to be considered from a liability standpoint. What if the client steps on my rake while I'm mowing the lawn? What if the dog dies the day after I sprayed the fruit trees? What if a sprinkler valve sticks open and saturates the hillside with water, causing a landslide? The attention given to legal liability probably now exceeds that given to tax liability, and the fear of a lawsuit is right up there with the fear of being audited for most businesspeople. Heck, even if you don't do *anything* wrong you may still have to defend yourself against a shotgun lawsuit in which the attorneys go after everybody they can in the hope of finding some deep pockets somewhere. They'll even sue people that they know didn't have a thing to do with the problem and then extort money from them on the grounds that a settlement will cost less than defending themselves. It's a nasty mess.

So what can you do to protect yourself against lawsuits? First, make sure that everything you do is completely legal. That way nobody can attack your integrity. Next, keep impeccable records of everything you do, say, and think: contracts and change orders, meeting notes, daily job sheets, emails, letters and memos, and more. Do the best quality work you possibly can and know in intimate detail all the laws, building codes, and regulations applying to that work. Check your jobs constantly to be sure no one has left an open trench, forgotten to do part of the job, or made an irresponsible statement to anyone. Keep your clients happy so that if a problem comes up they'll work with you and not just sic their lawyers on you right off the bat. Go over your situation periodically with your attorney to see if you're sticking your neck out somewhere. Finally, buy lots of insurance.

These strategies take a lot of the spontaneity out of being in business, but they're a whole lot better than ending up in court, because whenever you go to court, you lose, even if you win. Ask anyone who's been there.

Here are a few examples of the pitfalls that await you. (*Warning:* The following situations are only examples and are not all-inclusive or complete, nor are they intended to inform you of all possible legal liabilities or obligations that may affect you or your business under various conditions and circumstances. These examples are fictitious and do not in any way depict actual legal cases or real people, living or dead. The author hereby assumes no responsibility of any kind whatsoever for the consequences of the use of the information hereunder by the reader or anyone else.)

The Oral Contract

Lacking a detailed written contract, the client may claim that you did less than you said you would or that you somehow violated an oral understanding, justifying nonpayment of the whole amount due. This isn't at all far-fetched or unusual; in fact, it happens every day. If you take someone to court and you don't have a written contract, your case will probably be dismissed, and you could be disciplined by the contractors' board for not complying with the law. As the old saying goes, an *oral contract* isn't worth the paper it's written on. Always, always have a written contract.

The Oral Change Order

During the job, the owner makes a number of requests for additional work. Naturally, you take care of these, and because the owner's a real good guy, you don't take the time to let him know how much these changes are going to cost, much less get written approval. At the end of the job, you total everything up and present your bill, being careful to itemize the changes. He's outraged at the additional charges and refuses to pay you. You lose the money and the client, with no recourse from the courts. Maybe you even have your contractor's license suspended for a while. Again, it happens every day. Get written change orders.

Omission of Information on Contract

The law has a lot to say about how home improvement contracts are worded. You may need to include things like a *Notice to Owner*, explaining the lien laws; a *Three-Day Notice of Cancellation*, giving the owner time to back out of a contract; a place for your license number; the address of the state contractors' board; and a lot more. Your state will have its own unique set of requirements. If you omit one, word it wrong, or even use the wrong-size type, you risk voiding the entire contract and losing the money for the work you did. Remember that the law is logical but sometimes crazy, and will deny you payment even if everyone agrees that the work is fine and by any reasonable reckoning you should be paid. It's not fair, but it's the way it is. That's why it's so important to follow the rules down to the last little nitpicking detail.

Work Not Done to Specifications

You complete a beautiful flagstone walkway, done just like you told the owner you'd do it. You bring the owner out and proudly show off your creation. She sniffs and hunches up her shoulders and says, "Well, this is not what I expected. Take it apart and do it over." Yikes! Not only is your ego heavily abraded, you've got a lot of work to do. Sometimes this situation occurs because the owner really did have a different expectation of the work. Other times, the owner is trying to jerk you around, to delay paying you for some reason—lack of funds, personal problems, or just plain orneriness. There are a lot of really vicious people out there. Either way, you failed to clearly spell out, through written *specifications* and *detail drawings*, exactly how this walk was going to be constructed, and, like it or not, you'll have to redo it. If you had something on paper, you could just point to it and say, "See? Just like I said it would be."

This problem can even come up in garden maintenance. I once had a persnickety client accuse me of cutting his hedge too far back, even though many of the stubs from the previous trimming were still present underneath the foliage. I spent more time settling him down than I spent trimming the hedge. (*Tip:* Talk to your clients a lot during the job. Get their approval on something every day. Explain what you're doing and why you're doing it. Come back after they're home from work if need be. Keep them informed and happy. It's worth the effort.)

Work Fails after Completion

You install a retaining wall; two years later it falls down. You're liable for replacement of the wall and for any consequential damages. Build things right the first time. If you don't know how to do something right, find out or hire a subcontractor who does; otherwise, just pass up the job.

Proximate Cause

You do a job that was designed by a landscape architect. It's obvious to you right from the first time you look at the plans that there are serious problems with the design. But, of course, you don't want to step on the architect's toes, so you keep quiet and install the job as it was designed. Later it fails, just like you thought it would. The owner comes after you. The owner wins a judgment against you, not against the offending landscape architect. Not fair? Well, the law says you should have said something, and by not doing so you became the *proximate cause*: the last professional to work on the project and therefore at least partially responsible for the problem.

The Faked Back Injury

One Friday afternoon, a new employee hobbles into the office in apparent pain. Off you go on a possibly phony injury claim that will cost you big bucks in worker's compensation insurance premiums. Typically, the insurance company will charge a couple hundred thousand dollars to your worker's compensation account to cover possible costs of an extended disability. Regardless of what they end up paying the employee, your rates go up because of the claim. There are attorneys out there who specialize in counseling employees in how to turn a little muscle cramp into a long vacation with generous pay, compliments of you-know-who. It doesn't look like this problem will get better any time soon.

Hold regular *safety meetings*, provide training for all new employees, and most important of all, screen new employees carefully for a history of injuries or claims. Then hope for the best. To be fair, legitimate injuries, especially back injuries, are common in this business, what with all the lifting and bending we do. Teach your people how to stay healthy, for their benefit and yours.

La Migra

La Migra is what the *U.S. Citizenship and Immigration Services ("USCIS")* is unaffectionately called by the millions of undocumented workers from Mexico and elsewhere who live and work in the United States. Landscaping businesses hire people from south of the border because they're usually far superior to our own workforce—hardworking, honest, faithful, decent, and willing to work for less. However you feel about this controversial issue, you need to be aware of your risks as an employer of undocumented workers. The USCIS regularly follows landscapers' trucks in the Southwest and beyond, and asks for employees' green cards. Roundups and deportations are common, and by law the employer can be subject to stiff fines for hiring illegals. Plus, it's no fun to find out that your entire crew is on a bus back to Mexico instead of on the job.

Well, I don't mean to scare you to death. Most of the time things go just the way you planned. Still, knowing that these things can happen is important to your success and even your survival. Now that you're aware of some of the problems, it'll be easier to avoid them.

09 The Long Haul

After the Work Is Done

Your work isn't over when you load the last tool on the truck at the end of the job. Remember that you've set up a living ecosystem for your client, and your ongoing expertise is needed to make it work properly. That means you have to follow up on your jobs and be available for questions, even if you aren't doing the maintenance on the project. A little of your attention now and then can prevent major problems that lead to dissatisfaction, failure of the work, and possible legal action against you.

I always offer free follow-up on all my jobs. Forever. I urge clients to call me any time they have a problem or a question, no matter how dumb it might seem. I ask that they call me within twenty-four hours if they notice a problem with a plant, so I can try to save it. If a leaf falls off, I'll try to tell them why it fell off. People do call, especially during the first few weeks after the job is done, and I'll go out anytime and look at things if I can't help them over the phone. I also drop by recently completed jobs now and then, because I can usually see developing problems before the owners or their gardeners can.

I'll be honest with you. For the first few years, I'd swear at least once a week that I was going to get out of this crazy business. "I don't need this!" I'd say to myself. "I'm going to get a real job." So, what's kept me in the saddle all these years? Well, one thing is that the thought of a "real" job is so distasteful to me that I'd rather do anything than fall into the ranks of the gainfully employed. Before I started doing landscaping, I fixed TVs for a living, and I got fired from my last "real" job in 1969. It was the best thing that ever happened to me because I realized that I didn't need to spend my life doing something I hated. So after I went into business for myself, when I would get discouraged, I'd just think back to my TV repair days and the present would look a lot better.

But that wasn't enough by itself to keep me going. What truly worked, and it took a long time, was that I gradually learned how to make my business run as smoothly as possible. I learned that, for me, the worst part of owning a business was waking up in the morning with a crushing burden of anxieties about what I had to do that day. I'd lie there in the dark and think about the phone calls that I hadn't returned, the equipment that I hadn't serviced, and the bids that were stacked up on my desk, and my heart would race until I had to jump up and do something, anything, just to keep from exploding.

I finally figured it out—it wasn't the business that was making me unhappy, it was me! By taking on too much work and not having systems set up to handle the work efficiently, I was constantly falling behind, getting people sore at me, and losing track of important details. You see, I didn't have a book like this one to help me, or a mentor who would gently suggest that I could make a few simple changes and improve both my business and my life. Then I looked around at other contractors and people in small service businesses like mine, and I realized that most of them were having exactly the same problems. I wasn't alone in feeling that I had given birth to a monster.

So let me be your mentor for just a moment. You were kind enough to buy this book, so it's the least I can do. These tips may help you stay on top of things, have more fun, and stick with your career because you want to, not because you're trapped.

1. Don't take on more work than you can handle.
2. Decide what you need to get done each day and don't quit until you've completed it all; otherwise, things get hopelessly backed up.
3. Keep everybody informed about what's going on.
4. Develop systems to make things go smoothly (the ones in this book or others that work for you) and follow them rigorously. Business is a discipline; learn to love it the way a Zen monk loves his meditation practice.
5. Give yourself time off. Take frequent hikes or go swimming or just goof off now and then.
6. Work odd hours if you prefer. You're the boss, remember?
7. Stay healthy: Exercise. Eat right. Rethink your relationship to cigarettes, alcohol, and drugs.
8. When you get discouraged, give yourself a pep talk.

Here are some of the things I try to say to myself at difficult moments:

- "This isn't really *that* bad, is it?" (A deep breath at this point helps a lot.)
- "Thanks for the advice, Mr. Discouraged Self, but you're not going to run

my life. Just go sit in the corner, please, and keep quiet." (I learned this one from my therapist.)

- "What, exactly, is the problem here?" I might make a list of things to do and then sort them in order of importance, then do them one at a time without thinking much or whining about it. If you're pulling weeds, you can look at each weed and feel pretty good, or you can look around at all the weeds and get pretty blue about how many there are. It's your choice.
- "I could be a [insert name of odious job you could be stuck in if you hadn't chosen to be a landscaper].

In short, I try to reframe my reality so that things don't look so bad. After all, at any given moment, you could usually say, "This is a big fat hassle!" or you could say, "This is a great challenge!" Which you choose determines how you feel about things.

Don't get me wrong. I still feel overwhelmed at times when these clever little mind games aren't working like they're supposed to. It's hard to run a business, and all the tips and positive self-talk in the world won't solve all your problems (oops, I mean challenges). But when things go smoothly most of the time, and when you're happy to answer the phone rather than afraid, when you can wake up bursting with enthusiasm instead of cringing with anxiety, you'll be really glad you went into business for yourself. The way to accomplish this is simple, really: Put every fiber of your being into keeping things working smoothly and never let up.

Someone once said that the secret of happiness is being responsible. Once you can accept that and practice it, you'll find that it's true. Give it a try.

Guarantees

To what degree you must stand behind your work is defined in a number of ways. The first is *statutory*—in some states the law defines the guarantee period for home improvement work. In addition, a more detailed guarantee will be included in your agreement with the owner. Often the landscape architect will specify the terms of the guarantee. If you're working under a contract prepared by a general contractor or developer, there will certainly be guarantee requirements coming from them. (*Tip:* Watch for unreasonable requirements in other people's contracts. If you can't live with them, negotiate to change them.) If you're doing design/build, it's your responsibility to develop a guarantee that will satisfy both you and the client.

Each kind of work is guaranteed in a different way and for different periods of time. It would be ludicrous to guarantee a planting of annual flowers for three years, but it's equally ludicrous to guarantee a deck for ninety days. Here's my standard boilerplate guarantee, just to give you an idea of the details:

GUARANTEE

GENERAL: Landscape Contractor guarantees all work to be free from defects in materials and workmanship. The duration of the guarantee is one year for sprinkler systems, hardscape construction, and low-voltage lighting systems, and ninety days for all other work, except as noted. CONDITIONS, LIMITATIONS, AND EXCLUSIONS: In the case of weed control, no guarantees of effectiveness of treatment or duration of treatment are made, and treatments are made with the express understanding that such work is done entirely at risk of Owner with regards to the effectiveness of treatment. The same limitation of effectiveness shall apply to renovation, fertilization, pest control, and other similar procedures. In the case of irrigation, Landscape Contractor shall guarantee adequate coverage for the purposes intended, with a minimum of overspray or dry spots. In the case of lawns, plants, and other living things, no guarantee of survival, vigor, ultimate size or appearance, or suitability to site conditions is made. Plants that die will be replaced one time at no expense to Owner, provided Owner's responsibilities for care and notification are fully met. Seeded lawns are not guaranteed to germinate and grow, as the success of a seeded lawn is chiefly determined by the watering and care given by Owner and is beyond the control of the Landscape Contractor. Sod lawns are guaranteed for fourteen days against infestation of pests and diseases; otherwise no guarantee is made, because watering and care are beyond the control of the Landscape Contractor. In all cases with living things, Owner must notify Landscape Contractor within twenty-four hours of noticing a problem. Allowing plants, lawns, etc., to die or reach an advanced state of decline before notifying Landscape Contractor automatically and without recourse voids all guarantees on that portion of the project. In no case shall Landscape Contractor honor any guarantee when evidence of abuse, neglect, vandalism, vertebrate, insect or other damage, disease, misuse, improper care, or any other condition beyond the control of the Landscape Contractor is found. Guarantees shall be effective only if the Owner has complied with all the terms and conditions, payments, and other provisions of the contract.

Notice that this guarantee does four things: It says what will be guaranteed, it establishes the guarantee period, it defines limitations on the guarantee, and it establishes responsibility (including the responsibilities of the client).

Guarantees boil down to this: You're responsible for defects in the materials and work that you provide and, if you designed the project, for defects in your design. If elephants stampede through the garden, that's not your fault. Also, because you're dealing with nature, you can't guarantee that plants will thrive or that weeds will die. After all, surgeons don't guarantee that their patients will live, only that they won't commit malpractice.

Still, when a plant dies within the first ninety days, it's good public relations to replace it, no questions asked. Maybe the client forgot to water or watered too much or the dog peed on it, but why make them feel bad by arguing about who screwed up? Just put a smile on your face and a fresh plant in the ground. You see, these clients paid you a lot of money to build them a nice garden, and they don't want to hear you whine about your problems. Nobody likes a whiner. (Besides, you did include something in your bid for warranty replacements, didn't you?)

By the way, if you're doing the maintenance on a job you installed, there's no question about replacements. If a plant dies or is looking bad during the maintenance period, you just replace it unless it was damaged by someone or something else or hammered by the weather. On the other hand, if you're doing maintenance on an existing garden, you're not responsible for plants dying unless you killed them.

Naturally, you have to budget something into your bids to cover the replacement of a reasonable number of plants. This cost doesn't show up as a line item on your bid, but you've got to allow for it in your planting price, because no matter how careful you are, plants *do* die, and you *will* be out there replacing them. Depending on the plant (some are harder to establish than others), you might allow 2 to 10 percent in your planting bid for replacement. The loss rate for small plants is higher than for larger plants, so if you're planting a lot of ground cover from flats, plan on coming back for sure. Specimen trees are a special case: Sometimes they're planted at a low markup with no guarantee; other times they're guaranteed for a year, but at a much higher price. After all, replacing a $1,000 tree is not trivial. Transplants are normally not guaranteed at all. (*Tip:* You normally replace plants only once because repeated failure is probably caused by a soil pathogen or other problem beyond your control. With subsequent replacements it's a good idea to bill the clients at your cost. They'll appreciate it. And hey, try to find out what is causing the problem so that you eventually find something that works.)

Finally, you should be aware that most states and courts enforce an extended period of liability for *latent defects*, that is, a concealed flaw such as an inadequate footing on a retaining wall, hidden from view, that caused the wall to overturn during a rainy period. The duration and extent of latent defects liability varies from one place to another, so talk to your attorney about this important matter.

Liability for Work

Your guarantees will hold up better if you've done the job right the first time. See the checklist that follows some of the problems that you should look for and avoid on any job. It presents examples of the most common and most important problems that landscapers and gardeners create. You'll undoubtedly discover others as you become more experienced. I've listed items in the order in which they're normally done on a typical landscaping job.

Long-Term Management

Managing Cash Flow

Your goal in managing cash flow is to always have just the right amount of money on hand—never too much or too little (If you're lucky enough to have extra cash, put it into an interest-bearing account or CD). To accomplish this, you need to keep good records, know the cash-flow pattern of your company, and project cash flow.

Re-read "The Cash Forecast" in chapter 3 to remind yourself how easy it is to get into financial trouble by neglecting your cash flow, and how easy it is to prevent this deadly problem by doing a *cash forecast* regularly—at least every month, especially if you're getting bigger jobs and more work than you've been accustomed to having.

There are some classic cash-flow pitfalls. Getting a big job means that you'll have to invest a lot of money up front in labor and materials, administrative expenses, and possibly even capital investments in new equipment to do the job. If you can't cover those costs by getting payments from your client, you'll have to dip into your reserves or get a short-term loan. If your cash isn't enough to cover the expenditures, you'll have a cash-flow crisis, which in turn means you'll be delinquent in paying your bills, which is a red flag for your creditors, who may put you on *C.O.D.* (*cash on delivery*)—no more charges. This kind of cash-flow crisis is often the start of a tailspin from which the small operator may never recover. After all, if you can't charge things, you can't buy the materials you need to do the job, let alone start the next job.

A short-term but deadly solution is to pay for the last job out of money that you collect in advance from the next job. In addition to digging you even deeper into the hole, such behavior (sometimes referred to as *commingling of funds*) may be illegal. Once you're in this deep, your business may be beyond saving. You might be able to limp along for a while, but unless something unusually wonderful happens, you'll eventually succumb to your financial weakness.

Even a steady-state business like maintenance can run into cash-flow problems if unusual expenses aren't anticipated or if clients quit paying you promptly. Let's say your faithful old truck finally breaks down. Do you have the money for a new one? Do you even have a down payment? If not, what are you going to do? So you have to plan ahead for future expenditures. (*Tip:* Set up an *equipment replacement fund* and pay into it every month. That way when you need something, you'll be able to pay cash for it, saving thousands of dollars in interest.)

Other sources of cash-flow problems include failure to anticipate upcoming tax liabilities, ignoring the cost of monthly loan payments, buying equipment you don't need and can't generate the income to pay for, having too much money tied up in inventory of materials that aren't allocated to any upcoming jobs, failing to anticipate seasonal slowdowns in business, and taking too large a draw for yourself.

How do you avoid these problems? One answer is to always run your business lean. Don't spend any more than you have to, don't fall for fancy geegaws, don't overinvest in fixed assets, and don't let salespeople talk you into unnecessary purchases. Don't buy your BMW too soon. On the income side, make sure you bill people on time and in full, and make sure they pay you on time and in full. Your first responsibility is to be sure you provide the resources that your business needs to run smoothly. Your second responsibility is to be sure the business lives within those resources. In business, there's a lot to be said for being a tightwad.

Seasonal Cash-Flow Management

Remember that even though business will be slow during part of the year, your fixed expenses go on. If you spend all the money you make during the busy periods, you won't have any money to pay the bills during the slow times. A year's cash forecasts will tell you how much you'll need to set aside in the bank to cover yourself during your slow time. Remember, you might feel pretty cocky if you have $30,000 on hand at the end of the busy season, but if you need $50,000 to carry you through the slow times, you'll be in for a shock. *Rule: Cash in the bank is not necessarily profit.* Part of it may be profit, but much of it is the *reserves* that you need for future expenses.

Estimate seasonal sales and expenses based on past experience (yours or other people's), modified by projected changes. My sales doubled every year for the first few years, then leveled off. Sales volume can vary with the state of the economy, price changes, your own marketing efforts, local business conditions, the weather, and other factors. A realistic sales projection takes these into account.

Problems Checklist

CONDITION	PROBLEM	SOLUTION
GRADING AND DRAINAGE		
Contact between soil and siding or framing wood of house or other untreated wood.	Causes dry rot, other structural problems.	Leave 6-inch gap between soil and untreated wood.
Runoff to inappropriate location (i.e., toward house, onto neighboring property).	Causes flooding, soil subsidence or expansion, property damage. May be illegal.	Establish minimum 2 percent grade to direct runoff to street or drainage system. Check all finish grades with sighting level and correct as needed.
Rainwater soaking into unstable soils (especially on slopes).	Can cause landslides.	Direct water away from slopes into drains or to street. Plant slopes with erosion control plants.
Runoff across paved areas on property, such as sidewalks and driveways.	Makes pavement slippery.	Direct water away from pavement.
Covering root systems and trunks of existing plants with soil.	Can kill plants, especially mature trees.	Avoid changing the grade around trees and mature shrubs.
Destruction of habitat or protected species.	Can be illegal.	Check with authorities before working in or near wildlife areas.
Contaminated imported soil.	Can kill plants. Costly to remove and dispose of as hazardous waste.	Buy from reputable dealers. Test soil before accepting.
IRRIGATION		
Pressure mains or valves located at top of slope.	Broken pipe can cause flooding and landslide.	Install pressure mains and valves at bottom of slopes.
Backflow devices missing or installed wrong.	Illegal; could contaminate water supply.	Install required devices in compliance with local building codes.
Pressure too high or too low for irrigation system.	Can affect system performance and survival of plants; high pressure can damage system.	Check pressure with gauge before bidding job.
Plants with different water needs on same valve.	Some plants will be overwatered, others underwatered.	Design planting in hydrozones, grouping according to water need.
Contact between copper and galvanized pipes.	Electrolytic action destroys pipes.	Use same kind of pipe or install dielectric union.
Sprinkler heads next to walks are installed above grade.	Trip hazard.	Use pop-up heads; install at or slightly below grade. Set heads at least 6 inches away from walks.

Problems Checklist (cont.)

CONDITION	PROBLEM	SOLUTION
IRRIGATION (cont.)		
Rigid, fixed riser heads installed in or near lawns or traffic areas.	Trip or injury hazard.	Use pop-up heads, keep away from traffic areas.
Overspray onto paved areas or buildings.	Causes slippery pavement; damages buildings.	Place spray heads so they point away from buildings; place spray heads at least 6 inches from buildings (impact heads 12 to 18 inches).
Low head drainage onto paved areas.	Causes slippery pavement.	Install check valves in low heads. Install heads away from pavement.
Digital controller on same circuit as large motor (e.g., washing machine, pool equipment).	Causes controller to malfunction, possibly overwatering plants.	Use a different circuit.
PLANTING		
Plants are too close together.	May stunt plants; causes unnecessary maintenance; creates greenwaste; wastes clients' money.	Give plants room to grow naturally; don't overplant.
Plants are too close to edges of walks, lawns, etc.	Plants need constant trimming.	Give plants room to grow naturally to mature size. Check mature size before planting.
Trees are planted too close to buildings, pavement, etc.	Damages foundations; lifts paving, causing trip hazard.	Keep trees away from buildings and paved areas.
Trees are planted over buried utilities (pipes, cables, etc.).	Roots can damage utilities and make repairs difficult.	Locate utilities before you plant.
Plants are planted in easements and rights of way.	Easement owner has right to remove plants.	Avoid permanent plantings in easements.
Using plants with invasive or surface roots.	Damages other improvements, could cause trip hazard.	Consider root system before specifying plant.
Poisonous plants.	Can injure or kill, especially children.	Avoid poisonous plants or provide written warning to client.
Highly flammable plants.	Can cause loss of structures in wildfire.	Avoid using highly flammable plants in high-fire-hazard areas.
Thorny plants near walkways.	Can cause injury.	Place thorny plants away from traffic.
Thick mulch around base of plants.	Can injure bark and kill plant.	Keep mulch at least 3 inches away from stems and trunks of plants.

Problems Checklist (cont.)

CONDITION	PROBLEM	SOLUTION
HARDSCAPE		
Single step on path.	Trip hazard (hard to see, unexpected).	Use ramp, or use three or more steps per location.
Poorly lighted steps.	Hazard at night.	Use low-voltage lighting at steps.
No handrails on steps.	Dangerous, may violate building code.	Use handrails on all steps.
Inadequate or blinding lighting.	May cause trip-and-fall injury.	Relocate or modify lighting.
Pavement displacement greater than ¼ inch.	Trip hazard.	Modify pavement to eliminate displacement.
Gaps in pavement or deck boards.	High-heeled shoes may catch in gap, causing a fall injury.	Eliminate gaps.
Slippery pavements.	May cause injury.	Use rough-textured paving materials, especially in shady locations.
Gravel or other loose materials near paved areas or lawns.	May cause slip-and-fall injury; gravel may be thrown by lawn mower.	Use different material or separate from lawn or pavement.
Sharp edges on materials.	May cause injury.	Round over or eliminate edges.
Work not complying with building codes.	May create liability in event of injury.	Check for and comply with applicable building codes.
Work not complying with fire codes (open decks, wood fences, etc.).	May create liability in the event of fire.	Check and comply with fire codes.
Work done without building permits or review process.	Against the law.	Comply with permit requirements.
Structures not engineered properly.	May fail and/or cause other damage.	Check for proper materials and design. Use an engineer where necessary.
MAINTENANCE		
Overwatering, especially near buildings.	May damage building, plants.	Manage water better.
Overpruning of trees and shrubs.	May injure or kill plants or cause safety hazards.	Prune correctly. Never top trees.
Broken sprinkler system flooding area.	May damage structures, injure or kill plants, make paved areas hazardous.	Test system regularly and repair as needed.
Misuse of pesticides and other chemicals.	Can cause injury or death to people, plants, pets, wildlife. Can contaminate soil, water, air.	Follow label instructions to the letter or use organic methods.

Some people work night and day during the summer, then kick back in the off season, happy to have enough money in the bank to get them through until spring. Others turn to other kinds of work in winter. Snow plowing is popular in colder climates, but there may be other opportunities in your community. Naturally, you could get an entirely different kind of job in winter, but why not use your entrepreneurial talents to do something related to your abilities, such as plowing snow, selling Christmas trees, repairing people's lawn mowers, or putting up gutters?

Accounts Payable Management

Pay bills marked "*2 percent 10th*" by the tenth of the month to get your discount. Pay bills on time to avoid late charges and interest (not to mention damage to your credit rating). Anticipate large or out-of-the-ordinary payments. Keep a running total of your payables: one total for everything in the *Invoices Unpaid* file and another for the *Accounts Payable* files. Always know how much you owe.

Accounts Receivable Management

The most important strategy is to pick credit-worthy clients, but there are other strategies. On big jobs, structure your progress payments so they cover anticipated expenses. Provide the client with a written schedule of progress payments along with the contract. Have a clause in your contract that makes failure to pay progress payments within three days of the due date a *material breach of contract*. Stipulate in writing that the final payment is due on completion of the work. Reinforce all this verbally when you present the contract to the client.

Get signed *change orders* for all changes, whether they increase or decrease the contract price or even if there's no price change. Keep track of all changes and payments on a *job ledger* so you can bill promptly for progress payments and at the end of the job. Present clients with understandable *invoices* and *progress billings* so they won't have reason to delay payment because of questions. Bill immediately on the schedule you agreed on when you signed the contract and on completion of the job. Hand deliver your bills on big jobs, and try to get payment on the spot. For all bills, provide a return envelope, addressed and stamped, for clients to send in payments, and consider taking credit cards so that you get your money faster.

Track the aging of all *receivables* and send notices to anyone who is thirty days past due. Better yet, give them a friendly reminder call on the phone. Comply with all requirements for protecting your lien rights, and file liens within the allotted time limits. Stop working for clients who are more than sixty days past due. Take clients who are seriously delinquent to small claims court. Keep a running total of current and past-due receivables; update it every week.

Cash Budgeting

In chapter 3 you learned how to do a *cash forecast*. Have another look at it. The cash forecast isn't just for the business plan; it's something you do regularly as part of your cash management. (*Tip:* A neat trick is to go back and compare your forecast with reality. To do this, just add another column for each month. One column is for projected figures, which you fill in before the fact, and the other is for actual figures, which you fill in from what really happened. Computerized bookkeeping systems will prepare this report for you in a jiffy. If you're too far off, you know you need to adjust future forecasts.)

Tax Planning

In addition to taking care of employee taxes, sales taxes, and other business taxes, you've got to deal with your own taxes. This is no place for an exhaustive treatise on income taxes, but a few tips are in order.

First, your tax situation will be very different when you're in business for yourself than it was when you were an employee. Before, the government (using your employer as an accomplice) just picked your pocket every week, and you got what was left over. At the end of the year, you probably filed a short-form tax return, maybe got a small refund, and that was that. Now, you'll be faced with a lengthy and complicated tax return, quarterly estimated tax payments (which also include social security contributions), and tax liabilities that may shock you if you don't anticipate them.

When you're in business, everything you do has tax consequences, and the prudent business owner thinks about taxes every time there's a decision to be made, no matter how small. He or she also visits the accountant toward the end of the year to estimate the taxes that will be due for the year. I go see my accountant in October or November, when there's still time to change my strategy if necessary.

Getting a Handle on Taxes

The IRS puts out a great, free book, revised annually and available online, called *Tax Guide for Small Business* (Publication 334) that gives you all the basics of income taxes for businesspeople. Get one and read it cover to cover. (*Tip:* The IRS has a website: www.irs.gov. It's got a whole section devoted to starting and operating a small business. It's friendly and it won't put you on hold.)

Who Has to File a Tax Return?

If your net earnings from self-employment exceed $400 in one year, you have to file a return, even if no taxes are due.

Tax Forms and Returns You Must Fill Out

You have to file the long Form 1040, U.S. Individual Income Tax Return, with some or all of these supporting schedules and forms. You may need others as well; check with your accountant.

- Schedule A: Itemized Deductions
- Schedule C: Profit or Loss from Business
- Form 4797: Sales of Business Property
- Form 8829: Expenses for Business Use of Your Home
- Form 4562: Depreciation and Amortization

Your state may require a separate set of tax returns, so check with them or your accountant. Visit http://www.irs.gov/Businesses/Small-Businesses-&-Self-Employed for great info on federal requirements.

What Kinds of Taxes Do You Have to Pay?

You'll pay federal (and possibly state) *income taxes* and federal *Self-Employment Tax* (the equivalent of social security tax, only you have to pay a much larger percentage than employees do).

Making Estimated Tax Payments

If you estimate that your combined federal taxes will exceed $1,000 in the current year, you have to pay *estimated taxes* every quarter. The payments are due April 15, June 15, September 15, and January 15. If your actual income is different from your estimated income, you have to adjust your payments accordingly. There are penalties for failing to pay estimated taxes and for underestimating them. Get IRS Publication 505, *Tax Withholding and Declaration of Estimated Tax* (www.irs.gov/pub/irs-pdf/p505.pdf) or talk with your accountant. Your state may also require estimated tax payments.

Planning for Growth

So many people who go into business fall for the notion that the only successful business is the one that gets big. Let me give you a piece of advice: Don't even think about getting big for at least three to four years. You'll learn a lot during that time and maybe your ideas about growth will change. If you still want to get big, come back and reread the following information.

The One-Big-Job Syndrome

Many's the contractor who was cruising along just fine when he or she decided to take on a Really Big Job. Maybe a good residential client offered the chance to bid on a shopping center development. Perhaps an opportunity came up to bid on a big commercial maintenance job. Whatever the source, big jobs are different critters than small ones, and they can be a death trap for the naive. Suddenly, the happy small businessperson is transformed into a panic-stricken basket case, unable to cope with his or her new responsibilities, to handle lots of employees, to control the quality of the work, to manage cash flow, or to complete jobs. Maybe he or she grossly underbid the job and got stuck with the consequences. Maybe something goes wrong—a serious accident, an unintentional legal transgression, or a major flaw in the work. Within days or weeks, the doors are closed, the business is bankrupt, and the entrepreneur is facing the loss of everything. It happens all the time, and it's not funny.

The Perils of Creeping Success

Even without a monumental opportunity coming your way, you may find your business growing faster than you can handle it, the result of all your fine work bringing you more new clients than you are really equipped to serve. It's easy to say yes to every job that comes along and one day find yourself buried and not keeping up with it all. Keep a constant eye on your workload and take on new work only if you are in a position to do it in a timely manner without shortchanging other clients.

Evaluating Your Ability to Get Big

Why do you want to get big? If it's to make a lot of money, be aware that it usually doesn't happen in this business. If you're good you'll make a nice living, but if you're looking to get rich, try some other line of work. If it's because you want to be a big shot, that's OK I suppose, but you've got to walk the walk, not just talk the talk. Bonafide big shots actually know how to run their operations; will you?

To get big, you've got to develop technical and management skills far beyond the basic ones that you've learned from this book. Believe me, you just have no idea how complex this business can be. Be prepared to go to school or spend a lot of time studying before you go beyond the cozy world of your little home-based, cottage-industry business.

You've also got to have access to plenty of money to get big, because you'll have to invest in equipment, increase your overhead, and finance those big jobs.

Finally, to make money on a big job, you've got to develop new, efficient methods for getting the work done in the least possible time. On a big job, there's little slack and little room for error. There's also no kindly, forgiving homeowner who'll let you slide when you screw up. If you swim with the sharks, you'd better have a good set of teeth. I'm not saying you shouldn't get big if you really want to; I'm just letting you know that the game changes and you need to be ready for it.

Planning for Retirement

I'm semi-retired these days. Yes, it's possible to retire from this business if you play your cards right and get a few lucky breaks along the way. I do a little design work, I teach professionals and give lectures to garden clubs and various other audiences, and I do some writing. I work a couple hours a day and putter in the yard and do volunteer work and loaf the rest of the time. I chuckle when I read what I wrote for this book so long ago now:

> To be honest, I haven't given much thought to retirement. For one thing, I'm not sure I could afford it! Besides, I love this business. It's more fun than anything I've ever done, and I just can't imagine quitting. I look forward to every new day, just to see what crazy thing is going to happen next. How do you beat that? Certainly not by sitting on the porch or watching soap operas! Then, too, I figure that by the time I'm sixty-five I'll just be getting good at this.
>
> Still, you do need to set aside some money for when you don't want to work any more, or can't. (*Tip:* You're not automatically protected by *disability insurance* the way employees are, so get yourself a good *disability policy*, just in case something awful happens.) Talk to your accountant about setting up an *IRA*, *Keogh Plan*, or *SEP IRA*, which are pension plans for the self-employed. Remember, too, that you're investing much of your money (maybe most of it) in a business that you can eventually sell.

That advice is still good. I've made it to 64, and at the moment I'm goofing off in the shade on my back patio on a weekday afternoon and feeling happy to be able to tell you that planning for a secure retirement does work and you can do it too. Just be prudent and don't live like a bigshot unless you've got some cash put aside for the future. I've lived a modest but very pleasant life, keeping my spending to a reasonable level, avoiding most of the temptations that come with success, and putting money aside for the future that I'm finally enjoying. I don't have (or want) a sailboat, a mountain cabin, or a fancy European sports car. I do have a little bit of security, a nice home that's all paid for, no debt, my health, and a pretty happy future to look forward to. That's enough for me.

In Conclusion

I'm sorry the book is finished because there's so much more I want to tell you. I know that if you've read this far, you really want to succeed, and I believe you will. I wish I could be there to help you on your great adventure and to share the excitement with you, because I remember the feeling, and it's the greatest thing in the world. I think it's best to conclude with a true story, one that happened to me a few years ago, that I will never forget. Maybe you'll enjoy it.

It was late Friday afternoon, and I had dragged myself out to a meeting with two of my best clients. It had been a pretty grueling week—a family medical emergency, the end of one job and the start of two others, car problems, a huge backlog of work, and no time for rest. I was exhausted and thought about canceling the meeting, but I went anyway.

These clients, both teachers, are some of the nicest people you'll find anywhere, and we had worked hard over a fifteen-year period to transform their property into a real showplace. Now, the flowers were blooming, the cats were running back and forth across the new footbridge, and the shade from the oak trees danced across the lawn. We were really enjoying our walk around the garden.

We paused down by the hammock, and Dennis said, "You know, recently Carolyn and I were both asked, independently of each other, where our favorite place was, and we both answered, without hesitation, 'Our garden!'" I remembered how their place looked the first time I saw it, and I knew why they appreciated it so much now.

I get that kind of feedback from people all the time, and it's always an emotional experience knowing that I helped people and made beautiful places for them to enjoy their lives. You'll get it, too, and I can't think of a better payoff for all your hard work. Learn your profession well, work hard, and have a great life. I'll be with you in spirit all the way. Good luck.

I'll close with a popular quote that has been misattributed to the great German writer Johann Wolfgang von Goethe (it's unclear exactly who first wrote this, as it appears to have been plagiarized several times over, but no matter, as it's a wonderful sentiment):

Until One Is Committed

> Until one is committed, there is hesitancy, the chance to draw back, always ineffectiveness. Concerning all acts of initiative (and creation) there is one elementary truth, the ignorance of which kills countless ideas and splendid

plans: that the moment one definitely commits oneself, then Providence moves too. All sorts of things occur to help one that would never otherwise have occurred. A whole stream of events issues from the decision, raising in one's favor all manner of unforeseen incidents and meetings and material assistance, which no man could have dreamed would have come his way.

Whatever you can do,
or dream you can, begin it.
Boldness has genius,
power and magic in it.

I love quotes, so I'll share a last one with you, from Henry Ford: "A business that makes nothing but money is a poor business." My personal philosophy has distilled down to three principles: Do some good, have some fun, make some money. That's it. You have to do all three, because if you skip one something important will be missing. Go forth, work hard, make money, do good, have fun, be happy, and make others happy. Your life will matter. Happy trails to you!

Appendix 1: Resources

Here are some knowledge tools for you to use in developing your career. There's a lot of information out there, too much to list in one place, but this section will give you a good sense of the kinds of information and resources that are available to you. You'll quickly see that you're not on your own, that there are lots of people you will never meet who are working hard to smooth your path and improve the odds of your success.

Trade and Professional Associations

The suppliers out our way have a saying: "When a landscape contractor is elected president of his trade association chapter, put him on C.O.D." That's a way of recognizing that people can get so wrapped up in doing volunteer work for their trade association that they ignore their business obligations, including paying their bills on time. Being a big fish in a small pond is seductive, and for some reason it's often more tempting to spend all day planning a conference than it is to spend it taking care of paying jobs. Still, trade and professional associations offer you a lot; you should join one and become involved as long as you can do so after you've taken care of your business responsibilities and not in place of them. The following organizations offer technical and management assistance, training, and certification programs; they conduct and promote research, publish magazines, print forms and contracts, promote the industry to the public and government, lobby to support favorable legislation, sponsor awards programs, and put on trade shows. Not all of these associations are on board with the latest in sustainable practices (some of them pretend to be while secretly supporting obsolete and environmentally harmful products and practices). I have indicated the organizations with a strong and proven commitment to sustainability by placing the word "DEEPGREEN" after the listing; that is a personal judgment call and is not meant to denigrate other organizations or to imply that they are bad guys (in some cases I may not have enough information to know for certain, and the missions of organizations change over time, sometimes in ways that are an improvement). Note that in addition to the associations listed below, most states have their own trade and professional associations, and many national associations have regional chapters.

For listings of international, national, and state associations on the Internet, see www.landscapeonline.com, dir.gardenweb.com/directory/nph-ind.cgi, or www.lawnandlandscape.com/AssociationSearch.aspx.

National and International Associations

Here are the prominent U.S. and Canadian national and international associations in the green industry. There are also organizations in nearly every state and numerous regional and local groups. If you're outside the United States and Canada, do a web search on "landscape association [name of region]." I've included the mission statements of the organizations so that you can get an idea of what they're up to. I've also included some non-profits that, while not membership groups per se, act on behalf of landscaping professionals in some way.

American Community Garden Association, (877) ASK-ACGA, www.communitygarden.org ("The Mission of the American Community Gardening Association is to build community by increasing and enhancing community gardening and greening across the United States and Canada.")

American Horticultural Society, (703) 768-5700, www.ahs.org ("Making America a nation of gardeners, a land of gardens.")

American Horticultural Therapy Association, (610) 992-0020, www.ahta.org ("The American Horticultural Therapy Association is the only U.S. organization committed to promoting and developing the practice of horticultural therapy.")

AmericanHort, (614) 487-1117, www.americanhort.org ("Our vision is to be the leading and unifying organization for the horticulture industry in order to cultivate successful businesses, and for our industry to enhance lives through the benefits of plants.")

American Rainwater Catchment Systems Association, (512) 617-6528, www.arcsa.org ("The mission of The American Rainwater Catchment Systems Association is to promote sustainable rainwater harvesting practices to help solve potable, non-potable, stormwater and energy challenges throughout the world.") DEEPGREEN

American Society of Consulting Arborists, (301) 947–0483, www.asca-consultants.org ("The American Society of Consulting Arborists (ASCA) is the industry's premier professional association focusing solely on arboricultural consulting.")

American Society for Horticultural Science, (703) 836-4606, www.ashs.org ("The mission of ASHS is to promote and encourage national and international interest in scientific research and education in horticulture in all its branches.")

American Society of Irrigation Consultants, (508) 763-8140, www.asic.org ("The mission of the society is to enhance the role of the independent professional irrigation consultant as the unbiased advocate of the client.")

American Society of Landscape Architects, (202) 898–2444, www.asla.org ("For more than 100 years, ASLA has promoted the practice of landscape architecture and advanced the profession through advocacy, education, communication, and fellowship.") DEEPGREEN

Association of Professional Landscape Designers, (717) 238-9780, www.apld.com ("Our mission is to advance the profession of landscape design and to promote the recognition of landscape designers as qualified and dedicated professionals.")

Canadian Nursery Landscape Association, (905) 875-1399, www.canadanursery.com ("The purpose of CNLA is to foster relationships and alliances, provide member certification and help its members function more effectively.")

Ecological Landscape Alliance, (617) 436-5838, www.ecolandscaping.org ("The Ecological Landscape Alliance is a nonprofit, member-based organization made up of professionals, businesses and pro-active community members who believe in using landscape practices that are environmentally safe and beneficial.") DEEPGREEN

International Erosion Control Association, (800) 455-4322, www.ieca.org ("The International Erosion Control Association (IECA) is the world's oldest and largest association devoted to helping members solve the problems caused by erosion and its byproduct—sediment.")

International Society of Arboriculture, (217) 355-9411, www.isa-arbor.com ("Through research, technology, and education, the International Society of Arboriculture promotes the professional practice of arboriculture and fosters a greater worldwide awareness of the benefits of trees.")

Irrigation Association, (705) 536–7080, www.irrigation.org ("IA is the leading membership organization for irrigation companies and professionals. We help our members grow with networking, education and certification, while working to protect your interests.")

National Arbor Day Foundation, (888) 448–7337, www.arborday.org ("We inspire people to plant, nurture, and celebrate trees.")

National Hispanic Landscape Alliance, (877) 260-7955, www.masverde.us ("The National Hispanic Landscape Alliance seeks to inform, encourage, and support its members so that they can become highly successful professionals, better-engaged leaders, and more effective advocates." Seems like a good group but hostile statements about "so-called environmentalists" put me off.)

NOFA Organic Land Care Program, (203) 308-2584, www.organiclandcare.net ("Organic Land Care, Naturally Beautiful") DEEPGREEN

Oregon Tilth Organic Land Care Accreditation Program, (503) 378-0690, www.tilth.org/partners/organic-land-care-accreditation-program ("The OLC program works to offer tools and market opportunities for landscape professionals to work under organic principles.") DEEPGREEN

Professional Grounds Management Society, (800) 609–PGMS, www.pgms.org ("The purpose of PGMS is to unite professional grounds managers and those interested in or providing service to the grounds management industry, to promote the dissemination of educational materials and reliable information pertinent to the execution of grounds management functions, and to assist in attaining and maintaining a high standard of business ethics.")

Professional Landcare Network ("PLANET"), (800) 395–2522, www.landcarenetwork.org ("To advance and communicate the interests of PLANET's members in the conduct of effective and environmentally responsible landscape services.")

Snow & Ice Management Association, (414) 375-1940, www.sima.org ("SIMA provides resources, leadership and support for snow removal and management professionals across North America. It is a non-profit trade association with a focus on training related to snow plowing, ice management, and business management.")

Tree Care Industry Association, (800) 733-2622, www.tcia.org ("Our mission is to advance tree care businesses.")

Schools

Many community colleges offer programs in *landscape horticulture* (also called *ornamental horticulture* or *environmental horticulture)* that will give you the basic skills you'll need to get started. More advanced programs are available at some state colleges and universities. There are also private educational institutions that have programs in horticulture. As far as I can tell there's no central directory of these programs, but a quick web search should turn up something in your area. Landscape architecture programs are offered at many universities; for a complete list visit www.asla.org/schools.aspx.

Trade Shows

Contact your trade association for information about *trade shows*. Companies and organizations that supply and support the profession have booths at these usually annual events. Going to a trade show is a great way to learn about new products, schmooze with salespeople and other contractors, pick everybody's brains, and have a good time. Anybody who doesn't take advantage of this resource, especially when starting a company, is missing an important business opportunity.

Magazines and Periodicals

There are so many resources available online these days that old-fashioned paper magazines seem irrelevant. But there's a lot to be said for using whatever educational resources are available, so don't discount magazines. And keep in mind that many if not most of the magazines listed offer digital editions. Here's a listing of prominent publications for professionals and general interest audiences.

Trade Magazines

Many trade and professional magazines are sent free to qualified companies in the hope that they'll buy lots of stuff from the advertisers. Others are paid subscriptions the same as regular magazines. Some will give you a free subscription even though they offer paid ones, so be sure to ask before you send in your money. In addition to the magazines listed, most trade and professional associations publish their own magazines; many of them are excellent. Most trade publications are now available online as well as in print. (*Tip*: Some of the articles in trade magazines are written by the companies who advertise in the magazine. Take the claims made with a grain of salt and realize that they're often thinly veiled advertising. Still, you can learn a lot, as long as you retain a healthy dose of skepticism.)

American Nurseryman, (802) 748-8908, www.amerinursery.com ("Covering commercial horticulture since 1904")

Arbor Age, (847) 720-5613, www.arborage.com ("*Arbor Age* targets arborists in the commercial, municipal and utility sectors.")

Arborist News; International Society of Arboriculture, (888) 472-8733, www.isa-arbor.com/education/publications/arboristNews.aspx ("*Arborist News*, a bimonthly ISA magazine, provides the latest in arboricultural news and education.")

Environmental Design & Construction, (248) 244–6258, www.edcmag.com ("The official magazine for the LEED Professional")

Erosion Control, (805) 682–1300, www.erosioncontrol.com ("Official journal of the International Erosion Control Association")

Green Industry Pros, www.greenindustrypros.com ("Products, Trends, and Strategies for Business Leaders")

Grounds Maintenance, www.grounds-mag.com ("Grounds Maintenance is the web's most popular source of information for grounds maintenance professionals.")

IPM Practitioner, (510) 524-2567, www.birc.org ("The IPM Practitioner focuses on management alternatives for pests such as insects, mites, ticks, vertebrates, weeds and plant pathogens.")

Landscape Architecture, (202) 898–2444, www.asla.org/lamsubscription.aspx ("The Magazine of the American Society of Landscape Architects")

Landscape Management, (847) 763-4942, www.landscapemanagement.net

Landscape Trades, (647) 723-5305, www.landscapetrades.com ("Canada's Premier Horticultural Trade Publication")

Lawn & Landscape, (800) 456-0707, www.lawnandlandscape.com ("For more than 30 years, *Lawn & Landscape* has equipped landscape contractors and lawn care operators with the critical information needed to grow their businesses.")

Total Landscape Care, www.totallandscapecare.com ("Our coverage of landscaping ideas, landscape design, how-to's, equipment, and business best-practices is focused on helping lawn and landscape professionals run their businesses more successfully and more profitably.")

Turf Magazine, (802) 748-8908, www.turfmagazine.com ("Serving Landscape and Lawn Care Professionals")

General Interest Gardening Magazines

These are available on the newsstand or by subscription. Although they're aimed at the general public, there's a lot of good information in them. Note that there are also a number of regional and local gardening magazines not listed here.

Common Sense Pest Control Quarterly, (510) 524-2567, www.birc.org ("Common Sense Pest Control Quarterly features least-toxic solutions to pest problems of the home and garden.")

Fine Gardening, (203) 426–8171, www.finegardening.com ("We're where plant lovers go to get the very best hands-on gardening advice, in-depth information and garden design inspiration.")

Garden Design, 855-624-5110; www.gardendesign.com ("The Magazine of Outdoor Design + Garden Aesthetics").

Garden Gate; (800) 341-4769, www.gardengatemagazine.com ("The Illustrated Guide to Home Gardening and Design®")

Horticulture, (513) 531-2690, www.hortmag.com ("The Art and Science of Smart Gardening").

Pacific Horticulture, (510) 849-1627, www.pacifichorticulture.org (". . . publishes quarterly with in-depth articles and regular departments focusing on plants, gardens, design, and concern for the environment.")

Southern Living, (205) 445-6000, www.southernliving.com ("Southern Living celebrates the best of life in the South.")

State-by-State Gardening, 888-265-3600, www.statebystategardening.com ("State by State Gardening publishes gardening magazines for 16 states or regions.")

Sunset, The Magazine of Western Living, (800) 777-0117, www.sunset.com ("Published monthly, Sunset shares the best of life in the West—from travel and food to home and garden—with our nearly five million readers.").

Books, Videos, and Software

Here is a basic list of books and other resources. The Internet dominates many people's reading these days, but books often contain information not found online, so don't overlook these valuable tools. Budget a little money each year to invest in books; they'll be some of your best friends in your business. Don't forget that you can check out a lot of these books from your public library at no cost, and then buy just the ones you feel you really need. Many titles are available as e-books at a lower cost than the print versions. Of course there are the mega-sites like Amazon and Barnes & Noble, but the resources listed here are more focused and often carry unique items. Try to buy from small local businesses when you can; remember, you are one.

Bookstores for Landscape Professionals

Here are some one-stop sources for a wide range of books and other information for landscapers. Check with your state or regional trade association for more possibilities including regional titles not available nationally.

American Nurseryman Publishing Co., www.amerinursery.com

California Landscape Contractors Association, (916) 830–2780, www.clca.org (Numerous publications at the store link of the "professional" section of their site.)

Landscape Management Bookshop, www.landscapemanagement.net/shop

Nilsson Books, (866) 280-2252, www.nilssonbooks.com ("Profit Building Books for Landscapers by Phil Nilsson.")

PLANET, (800) 395-2522, www.landcarenetwork.org (Go to "marketplace.")

San Luis Video Publishing, www.horticulturevideos.com

University of California Agriculture & Natural Resources, (530) 750-1370, http://www.ipm.ucdavis.edu/IPMPROJECT/pubsmenu.html (Loads of info on integrated pest management and related topics. Not just for California.)

Vander Kooi & Associates, (303) 697-6467, www.vanderkooi.com/books.htm (Industry consulting firm offering a wide variety of management resources. Nothing else like it, and well worth a look.)

Bookstores for the Construction Industry (most with sections on landscaping)

BNI Building News, (888) 264-2665, www.bnibooks.com

Book Depository.com, www.bookdepository.com/category/1066/Construction-Industry

Bookworkz, (800) 997-2922, www.bookworkz.com

Builders Book Depot, (800)284-3434; www.buildersbookdepot.com.

Builders Bookloft. (888) 810-8296, www.nwbuildnet.com/stores/bookloft

Builders Booksource, (800) 843-2028, www.buildersbooksource.com

Construction Book Express, (888) 264-2665, www.constructionbook.com

Bookstores for General Business Management

American Management Association, (212) 903-8416, www.amaconferencecenter.org/bookstores.htm

Entrepreneur Bookstore, (800) 421-2300, https://bookstore.entrepreneur.com

Project Management Bookstore, www.projectmanagementbookstore.com

Bookstores for Gardening and Landscaping

Chicago Botanic Garden, (847) 835-8336, shop.chicagobotanic.org/a551/?product_type=185

Garden Gate Bookstore, (800) 341-4769, www.gardengatestore.com/books

Hennesssey & Ingalls, (310) 458-9074, www.hennesseyingalls.com/Landscape.aspx

Northshire Bookstore, (800) 437-3700, www.northshire.com/gardening

Powell's City of Books, (800) 878-7323, www.powells.com/subjects/home-and-garden/gardening

State-by-State Gardening Bookstore, (318) 255-3149, statebystategardening.com/shop

Taunton Store, (866) 325-2495, www.tauntonstore.com/gardening.html

Timber Press, (800) 327-5680, www.timberpress.com

Management Books for the Landscaping Industry

Bass, Anthony C. *The E-Myth Landscape Contractor*. Carlsbad, CA: Prodigy Business Books, http://www.prodigybusinessbooks.com/e-myth-books/the-e-myth-landscape-contractor.html.

California Landscape Contractors Association. *Landscape Data Manual Revised Edition (2000)*. Sacramento, CA: California Landscape Contractors Association, 2000; www.clca.org. (Excellent set of all kinds of tables you'll use every day—soil volumes for different size holes; coverage for plants, mulches, and so forth; time studies; capacities of equipment; lots more. Must have.)

Cohan, Steven M. PhD. *Business Principles of Landscape Contracting, 2nd Ed*. Professional Landcare Network, Inc., www.isgweb.landcarenetwork.org/isgweb/Purchase/ProductDetail.aspx?Product_code=RB-0106.

Fee, Sylvia Hollman. *Means Landscape Estimating Methods, 5th Edition*. Hoboken, NJ: John Wiley & Sons, Inc., 2007; www.wiley.com. (Good bidding information for beginners and veterans.)

Hensley, David L. *Professional Landscape Management*. Champaign, IL: Stipes Publishing, LLC, 2010, http://www.stipes.com/catalog/horticulture/professional-landscape-management/29.

Lerner, Joel. *Landscape Professionals Marketing and Sourcebook*. Chevy Chase, MD: Joel M. Lerner Environmental Design, www.gardenlerner.com/books.html.

PLANET. *2010 Employee Compensation Report*. Professional Landcare Network, Inc., 2010, www.landcarenetwork.org.

———. *Blueprint for Success: Proven Systems Design/Build*. Professional Landcare Network, Inc., 2003, www.landcarenetwork.org.

———. Guide to Growing a Successful Landscape Maintenance Business. Professional Landcare Network, Inc., 2004, www.landcarenetwork.org.

———. Guide to Growing a Successful Lawncare Business. Professional Landcare Network, Inc., www.landcarenetwork.org.

Professional Grounds Maintenance Society. *Grounds Maintenance Estimating Guideline, 8th Edition*. Baltimore, MD: Professional Grounds Maintenance Society, www.pgms.org/online-store.

———. *Grounds Maintenance Management Guidelines*. Baltimore, MD: Professional Grounds Maintenance Society, www.pgms.org/online-store.

———. *Grounds Management Forms and Job Descriptions Guide*. Baltimore, MD: Professional Grounds Maintenance Society, www.pgms.org/online-store.

R.S. Means. *Site Work & Landscape Cost Data 2014*. Norwell, MA: R.S. Means, 2014, www.rsmeans.com. (Expensive, definitive cost data for the landscaping industry.)

Thomsett, Michael C. *Builder's Guide to Accounting Revised.* Carlsbad, CA: Craftsman Book Co., www.craftsman-book.com. (Many other titles available from this publisher.)

Walker, Nathan, Edward N. Walker, and Theodor K. Rohdenburg. *Legal Pitfalls in Architecture, Engineering and Building Construction.* New York: McGraw Hill Book Co., 1979. (Out of print, but worth looking for.)

Whitten, Bob R. *Building Partnerships: How to Work with Trade Contractors.* NAHB Builder Books, 1999, www.builderbooks.com.

Books on General Business Management

Try searching online for "best business books." You'll find an almost overwhelming number of titles. Here are some that have helped me, or that are well-received by others. Keep in mind that managing a small business is much different from managing a big corporation, so don't bother with books aimed at the big operations.

Brabec, Barbara. *Homemade Money: Bringing in the Bucks! A Business Management and Marketing Bible for Home-Business Owners, Self-Employed Individuals and Web Entrepreneurs Working from Home Base.* New York: M. Evans and Company, Inc., 2003, www.barbarabrabec.com/homemade_money.htm.

Entrepreneur Media. *Start Your Own Business: The Only Book You'll Ever Need, 5th Edition.* Irvine, CA: Entrepreneur Press, 2010, www.entrepreneur.com/entrepreneurpress.

Fishman, Stephen. *Deduct It!: Lower Your Small Business Taxes, 10th Edition.* Berkeley, CA: Nolo Press, 2013, www.nolo.com.

Harroch, Richard D. *Small Business Kit for Dummies.* Hoboken, NJ: Wiley Publishing, Inc., 2004, www.dummies.com.

Hawken, Paul. *Growing a Business.* New York, NY: Simon and Schuster, 1988, www.simonandschuster.com/search/books. (An inspiring classic from a fine thinker.)

Kamoroff, Bernard. *Small Time Operator, 13th Edition.* Boulder, CO: Taylor Trade Publishing, 2013, www.rowman.com/TaylorTrade. (Classic book on starting a small business. Must have.)

Levinson, Jay Conrad. *Guerrilla Marketing: Secrets for Making Big Profits from Your Small Business, 4th edition.* New York: Mariner Books, 2007, www.gmarketing.com/gm-store.

Phillips, Michael, and Salli Rasberry. *Marketing Without Advertising, 6th edition.* Berkeley, CA: Nolo Press, 2008, www.nolo.com.

Steingold, Fred S. *The Legal Guide for Starting and Running a Small Business, 13th edition.* Berkeley, CA: Nolo Press, 2013, www.nolo.com.

Strauss, Steven D. *The Small Business Bible: Everything You Need to Know to Succeed in Your Small Business, 3rd Edition*. Hoboken, NJ: Wiley Publishing, Inc., 2012, www.wiley.com.

Tyson, Eric, and Jim Schell. *Small Business For Dummies, 4th Edition*. Hoboken, NJ: Wiley Publishing, Inc., 2011, www.dummies.com. (Check out the many excellent small business books in the Dummies series.)

Weltman, Barbara. *J.K. Lasser's Small Business Taxes 2015: Your Complete Guide to a Better Bottom Line*. Hoboken, NJ: J.K. Lasser, 2015, www.jklasser.com.

Whitmyer, Claude, Salli Rasberry, and Michael Phillips. *Running a One-Person Business, 2nd edition*. New York: Ten Speed Press, 1994, www.crownpublishing.com/imprint/ten-speed-press. (Out of print; available used.)

Books on Horticultural and Landscaping Subjects

There is so much out there to choose from that it's hard to know where to start. Here is a list of some of my favorites.

Booth, Norman K. *Basic Elements of Landscape Architectural Design*. Long Grove, IL: Waveland Press, 1989, www.waveland.com.

Brown, George E., and Tony Kirkham. *The Pruning of Trees, Shrubs and Conifers*. Portland, OR: Timber Press, 2004, www.timberpress.com.

Creasy, Rosalind. *Edible Landscaping*. Berkeley, CA: Counterpoint Press, 2010, www.rosalindcreasy.com.

Dannenberger, T. Karl PhD. *Turfgrass Ecology and Management*. Valley View, OH: Lawn & Landscape Magazine, www.lawnandlandscape.com.

Dell, Owen E. *Sustainable Landscaping for Dummies*. Hoboken, NJ: Wiley Publishing, Inc., 2009, www.dummies.com. (Overview of sustainable landscaping practices, with plenty of technical details. My very favorite book on sustainable landscaping.)

Dirr, Michael. *Manual of Woody Landscape Plants, 6th edition*. Champaign, IL: Stipes, 2009, www.stipes.com.

Goodnick, Billy. *Yards: Turn Any Outdoor Space Into the Garden of Your Dreams*. Pittsburgh, PA: St. Lynn's Press, 2013, www.stlynnspress.com. (Humorous introduction to garden design that will set you on the right path.)

Hemenway, Toby. *Gaia's Garden Second Edition: A Guide to Home-Scale Permaculture*. White River Junction, VT: Chelsea Green Publishing, 2008, www.chelseagreen.com.

Hopper, Leonard J. *Landscape Architectural Graphic Standards*. New York: John Wiley & Sons, Inc., 2006, www.wiley.com. (Pricey but hugely valuable collection of construction details, standards, and other essential information. You'll learn a lot.)

Horticopia. *Horticopia* (several versions on CD/Flash Drive). Harwood, MD: Horticopia, Inc., various dates, www.horticopia.com. (Plant images and other information.)

Jabbour, Niki. *Groundbreaking Food Gardens: 73 Plans That Will Change the Way You Grow Your Garden*. North Adams, MA: Storey Publishing, 2014, www.storey.com.

Kourik, Robert. *Designing and Maintaining Your Edible Landscape Naturally*. Occidental, CA: Permanent Publications, 2004, www.robertkourik.com.

———. *Drip Irrigation for Every Landscape and All Climates, 2nd Edition*. Occidental, CA: Metamorphic Press, 2009, www.robertkourik.com.

———. *Roots Demystified*. Occidental, CA: Metamorphic Press, 2008, www.robertkourik.com.

Kramer, Richard, PhD. *Lawn and Landscape Technician's Handbook*. Valley View, OH, Lawn & Landscape Magazine, www.lawnandlandscape.com.

Lancaster, Brad. *Rainwater Harvesting for Drylands and Beyond* (3 volumes). Tucson, AZ: Rainsource Press, 2006-08, www.harvestingrainwater.com.

Landscape Contractors Association. *Landscape Specification Guidelines, 6th Edition*. Rockville MD: Landscape Contractors Association, 2000, www.lcamddcva.org/about/publications.cfm. (Standard reference for landscape construction. Available at Amazon.com.)

Ludwig, Art. *Create an Oasis with Greywater, 5th Edition*. Santa Barbara, CA: Oasis Design, 2006, www. oasisdesign.net.

———. *Principles of Ecological Design*. Santa Barbara, CA: Oasis Design, 2003, www.oasisdesign.net.

———. *Water Storage: Tanks, Cisterns, Aquifers, and Ponds*. Santa Barbara, CA: Oasis Design, 2007, www.oasisdesign.net.

Marrow, Rosemary. *Earth User's Guide to Permaculture, 2nd Edition*. Permanent Publications, 2006, http://permanentpublications.co.uk.

McHarg, Ian. *Design With Nature*. John Wiley & Sons, Inc., 1995, www.wiley.com. (Considered by many to be the most important book on landscape design. For landscape architects, but you'll get a good education on ecological design from this classic.)

Melby, Pete. *Simplified Irrigation Design, 2nd edition*. New York: John Wiley & Sons, Inc., 1995, www.wiley.com. (Everything you need to know about irrigation design and installation.)

Mollison, Bill, and R. M. Slay. *Introduction to Permaculture*. Sister's Creek, Tasmania,

Australia: Tagari Publications, 1997, www.tagari.com. (Basic reference on this important topic.)

———. *Permaculture: A Designer's Manual.* Sister's Creek, Tasmania, Australia: Tagari Publications, 1997, www.tagari.com. (Massive, definitive reference on permaculture.)

Nelson, Lewis S. *Handbook of Poisonous and Injurious Plants.* New York: Springer U.S., 2007, www.springer.com. (Always screen your planting designs for poisonous plants and inform the client in writing if you plan to use any. This book will help.)

Reid, Grant. *Landscape Graphics.* New York: Crown Publishing, 2002, www.crownpublishing.com. (How to draw landscape plans like a pro.)

Sauter, David. *Landscape Construction, Second Edition.* Independence, KY: Cengage Learning, 2005, www.cengage.com.

Schuttner, Scott. *Building and Designing Decks (For Pros by Pros).* Newtown, CT: Taunton Press, 1998, www.taunton.com.

Sunset Western Garden Book. Menlo Park, CA: Sunset Books, Inc., 8th Edition, 2007, www.sunset.com. (Focus is on plants and basic gardening techniques. The bible of western gardeners. Must have if you live in the west. Also available: *Sunset National Garden Book,* 2001, and *Sunset Northeast Garden Book,* 2001.)

Sunset Western Landscaping Book, 2006 Revised Edition. Menlo Park, CA: Sunset Books, Inc., 2006, www.sunset.com. (Focus is on basic landscape design and construction, and design ideas. Also available: *Sunset Midwestern Landscaping Book,* 2001, *Sunset Northeast Landscaping Book,* 2000.)

Thompson, J. William, and Kim Sorvig. *Sustainable Landscape Construction, 2nd Edition.* Washington, D.C.: Island Press, 2007, www.islandpress.com. (The latest information on ecologically sound landscaping practices. Essential reading.)

Tukey, Paul. *The Organic Lawn Care Manual.* North Adams, MA: Storey Publishing, LLC, 2007, www.storey.com.

Wang, Thomas C. *Plan and Section Drawing.* New York: John Wiley & Sons, Inc., 1996, www.wiley.com. (Classic drafting reference. See also *Pencil Sketching,* 2001.)

Wyman, Donald. *Wyman's Gardening Encyclopedia.* New York: Simon & Schuster, 1987, www.simonsays.com. (Thorough, concise, easy to use.)

Software

As with most aspects of modern life, there is plenty of software out there that claims to help you run your landscaping business more efficiently and make more money. I can't claim to be an expert on this subject, but I do want you to have access to some of the major players in this game. I offer the following information without any endorsement of the products mentioned. Thoroughly evaluate any software before you buy it, particularly if it is something like a complete management package that will be central to your operation. Some of these products are pricey; consider the overall cost, taking into account the cost of doing things manually versus automating. It's worth it to invest big bucks in something if it improves service and fattens up the bottom line, but you can't be sure if that will be the case. Work with a demo version before buying.

"Best of" Reviews

Here are some sites that gather up products they feel are worthy of consideration. My experience has been that the .com sites sometimes offer paid reviews and therefore are not always entirely credible; however, I include them because they provide quick access to some of the players in the field, including some potentially worthy products that I don't mention in the Individual Vendors section below, and some of these sites may indeed be objective. Use your own judgment.

American Society of Landscape Architects, www.asla.org/software.aspx (An array of design software for pros.)
Landscape Design Advice, www.landscape-design-advice.com/best-landscape-design-software.html#.VHYCJ1fF-7Y (Reviews of design software.)
Software Advice, www.softwareadvice.com (Reviews of management packages.)
Top Landscape Software Products, www.capterra.com/landscape-software
Top Ten Reviews, http://landscaping-software-review.toptenreviews.com

Individual Vendors

Boss LM (The Integra Group, www.bosslm.com) Management package.
Canvas (Canvas Solutions, Inc., www.gocanvas.com) Packages for many industries, including landscaping.
Dynascape Manage360 (Dynascape, www.dynascape.com/manage360)
GardenSoft (GardenSoft, www.gardensoft.com). Plant selection software.
Gopher (Ditech, www.gophersoftware.com) Billing and scheduling software.
Groundskeeper (Adkad Technologies, www.adkad.com) Automated package for all segments of the landscaping business.
Jobber (Octopusapp, Inc., www.getjobber.com/industry/landscaping) Scheduling and invoicing.
LandF/X (Ecografx, Inc., www.landfx.com) Landscape and irrigation design software.

Landscape Management Network (Landscape Management Network, www.golmn.com) Another broad-spectrum package.
ProLandscape Design Software (Draftix Software, Inc., www.prolandscape.com)
QXpress & EverGreen (Marathon Data Systems, LLC, www.marathondata.com/lawn-landscape)
Realtime Landscaping (Idea Spectrum, www.ideaspectrum.com) Design software.
Service Autopilot (Backtell, LLC, www.serviceautopilot.com/landscaping-software) Management package.
SlicePlus (Slice Technologies, www.sliceplus.com) Management package.
Yardbook (Enercloud, LLC, www.yardbook.com) Management package.

Internet Resources

Oh, the Internet. What a bottomless cornucopia of valuable information and utter nonsense! We can't live without it, and you will find much of value to you as a landscape professional and entrepreneur. Here are some websites that I've found helpful or intriguing. Be sure to pay special attention to the "links" listings because they contain far more resources than it's possible to publish here.

Business Internet Resources

Don't stop with this book. Your development as a business owner is a never-ending journey. There's a lot of stuff on the web for business people. Some of it is geared for the corporate world and won't be of much use to you. Some of it is exploitative or just pure nonsense. But there are plenty of useful sites for little guys like us.

Web Resources for Small Business

AboutMoney, http://sbinformation.about.com/od/bizopportunities/a/startup101.htm
All Business, www.allbusiness.com
BusinessUSA, www.business.usa.gov
Entrepreneur, www.entrepreneur.com
Entrepreneur Resources, www.entrepreneur-resources.net
Entrepreneurship.org, www.entrepreneurship.org
National Federation of Independent Business, www.nfib.com
Nolo Press, www.nolo.com/legal-encyclopedia/start-own-business-50-things-30077.html
Service Corps of Retired Executives ("SCORE"), www.score.org
U.S. Department of Labor Small Business Resource Center, www.dol.gov/oasam/programs/osdbu/sbrefa/main.htm

U.S. Environmental Protection Agency, www.epa.gov/compliance/resources/publications/incentives/smallbusiness/smallbusresources.pdf

U.S. Internal Revenue Service Small Business and Self-Employed Tax Center, www.irs.gov/Businesses/Small-Businesses-&-Self-Employed/Small-Business-and-Self-Employed-Tax-Center-1

U.S. Occupational Health & Safety Administration ("OSHA"), www.osha.gov/dcsp/smallbusiness

U.S. Small Business Administration, www.sba.gov

Small Business & Entrepreneurship Blogs

BigCommerce, http://blog.bigcommerce.com/17-marketing-blogs-every-small-business-owner-should-read

Blogrank, www.blogmetrics.org/small_business (Blogs ranked by popularity.)

Business Insider, www.businessinsider.com/24-must-read-blogs-for-entrepreneurs-2012-6#quora-1

FitSmallBusiness, http://fitsmallbusiness.com/small-business-blogs (List of "best" blogs.)

Small Business Trends, http://smallbiztrends.com/2012/09/blogs-small-business-should-read.html

Landscaping Business Blogs

Landscape Leadership, www.landscapeleadership.com/blog

Landscape Management Network, www.golmn.com/blog

Voice of the Green Industry, www.voiceofthegreenindustry.org/blog

Landscaping and Horticultural Internet Resources

Sites with Great Links

American Society of Landscape Architects, www.asla.org/ppnlinks.aspx (Impressive resources for designers.)

BuildingOnline, www.buildingonline.com (Mainly a building industry site with some landscaping links.)

Gardens.com, www.gardens.com

Green Pages: The Global Directory for Environmental Technology, www.eco-web.com (Environmental products and services from 136 countries.)

Green Media Online, www.greenmediaonline.com (A commercial site with a lot of advertising, comprehensive links page.)

Landscape Management, http://landscapemanagement.net/resources/industry-links (Industry site.)

San Marcos Growers, www.smgrowers.com (A wholesale nursery with extensive links on their resources page.)
The WWW Virtual Library for Gardening, www.gardenweb.com/vl (Thorough listings by subject, discussion groups, association listings.)

Sites for Specific Categories

This list will give you an idea of some good sites in some key categories. There are lots more, so don't limit yourself to these.

General Gardening Sites

Many of these websites are oriented toward the home gardener, but there is good information for professionals, too, especially those who are just starting out.

About.com, http://gardening.about.com
American Gardener, www.ahs.org/gardening-resources/gardening-publications/the-american-gardener
Brooklyn Botanic Garden, www.bbg.org/gardening
Cornell University, www.gardening.cornell.edu
Dave's Garden, www.davesgarden.com
GardenWeb, www.gardenweb.com
HGTV, www.hgtv.com/design/topics/gardening
Houzz, www.houzz.com/ideabooks/Gardening
Master Gardening Programs, www.ahs.org/gardening-resources/master-gardeners
Missouri Botanical Gardens, www.missouribotanicalgarden.org
National Gardening Association, www.garden.org
Organic Gardening Magazine, www.organicgardening.com
Pinterest, www.pinterest.com/all/gardening
Reddit Gardening, www.communitygarden.org
Sunset Magazine, www.sunset.com
USDA Home and Garden Bulletins, www.nal.usda.gov/ref/USDApubs/hgb.htm

Landscaping Idea Sites

These are about ideas for creating and managing landscapes.

Better Homes and Gardens, www.bhg.com/gardening/landscaping-projects
Country Living, www.countryliving.com/outdoor/garden-tours/landscaping-ideas#slide-1
DIY Network, www.diynetwork.com/topics/landscaping/index.html

Energy.goc, www.energy.gov/public-services/homes/landscaping
HGTV, www.hgtv.com/design/topics/landscaping
Homedit, www.homedit.com/30-wonderful-backyard-landscaping-ideas
Houzz, www.houzz.com/photos/landscape
Landscaping Ideas Online, www.landscapingideasonline.com
Landscaping Network, www.landscapingnetwork.com
Pinterest, www.pinterest.com/Remodelaholic/landscape-ideas
Southern Living, www.southernliving.com/home-garden/gardens/10-best-yard-landscaping-ideas
Sunset Magazine, www.sunset.com/garden/landscaping-design

Lawn Care

Some of these websites have great material on natural and organic lawn care, something that the industry as a whole still pretty much ignores.

Eartheasy: Solutions for Sustainable Living, www.eartheasy.com/grow_lawn_care.htm (Good tips.)
Natural Lawn of America, www.naturalawn.com (Franchise lawn care company.)
NOFA, www.organiclandcare.net/education/introduction-olc#just%20lawn%20and%20turf (Lots of articles, videos, books, and an accreditation program. Kinda awesome!)
North Carolina State University-TurfFiles, www.turffiles.ncsu.edu (NC-centric but good info for all areas)
Organic Gardening, www.organicgardening.com/learn-and-grow/organic-lawn-problem-solver
Planet Natural, www.planetnatural.com/organic-lawn-care-101 (Useful basics for homeowners.)
Safelawns.org, www.safelawns.org/blog (Great advocacy site.)
Seattle Public Utilities Natural Lawn Care Program, www.seattle.gov/util/environmentconservation/mylawngarden/lawncare (Some good links.)

Irrigation and Water Management

Here are some training sites to help you design irrigation systems and manage water properly. Don't overlook the sites of the major irrigation manufacturers like Toro, Rainbird, Hunter, and so on; they offer essential information on system design.

Alliance for Water Efficiency, www.allianceforwaterefficiency.org (Look in Resource Library for "Landscape and Irrigation.")

American Rainwater Catchment Systems Association, www.arcsa.org (Good info on rainwater harvesting.)
Irrigation Association, www.irrigation.org (Trade group for irrigation pros. Offers certification programs.)
Irrigation Training & Research Center, www.itrc.org (Cal Poly University's comprehensive irrigation site.)
Jess Stryker's Landscape Irrigation Tutorials, www.irrigationtutorials.com (Very helpful online training.)
LSU Ag Center, www.lsuagcenter.com/en/our_offices/departments/Biological_Ag_Engineering/Features/Extension/Agriculture_and_Environment/Irrigation/Irrigation-Basics-for-Irrigation-Landscape-Contractors_seriespage-2.htm (Irrigation basics with good graphics. From Louisiana State University.)
Rainbird Academy, www.rainbirdservices.com (Training programs from major irrigation manufacturer.)
Water Educational Training Services, www.wetscourses.com (Private training institute.)
Wateright, www.wateright.org (From the Center for Irrigation Technology in California.)
Watersense, www.epa.gov/watersense/outdoor/irrigation_professionals.html (A professional certification program of the U.S. Environmental Protection Agency.)

Soils and Composting

These websites offer soil management information and guidance on how to make and use compost. Check with your state's Cooperative Extension Service for localized resources.

City Farmer, www.cityfarmer.org (Lots of good info on this subject and more. See also their newer site at www.cityfarmer.info.)
Landscape for Life, www.landscapeforlife.org/soil (Part of Sustainable Sites Initiative.)
Composting Council of Canada, www.compost.org
Cornell Waste Management Institute, http://cwmi.css.cornell.edu
Natural Resources Conservation Service USDA Soil Quality Institute, www.nrcs.usda.gov/wps/portal/nrcs/main/soils/health
Soil Foodweb, Inc, www.soilfoodweb.com (Website for soil scientist Dr. Elaine Ingham, who knows a lot about soil biology.)
Soil Science Society of America, www.soils.org

Pest and Disease Control

These sites can help you explore integrated and organic pest management, biocontrol, and alternatives to pesticides, and the politics surrounding them.

Bio Integral Resource Center, www.birc.org (IPM pioneers.)
IPM Access Integrated Pest, www.ipmaccess.com
Mother Earth News, www.motherearthnews.com/organic-gardening/organic-pest-control-zmoz11zsto.aspx (Interesting article on which organic methods work best.)
National Pesticide Information Center, www.npic.orst.edu
Northwest Center for Alternatives to Pesticides, www.pesticide.org
Organic Gardening Magazine, www.organicgardening.com/learn-and-grow/organic-pest-control-techniques
Pesticide Action Network, www.panna.org

Plants

Some of the best resources for information on plants are the websites of wholesale growers. Just search on the name of the grower (Hines, Monrovia, etc.). I like to do an image search on Google's image search engine (www.google.com choose "images" in the upper left hand corner) using the scientific name of the plant I'm looking for. This turns up lots of interesting information and great photos that can be forwarded to clients via email, using the link to the site. (*Tip*: You can get copyright-free images by selecting "Labeled for Reuse" under Google's "search settings." You can use those images without worrying about violating the maker's copyright.) Keep in mind that plant information is regional, so a little creative searching using your region as one of the keywords ("Midwest," "Southwest," etc.) will help you find resources suited to your conditions. Regional botanical gardens often have lots of useful information on their websites.

Better Homes and Gardens: Deer Resistant Plants for Your Region, www.bhg.com/gardening/pests/animal/the-top-deer-resistant-plants-for-your-region
Dave's Garden, www.davesgarden.com (Lots of plants, lots of ideas.)
Humane Society of U.S., www.humanesociety.org/animals/resources/tips/plants_poisonous_to_pets.html (List of garden plants that are bad for pets. You need to take this into account when designing. Also see "Books on Horticultural and Landscaping Subjects" above for a reference on plants that are poisonous to humans.)
Missouri Botanical Garden, www.missouribotanicalgarden.org (One of the better botanical garden websites, with reliable information on a large variety of landscape species.)

National Gardening Association Weed Library, www.garden.org/weedlibrary

National Invasive Species Information Center, www.invasivespeciesinfo.gov (Check your designs for invasive plants.)

PLANTS Database (USDA), plants.usda.gov

Plant Search, www.plantsearch.com (Plant locating service.)

Plants for a Future, www.pfaf.org (Interesting information on the uses of plants.)

Selectree, www.selectree.calpoly.edu (Cal Poly University; species are mainly for California)

Watersense, www.epa.gov/watersense/outdoor/what_to_plant.html (Water-effi cient landscape plants for all regions of the U.S.)

Sustainable Landscaping

Here you find the new face of horticulture. These are cutting-edge websites with loads of good information and lots of links.

American Society of Landscape Architects, www.asla.org/sustainablelandscapes

Center for Regenerative Studies, www.csupomona.edu/~crs (Cal Poly Pomona)

City Farmer, www.cityfarmer.org (urban agriculture)

Forest Stewardship Council, www.us.fsc.org (Certified sustainably harvested wood.)

Landscape for Life, http://landscapeforlife.org (Based on Sustainable Sites Initiative.)

Landscaping Network, www.landscapingnetwork.com/landscape-design/sustain-able (Great links.)

Owen Dell and Associates, LLC, www.owendell.com (I've got some interesting articles and information on various sustainability topics.)

Sustainable Architecture, Building & Culture, www.sustainableabc.com (Some good links.)

Sustainable Sites Initiative, www.sustainablesites.org (Comprehensive, reliable information on sustainable landscaping practices.)

University of Minnesota Extension, www.extension.umn.edu/garden/landscaping

Miscellaneous Topics

Edible Landscape Design, www.edible-landscape-design.com

Firewise Communities, www.firewise.org (How to landscape safely in high fire risk areas.)

National Wildlife Federation, www.nwf.org/Home/How-to-Help/Garden-for-Wildlife.aspx (Gardening for wildlife.)

North American Butterfly Association, www.nababutterfly.com (Butterfly habitat gardens for North America.)
Rosalind Creasy Edible Landscaping, www.rosalindcreasy.com (Info on edible landscape plants.)
Therapeutic Landscapes Network, www.healinglandscapes.org (All about healing gardens and horticultural therapy.)

Blogs

There are tons of blogs out there on all aspects of gardening, landscaping, and related topics. Here are some that I think are pretty cool and would be useful to you. Gardening blogs aimed at home gardeners offer the professional a window into current trends and the desires of the public, which helps when marketing and also inspires the designer in you with current ideas. Some garden blogs are produced by amateurs and others by professionals; the latter are usually more substantial and worthwhile. For more, check out http://garden-bloggers-conference.com/lists-of-top-garden-blogs, www.pallensmith.com/articles/10-great-garden-blogs, and www.blogmetrics.org/gardening.

Danger Garden, www.dangergarden.blogspot.com (Luscious plants, mostly spiky, make up this quirky site.)
Digging (Pam Penick), www.penick.net/digging (Garden design out of Austin, TX.)
Earthworm's Lair, The (Owen Dell), www.owendell.com/blog (Wacky humor, spoofs, serious talk about sustainability and the meaning of gardens and landscaping.)
Eden Makers (Shirley Bovshow), www.edenmakersblog.com (Diverse topics from a media pro.)
Everyday Gardener (Meleah Maynard), www.everydaygardener.com (Eclectic blog out of Minnesota.)
Evolve: Professional Landscape Management, http://evolveyourlawn.com (Good stuff for landscape pros. Click on the blog link.)
Garden Rant: Uprooting the Gardening World, www.gardenrant.com (Popular, diverse collection of writers and provocative ideas.)
Gardening Gone Wild (Fran Sorin, Debra Lee Baldwin, Saxon Holt), www.gardeninggonewild.com (Classy stuff, by leading lights of the horticulture world.)
Gardenista, www.gardenista.com (Trendy garden design and garden history.)
Grounded Design (Thomas Rainer), www.landscapeofmeaning.blogspot.com (Thoughtful essays and other info from self-described "horticultural futurist.")

Miss Rumphius' Rules (Susan Cohan), www.susancohangardens.com/blog (Visits to amazing gardens and buildings all over the place.)

North Coast Gardening (Genevieve Schmidt), www.northcoastgardening.com (Knowledgeable information for Pacific Northwest gardeners.)

Thinking Outside the Boxwood, www.thinkingoutsidetheboxwood.com (High design, good ideas from an Ohio-based landscaper.)

Veggie Gardening Tips, www.veggiegardeningtips.com (Tips about . . . veggie gardening!)

Appendix 2: Business Plan Worksheet and Other Forms

Instructions

Use this worksheet to develop the information for your business plan. Don't submit it as a finished business plan, however; it's just a set of questions to help you gather information. Type up the plan itself and have it printed on good-quality paper and bound into booklet form. Make it look as professional as possible. If you've got a company logo, use it. Have someone else read your plan to be sure it's understandable and contains adequate information. Refer to chapter 3 on writing a business plan and to the business plan books listed in Appendix 1 for additional information. (*Tip:* When asked to come up with figures, such as the size of the present market for your services, don't guess. Use the techniques suggested in the book to research and come up with meaningful statistics; otherwise, you're shooting in the dark.)

Step One: Statement of Purpose

(35 words or less if possible)

Things to think about:

- What does your business do?
- What clientele does it serve?
- What does it offer to clients, employees, the community, the environment?
- What values are embodied in the operations of your business?
- What else do you want to convey in your statement of purpose?

Step Two: General Information

1. What classes of service do you offer?

☐ Maintenance ☐ Landscape Design

☐ Landscape Installation ☐ Other (explain)

____

____

____

2. Where will your business be located?
3. Who will own it?
4. Form of Business:

   ☐ Sole Proprietorship ☐ Partnership ☐ Corporation

   If corporation, type: ______________________________
5. Name(s) and Address(es) of Owner(s):

   ____

   ____
6. Proposed Starting Date of Business: ______________________
7. Proposed Name of Business: ______________________

Step Three: Background of Owner(s) and Key Employees

OWNER #1:

1. Name: ______________________________
2. Education:

   College Degrees/Certificates ______________________

   Seminars Attended ______________________

   Other Formal Training ______________________
3. Work Experience: List related employment and work experience. Include work outside of horticulture that provided you with management or other business experience.

DATE	EMPLOYER	TYPE OF WORK

4. Volunteer Work Experience

DATE	PROJECT	TYPE OF WORK

5. Horticultural Interest: How did you come to be interested in horticulture?

6. Business Interest: Why are you interested in going into business?

7. Licenses Held: What licenses do you have or plan to obtain?

☐ Contractor's License ☐ Pest Control Operator's License
☐ Pest Control Adviser's License ☐ Other

OWNER #2:

1. Name: ______

2. Education:

College Degrees/Certificates ______

Seminars Attended ______

Other Formal Training ______

3. Work Experience: List related employment and work experience. Include work outside of horticulture that provided you with management or other business experience.

DATE	EMPLOYER	TYPE OF WORK

4. Volunteer Work Experience

DATE	PROJECT	TYPE OF WORK

5. Horticultural Interest: How did you come to be interested in horticulture?

____

____

____

6. Business Interest: Why are you interested in going into business?

____

____

____

7. Licenses Held: What licenses do you have or plan to obtain?

   ☐ Contractor's License ☐ Pest Control Operator's License

   ☐ Pest Control Adviser's License ☐ Other

KEY EMPLOYEE #1:

1. Name: ______________________________
2. Education:

   College Degrees/Certificates ______________________________

   Seminars Attended ______________________________

   Other Formal Training ______________________________
3. Work Experience: List related employment and work experience. Include work outside of horticulture that provided you with management or other business experience.

DATE	EMPLOYER	TYPE OF WORK

4. Volunteer Work Experience

DATE	PROJECT	TYPE OF WORK

5. Horticultural Interest: How did you come to be interested in horticulture?

___

___

___

6. Business Interest: Why are you interested in going into business?

___

___

___

7. Licenses Held: What licenses do you have or plan to obtain?

☐ Contractor's License ☐ Pest Control Operator's License

☐ Pest Control Adviser's License ☐ Other

KEY EMPLOYEE #2:

1. Name: ___

2. Education:

   College Degrees/Certificates ___

   Seminars Attended ___

   Other Formal Training ___

3. Work Experience: List related employment and work experience. Include work outside of horticulture that provided you with management or other business experience.

DATE	EMPLOYER	TYPE OF WORK

4. Volunteer Work Experience

DATE	PROJECT	TYPE OF WORK

5. Horticultural Interest: How did you come to be interested in horticulture?

6. Business Interest: Why are you interested in going into business?

7. Licenses Held: What licenses do you have or plan to obtain?
   - ☐ Contractor's License
   - ☐ Pest Control Operator's License
   - ☐ Pest Control Adviser's License
   - ☐ Other

Step Four: Services Offered

1. Describe in detail the services or products you plan to offer. (Refer to the chart in chapter 3 for a list of possibilities.)

2. Describe any unique services or products you plan to offer.

3. What is the proposed geographical service area you plan to cover?

Name of Area Radius from Office (miles)

____

Step Five: Markets

1. Categories of Proposed Clients (check as many as apply):

__ Homeowners
__ General Contractors
__ Property Managers
__ Developers
__ Architects
__ Landscape Architects
__ Realtors
__ Spec House Builders
__ Apartment House Owners
__ Commercial Property Owners
__ Government
__ Other (describe) ____________

2. Classes of Proposed Clients (check as many as apply):

__ Young Families
__ Middle-Aged Homeowners
__ Retired Homeowners
__ Small Commercial
__ Medium Commercial
__ Large Commercial
__ Public Developments
__ Other (describe) ____________

3. Income Level of Proposed Clients (check as many as apply):

__ Low __ Middle __ Upper Middle __ Upper

4. Size of Potential Market:

(How many potential clients of each type are within your proposed service area?):

_______ Homeowners
_______ General Contractors
_______ Apartment House Owners
_______ Commercial Property Owners
_______ Property Managers
_______ Developers
_______ Architects
_______ Landscape Architects
_______ Realtors
_______ Spec House Builders
_______ Government
_______ Other (describe)

5. Market Penetration:

What is the size of the current market for your services in your proposed service area(s)? That is, how much money is being spent on services you plan to offer (dollars per year)?

____

What percentage of this business do you intend to take within the following periods?

1 year ____ 2 years ____ 3 years ____ 4 years ____ 5 years ____

6. Growth Trends:

What are the growth trends in your area for the type of work you propose to offer? Is the market growing or shrinking? Why? (Be specific and base your answers on statistically verifiable facts, not speculation.)

Step Six: Competition

1. How many competing companies exist in your proposed service area?
2. What is the sales volume, in dollars per year, of these companies? (List the number of companies in each category.)

   $10,000 or less ____ $10,001–20,000____

   $20,001–40,000 ____ $40,001–60,000____

   $60,001–90,000____ $90,001–120,000____

   $120,001–150,000____ $150,001–200,000____

   $200,001–300,000____ $300,001–500,000____

   $500,001–900,000____ $900,001 or more____
3. How many employees do these companies have? (List the number of companies in each category.)

   0–1 ____ 2–4 ____ 5–8 ____ 9–12 ____

   13–15 ____ 16–20 ____ 21 or more ____
4. How many people are employed in your business in your service area?
5. List the major services being offered in your service area:

6. Check off the major client categories in your service area:

- ☐ Homeowners
- ☐ Property Managers
- ☐ Architects
- ☐ Realtors
- ☐ Apartment House Owners
- ☐ Government
- ☐ General Contractors
- ☐ Developers
- ☐ Landscape Architects
- ☐ Spec House Builders
- ☐ Commercial Property Owners
- ☐ Other (describe)

7. What are the most popular services being offered?

____

____

____

____

8. Which competitors are the most important to you and why?

____

____

____

____

9. How do you plan to draw business away from your most important competition?

____

____

____

____

10. Why will your business be more attractive than your competitors' to potential clients?

____

____

____

____

Step Seven: Marketing

1. Pricing: Describe your pricing strategy (special offers, price structure, pricing position relative to competition).

____

____

2. Advertising: List and describe the advertising methods you will use to attract business.

Door-to-Door Solicitation ______________________________

Direct Mail ______________________________

Flyers ______________________________

Print Advertising ______________________________

Directory Advertising ______________________________

Radio Advertising ______________________________

Other Media ______________________________

Home Shows ______________________________

Alternative Marketing ______________________________

Describe any unique methods you plan to use to attract business.

____

____

____

____

3. Projected Budget: What is your proposed budget for marketing and advertising in the first five years?

Year 1 ________ Year 2 ________ Year 3 ________

Year 4 ________ Year 5 ________

4. Projected Results: What return, in sales dollars, do you expect to generate with the aforementioned advertising expenditure?

Year 1 ________ Year 2 ________ Year 3 ________

Year 4 ________ Year 5 ________

Step Eight: Company Organization

1. Field Employees: List the number and duties of field employees for Years 1 through 5. Indicate whether full time (FT) or part time (PT).

	NUMBER	DUTIES	FT/PT
Year 1			
Year 2			
Year 3			
Year 4			
Year 5			

2. Office Employees: List and describe the duties of office and managerial employees for Years 1 through 5. Indicate whether full time or part time.

	NUMBER	DUTIES	FT/PT
Year 1			
Year 2			
Year 3			
Year 4			
Year 5			

3. List projected wage rates for employees. Include labor burden.

Field Employees

	LABORER	FOREMAN	OTHER
Year 1			
Year 2			
Year 3			
Year 4			
Year 5			

Office Employees

	BOOKKEEPER	OFFICE MANAGER	OTHER
Year 1			
Year 2			
Year 3			
Year 4			
Year 5			

4. Benefits: Describe proposed employee benefits.

   Health Insurance ______________________

   Sick Leave ______________________

   Vacations ______________________

   Holidays ______________________

   Profit Sharing ______________________

   Bonuses ______________________

   Company Vehicle ______________________

   Other (describe) ______________________

5. Employee Training: Describe proposed employee training programs.

   ____

   ____

   ____

   ____

   ____

6. Subcontractors: Describe kinds of subcontractors you plan to use and whether you have specific subcontractors selected.

   ____

   ____

   ____

7. Outside Services: Describe other kinds of outside services you plan to use (mechanics, payroll services, bookkeeping services, etc.).

____

____

____

____

Step Nine: Facilities and Equipment

1. Purchased Field Equipment and Vehicles: For Years 1 through 5, list the field equipment you plan to purchase and whether it will be new or used. Also list the projected cost of each piece of equipment. Do not include small tools and other minor purchases; list only major equipment such as rototillers, mowers, trucks, tractors, and so forth.

	TYPE OF EQUIPMENT	NEW/USED	COST
Year 1			

	TYPE OF EQUIPMENT	NEW/USED	COST
Year 2			

Year 3

Year 4

Year 5

2. Leased Field Equipment and Vehicles: For Years 1 through 5, list the field equipment you plan to lease and whether it will be new or used. Also list the projected cost of each piece of equipment. Do not include small tools and other minor purchases; list only major equipment such as rototillers, mowers, trucks, tractors, and so forth.

	TYPE OF EQUIPMENT	NEW/USED	COST
Year 1			

Year 2

Year 3

Year 4

Year 5

3. Office Equipment: For Years 1 through 5, list the office equipment you plan to purchase and whether it will be new or used. Also list the projected cost of each piece of equipment. List only major purchases.

	TYPE OF EQUIPMENT	NEW/USED	COST
Year 1			

Year 2

Year 3

Year 4

Year 5

4. Facilities: For Years 1 through 5, describe your projected needs for office and yard space. Describe the location (home or elsewhere) and the projected cost in rent or purchase price per year.

Year 1

Year 2

Year 3

Year 4

Year 5

Estimated Start-up Costs

Fixtures and Equipment (tools, trucks, etc.)	$ ________
Materials and Supplies (parts, etc.)	$ ________
Office Supplies	$ ________
Decorating and Remodeling	$ ________
Legal and Professional Fees	$ ________
Licenses and Permits	$ ________
Initial Advertising	$ ________
Operating Cash	$ ________
Owner's Draw Prior to Start-Up	$ ________
Contingency	$ ________
TOTAL	$ ________

Step Ten: Financial Projections

1. Start-up Costs: List the cost of the things you'll need on your first day in business. (Refer to the Financial Projections section of chapter 3 for help with the details.)

 ____

 ____

2. Sales Projections: What is the projected dollar volume of your sales in the first five years?

Year 1 ____
Year 2 ____
Year 3 ____
Year 4 ____
Year 5 ____

3. Profit-and-Loss Projections: List your projected income and expenses for the first five years. (See Sample Profit-and-Loss Projection Sheet later in this appendix.)

4. Cash Forecast: Provide a month-by-month cash forecast for the first five years. (See Sample Cash Forecast Sheet later in this appendix.)
5. Balance Sheet: Provide balance sheets for the first five years. (See Sample Balance Sheet later in this appendix.)
6. Description of Accounting Systems: Describe proposed bookkeeping and accounting systems.

____

____

____

____

____

____

____

7. Financing Requirements: If you're seeking equity or debt capital to start up or help run the business during the first five years, describe the amounts needed and the way you plan to use it.

	AMOUNT	PURPOSE
Year 1		
Year 2		
Year 3		
Year 4		
Year 5		

Describe your plans for paying back this money (debt financing only).

____

____

____

Describe the equity position of the investor(s) (equity financing only). What percentage of the business will they own as a result of their investment? Will they have management interest or be silent partners? Are there limitations on their interest in the business?

Sample Profit-and-Loss Projection Sheet

	YEAR 1	YEAR 2	YEAR 3	YEAR 4	YEAR 5
INCOME					
Sales, Landscaping	$ ________	$ ________	$ ________	$ ________	$ ________
Sales, Maintenance	$ ________	$ ________	$ ________	$ ________	$ ________
Sales, Other	$ ________	$ ________	$ ________	$ ________	$ ________
TOTAL INCOME	$ ________	$ ________	$ ________	$ ________	$ ________
COST OF SALES					
Dump Fees	$ ________	$ ________	$ ________	$ ________	$ ________
Equipment Rental	$ ________	$ ________	$ ________	$ ________	$ ________
Labor	$ ________	$ ________	$ ________	$ ________	$ ________
Materials & Supplies	$ ________	$ ________	$ ________	$ ________	$ ________
Miscellaneous	$ ________	$ ________	$ ________	$ ________	$ ________
Outside Services	$ ________	$ ________	$ ________	$ ________	$ ________
TOTAL COST OF SALES	$ ________	$ ________	$ ________	$ ________	$ ________
GROSS PROFIT (income minus cost of sales)	$ ________	$ ________	$ ________	$ ________	$ ________
GENERAL OVERHEAD					
Accounting	$ ________	$ ________	$ ________	$ ________	$ ________
Advertising	$ ________	$ ________	$ ________	$ ________	$ ________
Bank Charges	$ ________	$ ________	$ ________	$ ________	$ ________
Car & Truck Expense	$ ________	$ ________	$ ________	$ ________	$ ________
Depreciation	$ ________	$ ________	$ ________	$ ________	$ ________
Dues & Subscriptions	$ ________	$ ________	$ ________	$ ________	$ ________
Entertainment & Meals	$ ________	$ ________	$ ________	$ ________	$ ________
Insurance	$ ________	$ ________	$ ________	$ ________	$ ________
Interest Expense	$ ________	$ ________	$ ________	$ ________	$ ________
Legal Expense	$ ________	$ ________	$ ________	$ ________	$ ________
Licenses & Permits	$ ________	$ ________	$ ________	$ ________	$ ________
Meetings & Seminars	$ ________	$ ________	$ ________	$ ________	$ ________
Miscellaneous	$ ________	$ ________	$ ________	$ ________	$ ________
Postage	$ ________	$ ________	$ ________	$ ________	$ ________
Professional Fees	$ ________	$ ________	$ ________	$ ________	$ ________
Rent/Real Estate	$ ________	$ ________	$ ________	$ ________	$ ________
Repairs & Maintenance	$ ________	$ ________	$ ________	$ ________	$ ________
Supplies, Office	$ ________	$ ________	$ ________	$ ________	$ ________
Taxes, Other	$ ________	$ ________	$ ________	$ ________	$ ________
Taxes, Sales	$ ________	$ ________	$ ________	$ ________	$ ________
Telephone	$ ________	$ ________	$ ________	$ ________	$ ________
Tools	$ ________	$ ________	$ ________	$ ________	$ ________
Travel & Lodging	$ ________	$ ________	$ ________	$ ________	$ ________
Uniforms	$ ________	$ ________	$ ________	$ ________	$ ________
Utilities	$ ________	$ ________	$ ________	$ ________	$ ________
Wages	$ ________	$ ________	$ ________	$ ________	$ ________
TOTAL GENERAL OVERHEAD	$ ________	$ ________	$ ________	$ ________	$ ________
NET PROFIT (LOSS) (gross profit minus overhead)	$ ________	$ ________	$ ________	$ ________	$ ________

Sample Cash Forecast Sheet

	JAN	FEB	MAR	APR	MAY	JUN	JUL	AUG	SEP	OCT	NOV	DEC
1. Cash in Bank (start of month)												
2. Petty Cash (start of month)												
3. Total Cash (add 1 and 2)												
4. Anticipated Cash Sales												
5. Anticipated Collections												
6. Other Anticipated Income												
7. Total Receipts (add 4, 5, and 6)												
8. Total Cash Receipts (add 3 and 7)												
9. All Disbursements												
10. Cash Balance (subtract 9 from 8)												

Sample Balance Sheet

ASSETS	
CURRENT ASSETS	
Cash:	
Cash in Bank	$ ________
Cash on Hand	$ ________
Petty Cash	$ ________
Accounts Receivable	$ ________
Less Allowance for Bad Debts	$ ________
Adjusted Accounts Receivable	$ ________
Prepaid Expenses	$ ________
Inventory	$ ________
TOTAL CURRENT ASSETS	$ ________
FIXED ASSETS	
Land	$ ________
Buildings	$ ________
Equipment & Fixtures	$ ________
Vehicles	$ ________
Less Allowance for Depreciation	$ ________
TOTAL FIXED ASSETS	$ ________
TOTAL ASSETS	$ ________
LIABILITIES	
CURRENT LIABILITIES	
Accounts Payable	$ ________
Notes Payable (due w/in one year)	$ ________
Payroll Taxes, Current	$ ________
Sales Taxes, Current	$ ________
TOTAL CURRENT LIABILITIES	$ ________
LONG-TERM LIABILITIES	
Notes Payable (due after one year)	$ ________
TOTAL LIABILITIES	$ ________
NET WORTH (Owner's Equity)	$ ________
LIABILITIES & NET WORTH	$ ________

DAILY TIME CARD

EMPLOYEE'S NAME ______________________________ DATE ______________

JOB NAME	DESCRIPTION OF WORK	IN	OUT	HOURS
TOTAL REGULAR HOURS				
TOTAL OVERTIME				
FOREMAN				

Sample Contact Form

DATE ______________ BY ________

PROJECT

Name

City/State/Zip

Contact

Address ______________

Phone ______________

Fax ______________

E-mail ______________

Type: Residential __________ Commercial __________ Other __________

OWNER

Name

City/State/Zip

Address ______________

Home Phone ______________

Work Phone ______________

E-mail ______________

LANDSCAPE ARCHITECT

Name

City/State/Zip

Contact

Address ______________

Phone ______________

Fax ______________

E-mail ______________

GENERAL CONTRACTOR

Name

City/State/Zip

Contact

Address ______________

Phone ______________

Fax ______________

E-mail ______________

DETAILS OF PROJECT

Drawing Nos./Dates/Revisions ______________

____

Specification Section No./Date ______________

Submit proposal to: Owner ________ L.A. ________ G.C. ________ Other ________

Bid date/time ______________

Date work to start ______________

Budget ______________

Getting other bids? Y ________ N ________

DESCRIPTION OF WORK

____

____

SUBCONTRACTOR BIDS REQUIRED

____

____

NOTES

____

____

Referred by ______________

Job Checklist

Job Name: ____________________

Job APN: ____________________

Client Name/Address: ____________________

Job Phone: ____________________

Client Phone: ____________________

Client E-mail: ____________________

Client Fax: ____________________

Other Contact Information: ____________________

Item	By	Date
☐ Initial contact		
☐ Referred by:		
☐ Thank you note sent to referrer		
☐ Info package sent to client		
☐ Job list sent to client		
☐ Approval from client to proceed with design work		
☐ Credit check OK		
☐ Background check OK		
☐ Scope of work discussed with client		
☐ Preliminary design fee estimate sent to client		
☐ Preliminary design fee estimate approved by client		
☐ Design contract sent to client		
☐ Design contract received from client		
☐ Retainer received from client		
☐ Gate code received from client		
CODE:		
☐ Site photos taken		
☐ Site measurement		
☐ Soil samples taken		
☐ Soil samples sent to lab		
Lab:		
☐ Soil testing completed		
By:		
☐ Survey completed		

Item	By	Date
☐ House plans received from client		
☐ Drainage testing		
☐ Geotechnical report		
☐ Other outside reports		
1.		
2.		
3.		
☐ Design package received from client Contents:		
☐ Preliminary landscape plan completed		
☐ Preliminary approval from building department		
☐ Preliminary approval from zoning		
☐ Preliminary approval from homeowners association		
☐ Preliminary approval/s other:		
☐ Preliminary plant list sent to client		
☐ Preliminary plant list received from client		
☐ Preliminary plant list approved by client		
☐ Final landscape plans completed		
☐ Final landscape plans approved by client		
☐ Final plans approved by agencies		
☐ Final plans approved by homeowners association		
☐ Final plans approved by others		
☐ Specifications prepared/delivered to client		
☐ House plans returned to client		
☐ Pre-budget meeting with subcontractors		
☐ Preliminary budget sent to client		
☐ Bid addendum sent to client		
☐ Preliminary budget approved by client		
☐ Subcontractors contacted for bids		
1.		
2.		
3.		
☐ Plans delivered to subcontractors		
1.		
2.		

Item	By	Date
3.		
☐ Bid forms delivered to subcontractors		
1.		
2.		
3.		
☐ Bids received from subcontractors		
1.		
2.		
3.		
☐ Insurance certificates from subcontractors current		
☐ Licenses from subcontractors current		
☐ Final bid meeting with client		
☐ Final bids approved by client		
☐ Construction contract sent to client		
☐ Construction contract approved by client		
☐ Subcontractors notified of approval		
☐ Starting dates approved by client		
☐ Starting dates approved by subcontractors		
☐ Deposit received from client		
☐ Building permit/s received		
☐ ABR approvals		
☐ Other agency approvals:		
☐ DigAlert called (Ticket No. ______________)		
☐ Site marked for DigAlert		
☐ DigAlert renewals		
1.		
2.		
3.		
☐ Utilities flagged by providers		
☐ Utilities located by client		
☐ Utilities located by contractor/s		
☐ Pre-construction photos taken		
☐ Toilet ordered		
☐ Toilet delivered		
☐ Pre-job meeting with client		

Item	By	Date
☐ Pre-job meeting with subcontractors		
1.		
2.		
3.		
☐ Permits posted at jobsite		
☐ Safety inspection/s completed		
☐ Preliminary notices filed		
☐ Toxic Substances Removal, bill for any charges		
☐ Progress billings from subcontractors received/approved		
1.		
2.		
3.		
4.		
5.		
6.		
☐ Progress billings sent/paid		
1.		
2.		
3.		
4.		
5.		
6.		
☐ Lien releases received from subcontractors		
1.		
2.		
3.		
4.		
5.		
6.		
7.		
☐ Lien releases given to client		
1.		
2.		
3.		
4.		

Item	By	Date
5.		
6.		
7.		
☐ Change orders approved by client		
1.		
2.		
3.		
4.		
5.		
6.		
☐ Progress photos taken		
1.		
2.		
3.		
☐ Building inspections		
1.		
2.		
3.		
4.		
5.		
☐ Approvals by client		
1.		
2.		
3.		
4.		
5.		
6.		
7.		
☐ Punchlist prepared and delivered to subcontractors		
☐ Punchlist items resolved		
☐ Record drawings received from subcontractors		
☐ Record drawings delivered to client		
☐ Final walkthrough with subcontractors		
☐ Final walkthrough with client		
☐ Client trained in controller operation		

Item	By	Date
☐ Client given verbal maintenance instructions		
☐ Client given written maintenance instructions		
☐ Final approval by client		
☐ Final building inspection		
☐ Final job accounting delivered to client		
☐ Final billing sent to client		
☐ Final lien releases from subcontractors		
1.		
2.		
3.		
4.		
5.		
6.		
7.		
☐ Final lien release sent to client		
☐ Final payment received from client		
☐ Toilet removed		
☐ Photos on completion		
☐ Thank you letter sent to client		
☐ Satisfaction survey sent to client		
☐ Satisfaction survey received from client		
☐ 14-day walkthrough with client		
☐ 30-day walkthrough with client		
☐ 60-day walkthrough with client		
☐ Collections action/s required		
1.		
2.		
3.		
☐ Record of warranty work done		
1.		
2.		
3.		
☐ Photos at maturity		
☐ Job posted to Web site		
☐ Job added to handouts		

Site Inspection Report (Landscaping)

Job Name ____________________

Job Location ____________________

Client's Name and Address ____________________

____

Client's Phone ____________________

Landscape Architect ____________________

General Contractor ____________________

Date Bid Due ____________________

Start Date ____________________ Completion Date ____________________

Access ____________________

Distance/Driving Time ____________________

Vehicle Parking ____________________

Suppliers Nearby ____________________

Water/Power/Temporary Improvements ____________________

Bathroom Facilities ____________________

Staging Area ____________________

Soil Conditions ____________________

Digging Conditions ____________________

Existing Grade ____________________

Weed Growth ____________________

Vertebrate/Other Pests ____________________

Existing Plants ____________________

Existing Structures ____________________

Other Considerations ____________________

____

____

MAINTENANCE REPORT
Prepared by
LISA'S GARDEN CARE, 560 W. CENTER STREET., GRASSVILLE, PA
(805) 555-3253

Needs Attention	Item	Area	Comments
	HOUSEKEEPING Cleanup		
	Trash Removal		
	Fire Hazards		
	PLANTS Trees		
	Shrubs		
	Perennials		
	Annuals		
	Ground Covers		
	Fruit Trees		
	Vegetable Garden		
	TURF		
	WEED CONTROL		
	PEST CONTROL		
	VERTEBRATE CONTROL		
	HARDSCAPE Paved Areas		
	Driveways & Parking Areas		
	Structures		
	SPRINKLERS Lawns		
	Beds & Borders		
	Slopes		
	Other:		
	DRIP IRRIGATION Regulator/s		
	Filter/s		
	Tubing		
	Emitters		
	Other:		
	IRRIGATION CONTROLLER Functioning		
	Program Settings		
	Backup Battery		
	MOISTURE SENSORS		

Needs Attention	Item	Area	Comments
	BACKFLOW DEVICE/S		
	PRESSURE REGULATORS		
	DRAINAGE Catch Basins		
	Downspouts		
	Drain Lines		
	Surface Runoff		
	Bench Drains		
	French Drains		
	Sump Pumps		
	Sediment Basins		
	EROSION CONTROL Jute Netting		
	Retaining Walls		
	Check Dams		
	Vegetation		
	LIGHTING Fixtures		
	Switching		
	Transformers		
	Timers & Photocells		
	WATERSCAPE Ponds		
	Pumps & Filters		
	Other:		
	PERSONNEL Punctuality		
	Attire		
	Blower Noise		
	Other:		
	EQUIPMENT Vehicles		
	Tools & Equipment		
	MISCELLANEOUS		

PROJECT NAME:	COMMENTS:
PROJECT ADDRESS:	
PREPARED BY:	
DATE:	

Index